THE BASEBALL ASTROLOGER

JOHN B. HOLWAY

THE BASEBALL ASTROLOGER

AND OTHER WEIRD TALES

TOTAL Sports Illustrated

KINGSTON, NEW YORK   NEW YORK, NEW YORK

For information about permission to reproduce selections from this book, please write to:

Permissions
Total/SPORTS ILLUSTRATED
100 Enterprise Dr.
Kingston, NY 12401

COVER DESIGN: DONNA HARRIS
INTERIOR DESIGN: ANN SULLIVAN
ILLUSTRATIONS: ROBERT PLACE

ISBN: 1892129-29-9
Library of Congress Catalog Card Number: 00-100102

Printed in the United States of America by R.R. Donnelly & Sons

To

Kristi, Sarah, Allie, and Jeremy

Other books by John Holway:

Japan is Big League in Thrills

Sumo

Voices From the Great Black Baseball Leagues

The Pitcher (with John Thorn)

Blackball Stars

Black Diamonds

Josh and Satch

The Sluggers

Josh Gibson

The Last .400 Hitter

Red Tails, Black Wings

The Complete Book of the Negro Leagues

Contents

ACKNOWLEDGEMENTS

The stories on John Agunga (chapters 33 and 36) and Steve Stone (chapter 38) previously appeared in slightly different form in *The Baltimore Magazine*. The Ron Cey story in chapter 35 previously appeared in *The Sporting News*.

Special thanks to Pete Palmer and Tim Joyce for their valuable statistical help on the astrology chapters, to Bill Deane for providing stories about called shots, and to Rosemary DeWitt for opening up this entire fascinating subject to me.

PART I

BASEBALL'S FIFTH DIMENSION

He can call his dreams fallacious
Who has searched and sought
All the unexplored and spacious
Universe of thought.

Henry Wadsworth Longfellow,
HERMES

*I'm on the border line of life and a greater realm
beyond, as though caught in the field of gravitation
betweeen two planets, acted on by forces I can't control, forces too weak to be measured by any means at
my command, yet representing powers incomparably
stronger than I've ever known.*

Charles A. Lindbergh
THE SPIRIT OF ST LOUIS

CHAPTER 1
A Roster of Oddities

♎ **A Message for Gehrig** ♎

IN 1939 FRED LIEB, the dean of American baseball writers who had been
covering the game since 1911, wrote a little-known but important book,
Sight Unseen: A Journalist Looks at the Occult. A close personal friend of
Lou and Eleanor Gehrig, Lieb reported spending an evening with the
Gehrigs playing with a ouija board.

An "entity" identified as Mark Antony spelled out the following message: "You soon will be called on to face the most difficult problem of
your life."

Two months later Lou learned that he had contracted the muscular
disease now known as "Lou Gehrig's Disease," an illness that would kill
him two years later at the age of 39.

✒ **Lucky Lohrke** ✒

In 1943 Jack Lohrke, a 19-year-old shortstop for Twin Falls,
Montana, was drafted into the army and put on a troop train to
California. The train ran off the rails and crashed, killing three men and
spewing scalding water over most of the rest, but Lohrke walked away
without a scratch. It was the first of his legendary escapes from death.

He would fight in Normandy and the Battle of the Bulge. Men died all
around him, but again he escaped without a wound. Back in the States
in '45, Lohrke boarded an army transport plane at Camp Kilmer, New
Jersey, for a flight home to California. "I was already in my seat," he says,
"when an officer climbed aboard with a priority and took my seat." The
plane crashed in Ohio, killing everyone on board.

Lohrke went to spring training in 1946 with San Diego of the Pacific
Coast League and was farmed out to Spokane, where he hit .345. On June
19 the players piled into their bus for the long trip across the Cascade
Mountains from Spokane to Bremerton. It was rainy and slick when they
pulled into a diner at Ellensburg, then filed onto the bus once more.

Just as Jack was about to climb aboard, the diner manager called him back to take a long distance call. It was the Spokane club owner, who told Lohrke he had just been recalled by San Diego. Did he want to return to Spokane and then fly to San Diego, or would he rather continue to Bremerton and leave from there? Jack said he'd rather go back to Spokane. So he waved goodbye to his buddies and watched the bus with 16 men pull onto the highway and disappear into the rain.

Twenty minutes later the driver was making a hairpin turn when he swerved to avoid a pair of oncoming headlights. The bus smashed into the guard rail and plunged over a 500-foot bank, rolling over and over. Men were thrown out the windows or trapped in flames inside. Nine players were killed. One received a broken neck. None ever played again.

Lohrke went on to play with the 1951 "Miracle Giants," who won the pennant on Bobby Thomson's playoff home run. "I'm a firm believer in fatalism," Lohrke said. "It just wasn't my turn to go. But I've often wondered how the Spokane owner knew we'd stop at the diner in Ellensburg to eat. That was pure fate. And what if he had called a few minutes later and missed us? I would have been on the bus."

✗ Lefty's Lucky Mutt ✗

From 1929 to '31 the Athletics were the kings of baseball behind their big ace, Lefty Grove. In 1929 Lefty led them to their first flag in 15 years with a record of 20-6. The A's repeated the next year behind Grove, who was 24-8. They made it three straight in 1931 as Grove had one of the best seasons in this century—31-4.

Then in April of '32 Lefty and the Athletics both stumbled. Grove won only one game against one loss, and the team was languishing in sixth place.

On the 26th Grove faced the woebegone Red Sox (111 defeats that year). Boston knocked him out of the box, pounding him for six runs in one inning. That made Lefty's record 1-2.

After one of his patented temper tantrums in the locker room, Lefty stalked out of the clubhouse to the garage where he kept his car,

---

popping pretzels as he went, when a stray dog came up, wagging his tail to mooch a snack. "Feed him, Lefty," the garage man said, "it'll bring you luck."

"I don't believe in that stuff," Grove growled, ignoring the drooling pooch.

In his next start, against Washington, Grove found his old stuff again. He was ahead 1-0 until, wrote James Isaminger of the *Inquirer*, "tragic events happened in the eighth."

Washington's Joe Cronin doubled. Carl Reynolds hit a short fly to center for a "spurious" single. Then the worst hitter on the team, Moe Berg (.234), hit a fly over Al Simmons' head in center to win the game 2-1. It was already Lefty's third loss of the season, compared to only four the year before.

The Athletics lost six out of their next eight and entrained for home, where Lefty was scheduled to face the fourth-place Indians and their unbeaten ace, Wes Ferrell (23-13 that year).

Grove drove to the park, munching on another bag of pretzels, and the same mongrel, tongue out and tail wagging, was waiting hopefully. Lefty slipped the pup a snack. That afternoon he whipped Wes, 15-3. He even got two hits himself in one inning. His record was now even at 3-3.

Grove beat the Indians in his next start 9-0, shut out sixth-place St. Louis 3-0, extended his scoreless streak to 23 innings against fifth-place Detroit, beat the first-place Yankees 4-2, and Washington 13-2.

That made six in a row, with an earned run average of 1.35. The great Grove was back in the groove. We don't know how long Lefty fed the dog, what became of it, or even what its name was. We do know that before encountering the dog, Lefty's record was 2-3. After he started feeding the dog, his record was 23-7. The Athletics finished second.

♉ The Strange Travels of Jim Busby ♉

Jim Busby was never a star—his lifetime batting average was just .262—but he stayed in the big leagues for 13 years (1950-62). He never played for a championship team. He was traded seven times. Yet, for some mysterious reason, Jim Busby was a winner. Almost every team he

joined suddenly spurted one or two positions higher in the standings. As soon as any team dealt him away, it fell back a notch or two again.

Jim's first full year was 1951 with the White Sox, who had finished sixth the year before. They rose to fourth.

The next year Chicago traded him to seventh-place Washington. Jim batted only .236, but the Senators improved to fifth place. In '55 Washington dealt him back to Chicago and fell back to eighth.

Busby went to second-place Cleveland in '56. The following year the Indians let him go and fell all the way to sixth.

Busby's new team, Baltimore, was an expansion club that had wallowed deep in the second division for all of its short life. In 1958, Busby was the focal point of an amazing occurrence. He batted only .237 with three home runs and just 19 runs batted in. Yet, with Jim in the lineup, the Orioles were the hottest team in either major league. They won 74 games and lost only 37 for a winning percentage of .667, compared to .597 for the champion Yankees of Mickey Mantle, Yogi Berra, and Whitey Ford.

But—and here's the rub—Busby was benched for 42 games, and Baltimore lost every one of them!

Unaware of Busby's magic, in 1959 the O's traded him to the Red Sox. Jim hit only .225 in Boston, and the Sox shipped him back to Baltimore—and fell from fifth to seventh.

With Jim, the Orioles soared from sixth to second, the highest they had been since coming into the league in 1954. In '62 the Orioles let him go to the new team in Houston and—that's right—plummeted back to seventh.

Why should Jim Busby, who didn't hit with either consistency or power, have had such a magic effect on almost every team he joined? Jim thinks it was all those fly balls he caught—he led the league in putouts four times. And each putout, he points out, saved his pitcher three or four pitches.

Busby's great glove was surely a factor. But 0-42 in games that he missed? That's pretty hard to explain by all the normal criteria.

♊ The Death of Clemente ♊

The afternoon before Roberto Clemente's fatal flight to Nicaragua in 1972, his young son, Roberto Junior, told his grandfather, "Daddy's going to Nicaragua, but he isn't coming back, because the plane is going to crash." The old man dismissed it as "a little boy talking."

But three hours later, several miles away, Clemente's father-in-law, Melchior, was also having "a terrible dream." He told the *Inquirer*: "I saw a plane crash into the sea, and I saw Roberto go down with it. There was no doubt that it was Roberto's plane. The dream was so clear." Not wishing to alarm anyone, Melchior and his wife decided to say nothing.

When Clemente's mother heard the two stories, she frantically phoned the airport. Her call was too late.

♑ Don Larsen and David Cone ♑

In 1998, David Cone pitched a perfect game on the same day that Don Larsen, the perfect World Series pitcher, was sitting in the stands with his old catcher, Yogi Berra. Coincidence?

This was the first game Larsen and Berra had attended together since Don retired from the Yankees some 75,000 games earlier. Since 1901 there have been about 150,000 major league games played, and 16 of them were perfect games. That means a perfect game comes up about once in 9,500 games. The odds that the two events would coincide by sheer luck were 9,500 x 75,000, or about one in 700 million. (They later attended another game together, thus cutting the odds to one in 350 million.)

Coincidence? Or could some unknown factor be at work? The only thing harder to swallow than an "X" factor is that it was sheer chance.

≈ The "X" Force ≈

All the stories in this book are true. They shouldn't be, perhaps, but they are. Were they just lucky coincidences? Any one of them

might have been. Probably two of them, possibly three, or even four or five. But all of them?

It's stretching a point to dismiss all of them as chance occurrences. Couldn't there be some mysterious "X" force, as yet unknown and not understood, that might account for the phenomena in this book? Science doesn't have all the answers. In fact, a real scientist is one who does not memorize answers, but rather asks questions.

When I was in high school my physics textbook taught that atoms were little solar systems, with a tiny sun, the nucleus, in the center and tiny planets, electrons, revolving around them. Years later when I helped my daughter with her science homework, I read that science now believes there are no particular tiny "planets" in orbits inside the atom; rather, there is a zone where invisible electrons are assumed to be found. What we had once been so certain of, we have now discarded. Will the new theory also be discarded in turn by still another newer one in our grandchildren's textbooks?

Western pragmatists scoffed at the Chinese claims of the power of acupuncture. Today no one snickers at it anymore. One hundred years from now, what other far-out ideas that science now ridicules will be accepted in the light of new discovery and insight?

What follows is not a book about superstitions. The word is too subjective: Other people have "superstitions." You and I, of course, have "firmly based convictions."

Also, I wanted to try to measure the effect of these non-normal phenomena. If Wade Boggs always eats chicken before a game, then how can we tell if the chicken effects his play or not? Therefore, I looked for reports that had clearly defined "before-and-after" episodes so that the two could be compared.

There are only two ways to live your life. One is as though nothing is a miracle. The other is as though everything is.

Albert Einstein

CHAPTER 2
Some Personal Experiences

I'VE ALWAYS BEEN WILLING TO EXPLORE possible explanations for events that were not found in my high school science textbook. Back when I was 14 I remember using a ouija board. My question was a profound one: Who will be the American League home run champion in 1944? My partner and I waited for many minutes, repeating the question, without getting a response. Suddenly, to our amazement and delight, the planchette did move! We certainly weren't pushing it but simply following where it led us. It spelled out the name "Dorr," which I, a Red Sox fan, naturally took to mean Bobby Doerr. Unfortunately, Bobby was drafted sometime after that and did not win the title, which went to the Yankees' Nick Etten.

About that same period in my life I had another experience that can be easily replicated by any reader. I was a counselor at a summer camp, and in the evening, the older boys got together at the lodge to hang around. One night one of the guys laid three kings from a deck of cards on a table and told us to concentrate on one of them. Then he left the room. When he returned, he unhesitatingly pointed to the right card.

Naturally we suspected a trick, such as a confederate or peeking. We took every precaution to prevent any chicanery, but he still picked the right card every time. He just smiled and said, "You can do it, too. Just concentrate on the three cards, and suddenly you'll know which one it is." We took turns, and quickly the other boys were also picking the right card time after time.

When it came my turn, my first try was a guess, and it was wrong. But on the second try, sure enough, one of the three cards seemed to vibrate or glow or grow larger. I knew that was it. And it was. Thereafter, I, too, did it again and again and again. We soon felt confident enough to do it with four cards. This is a good party game. The more people concentrating, the easier it is to do. They say young people are more successful at it than we older fogeys.

How often have we had a "hunch" to check something, but failed to and then regretted it? Can you tell who is on the phone before you pick

up the receiver? My wife often breaks silences by mentioning a subject that I'm thinking of; other couples say they can do the same thing. People I trust have told me about other experiences that happened to them, and I have to be open-minded until I see evidence to the contrary.

My mother says that when she was a college student in the '20s, the girls in her dorm were trying to levitate each other. She lay on a table as the other girls held their hands a few inches above her, breathed in unison, and raised their hands upward together. My mother says she floated up about six feet and stayed there for three or four seconds while the others screamed in fright, until she floated softly back down.

We lived in Japan in the late 1940s, and the ghost of a cat apparently inhabited the maid's room, and everyone who was hired refused to sleep there. A Shinto priest was called in to exorcise the spirit, and the maids slept untroubled from then on.

During that same time, our house in New Hampshire seemed to be haunted by the ghost of my great-grandfather, who was presumably unhappy with the tenants who lived there while we were away. They reported odd noises and the like, and when we returned, the phenomena continued. "Just a man walking around the house," my mother said—"a few steps here, then a few steps somewhere else."

My brother was painting furniture in the basement one night when he was called away. On returning, he found that the brush and rags had been picked up and piled neatly.

On a snowy night, my parents heard the sound of a shovel scraping on the roof. In the morning, the new snow had been thrown off the roof, and lay "in spadefuls" too far away from the eaves to have simply slid off by itself. And new snow still covered all the other roofs in town.

When my father was away, my mother and a woman friend lived together for a few weeks. They couldn't understand why they continually found the toilet seat up.

My sister was once about to leave on a trip, discovered she had forgotten a belt, and went back into the house to get it. She couldn't find it, but as she left, the belt came flying through the air and hit her on the shoulder.

My family called a psychic to get in touch with Gramp. After

reporting no success, they got up to leave, and an ashtray flew across the room and shattered on the wall.

I never saw Gramp myself, but as the old New England story goes, "I had a dog who did." Jeep and I were alone in the living room after the others had gone to bed. Suddenly Jeep got up, hackles standing up on his spine, and paced restlessly into every corner, sniffing and growling. He kept prowling like that for several minutes, then quietly hopped onto the sofa, curled up, and went to sleep.

Years later my friend, Rosemary Dewitt, and I visited a psychic, who asked me if I wanted to get in touch with anyone "on the other side." My father, I replied. The medium put her hand to her forehead and concentrated for a moment. At length she said, "I'm sorry, I can't seem to reach your father. But who is this jolly old gentleman with a mustache who keeps trying to come in?"

I suggested it might be my Gramp. She tilted her head as though listening, smiled, and then reported, "He says he wishes he were alive today, because he wouldn't have to wear those stiff collars." (My mother later confirmed it: "That's right, he hated stiff collars.") Then the medium suddenly asked, "Who is Julia?" "The only Julia I know," I said, "was my great-grandmother." "Maybe that's who it is," the psychic said. "She says she just wants to say hello, too."

Naturally on guard, I thought I might possibly have mentioned Gramp to Rosemary, who could have told the medium before we arrived. However, even I had never heard about the collars until my mother told me, and I am quite sure I never mentioned my great-grandmother, who died when I was two years old.

On another occasion I visited a Washington psychic. Before entering his office, I wrote on a 3x5 card the names of three persons "in spirit" I wanted to contact. I named John Adams, Thomas Jefferson, and Adlai Stevenson, folded the card, held it in one fist, and took a seat across the desk. The psychic held his hands over mine and began chatting. Midway through the session, he stopped. "I see Monticello," he said. "I see the front door opening, and someone is beckoning to you to come in. Does this make any sense to you?" I gave a noncommittal nod. A moment later, he said, "And I see John Adams—*the* John Adams—standing right behind you."

He never picked up on Stevenson, but as I stood to leave, he asked, "What is this big O that keeps coming in and out?" The old Negro League baseball star, Oscar Charleston, had that morning been elected to Cooperstown, and I had just mailed an article on him to an editor. The title of my article was "The Big O."

Other strange things have occurred to members of my family. One night in New Hampshire, about 1963, my mother shook my father and sister awake and led them to the window at the front of the house. In a field across the street, above some electric wires, they saw a UFO some 50 yards away. "It was lit from the inside," my mother told me, "not quite as big as a trolley car" and shaped "like a hot dog roll." When I asked her to repeat the story at the age of 92, her memory was gone. But here is how my sister Jane remembered it:

"Mother first saw it, a bright light coming up the road in the middle of the night, about two o'clock, I'd guess. She said, 'Get up and look at the UFO.' It was over the telephone wires across the street, about eye-high from the upstairs window. It was machine-made, like hammered metal, a khaki-brown color. It was the length of a school bus, maybe as thick. Cigar-shaped... with a little turret. I could see the windows in the turret revolving. It made a whining sound.

"It was scary," Jane continued. "I've never seen anything like it, ever. I've seen everything that's come out of Pease Air Force Base, but that didn't come out of Pease. It wasn't a helicopter. It wasn't earthly. It was eerie. Here was that damn thing, that close.

"Mother wanted to go outside. Daddy said, 'No, don't go out there.' It stayed about five minutes, hovered over the lines, and then it sort of moved to the field. I thought the damn thing was going to land, but it didn't. It changed its mind and went over the house slow enough so I could walk from the front to the back following the noise. We watched it disappear over the woods."

Apparently "non-normal" experiences such as these cross natural and cultural borders; nearly every society has traditions of ghosts, UFOs, prophetic dreams, and other unexplainable things. Perhaps you, or friends of yours, have reported similar phenomena.

It would be difficult to write [psychics] off entirely.
The Scriptures say there will be such people.

Ronald Reagan

CHAPTER 3
Getting Into Psychic Sports

♂ Horse Racing ♂

THE UNLUCKIEST HORSE IN HISTORY WAS BURGOO KING, winner of the 1932 Kentucky Derby. Three jockeys who rode him came to tragic ends. One drowned, one shot himself, and the third leaped to his death from a window.

A happier story is that of Risen Star, the 6-1 long-shot running with an injured ligament, who won the 1988 Preakness by 20 lengths in near-record time. Far away in New Orleans, the Little Sisters of the Poor prayed and screamed and hugged each other in front of the TV. The horse's born-again owner, Louie Roussel, had dedicated all winnings—more than a million dollars—to the Little Sisters, who used it to renovate their day-care center for 100 old people. It was the last race Risen Star ever ran.

"The Lord asks us to ask for whatever we need," said Sister Mary Vincent, the Mother Superior. "God loves the poor... and God will never be outdone in generosity."

♋ Golf ♋

Golf is a mental game, and those who play it sometimes speak of it as a psychic, even spiritual, game. In his delightful book, *Golf in the Kingdom,* Michael Murphy, one of the most poetic writers on the sport, described it this way:

"As you practiced this skill of the inner eye, you would develop a capacity which put forth 'streamers of heart power for the ball to fly on.' At times it seemed that my mental picture has changed the direction of a shot after it has left the ground, as if I were steering it from afar."

Or Jack Nicklaus: "I never hit a shot, not even in practice, without having a very sharp, in-focus picture of it in my head. It's like a color movie. First I 'see' the ball where I want it to finish, nice and white and sitting up high on the bright green grass. Then the scene quickly

changes, and I 'see' the ball going there: its path, trajectory, and shape, even its behavior on landing. Then there is sort of a fade-out, and the next scene shows me making the kind of swing that will turn the previous images into reality."

♀ **Soccer** ♀

"Macumba"—magic—is all over the field when Brazil, Cameroon, Honduras, Algeria, and even Western European countries send their teams into the World Cup. In Rio de Janeiro especially, the cultists beat the drums, roll the cowrie shells, go into trance, and ask their Exu demon gods for help. Sacred cult centers all over the country are filled with lighted candles, sacrificial chickens, and baptismal rum bottles.

One of the most famous practitioners a decade ago was Eduardo Santana, who called himself the "instrument of the demon Exu," or "Cross of Souls." Dressed in a black cape, on his knees on a dirt floor, he'd light 32 white candles, three black ones, and four yellow ones around a Brazilian flag. Brazil would win, he predicted, because one of its stars, Toninho Cerezo, was "an unconquerable medium."

Santana once assured a national championship by predicting that the great Pele would not play for the other team. Pele twisted his ankle descending from the plane before the game. He also recalled once placing a pig's head at the entrance to the office of the other team, Flamengo. "I was already lighting the candles when I was discovered," Santana said. "I had to leave running, with a band of Flamingoists after me, some even shooting with a revolver."

In Africa teams would rather take the field without a goalie than without a witch doctor. Kenya's Serif Omar Abubakar was one of East Africa's most famous witch doctors of 20 years ago. Wearing a flowing *kansu,* or robe, he counted the top teams of Kenya, Uganda, and Tanzania among his clients. They paid up to $250 a game, and his office walls were adorned by pictures of him surrounded with trophies won by his teams.

Serif considered himself a healer, astrologer, and soothsayer, treating 100 people a week with requests to cure sick relatives, trace stolen

property, and remove hexes. "All my powers come from God," he said, adding that he received his knowledge from holy books, prayers, and dreams. To appease the angels, Serif said it was sometimes necessary to sacrifice a goat, and that players also had to purify themselves: "That means no beer and no women." He gave them potions—secret herbs, roots, and powdered animal and snake skins—to eat, wear, throw into the back of the goal, or just to leave around the other team's dressing room.

"The other team may have better players," Serif said, "but I can make weird things happen. The football can go wide, go over the goal, fall short, and so forth." In the Kenya Cup final in 1968, the goalie for the team that Serif was hexing let in three easy goals, which cost his club the championship. "I kept seeing snakes," the goalie said. "The ball turned into a snake."

When two great shamans face each other, the game can get wild. In one game Serif's Abaluhya team picked up the opposing goalie's cap and found an old penny, a needle, some pieces of animal skin and bones, a horn, and some roots. A riot broke out, and the game had to be replayed—without the hat.

♉ Martial Arts ♉

The Chinese call this power chi, the force or spirit that flows through our bodies. Among other things, it tells acupuncturists where to insert their needles. Focusing chi is the object of tai chi exercises. Projecting it is the key to karate, tae kwon do, kung fu, aikido, and other martial arts. In Tokyo's great judo-kan, the Madison Square Garden of judo, I once watched an elderly master kneel on one knee and easily flip young men who rushed at him from left and right, giving each a soft, quick cuff behind the head.

Many volumes have been written about this subject. Bruce Lee could reportedly stagger a foe with a one-inch punch. Other masters reportedly can do it by simply pointing.

♉ **Some Unsolved Puzzles** ♉

Once I attuned myself to pick up reports such as these, I found they came rushing at me. Some, however, led nowhere.

Ty Cobb had a Negro mascot named Rastus, and it would be thrilling to find that Ty's batting average went up when Rastus was around and down when he wasn't. But as far as I can tell, there was no connection.

Bill Stern, the old sportscaster, once told of a catcher with the Runyonesque name of "Evil Eye" Billy Earle, who played a century ago. Earle was a pretty good hitter, with a lifetime .286 average. Yet in five years he was shunted to five different teams and finally allowed to drift out of the major leagues completely, though he was batting .348 when he left, in 1894. The rap on Earle was that his evil eye was upsetting his teammates. Unfortunately, after a century, the trail on Evil Eye has grown too cold to follow.

I was also excited about a character named "Evil Eye Finkle," whom the Chicago Cubs reportedly hired in the 1930s and '40s to jinx the Cubs' foes. But I have so far not been able to track "Evil Eye" down; even the Cubs' front office couldn't remember that far back.

I welcome any help from readers on these and other phenomena to investigate.

♎ **What Is It?** ♎

What should we call this phenomenon? I've already rejected "super-stition." "Witchcraft" carries too much emotional baggage. "Abnormal" or "paranormal" aren't quite right, because if it does happen, then it is normal. "Psychic sports," maybe? Duke University, which pioneered research in this area, used an umbrella term, "psi." Perhaps the term "non-ordinary reality" is the most satisfactory.

There are three reasons for studying this side of sports.

1. Curiosity. These phenomena are reported outside the playing field. The theater, for instance, has a rich body of lore concerning ghosts. And how many credible people (Winston Churchill, Queen Wilhemina of the Netherlands) say they have seen Abraham Lincoln's spirit? Lincoln

attended seances and foresaw his own death in a dream. Jimmy Carter claimed to have seen a UFO. Surely these phenomena must be happening on the field, too.

2. Sports can help psi investigators. It's a perfect laboratory. In everyday life, how do we measure "good" days and "bad" days? It often has to be subjective. But in sports, one wins or loses, gets a hit or makes an out, scores a goal or misses the net. So parapsychologists can collect data.

3. Psi investigators can help sports. All other things being equal—physical, mental, coaching, equipment—victory may go to the side that makes best use of this still under-used tool.

⚐ Psychics Can Strike Out, Too ⚐

I do not include many instances of failure in these pages, though there must be many. The principal reason, of course, is that failures generally do not reach the newspapers, so there's no way for me to follow up on them. However, some stories I looked into did not stand up to investigation.

One woman written up in *The New York Times* reportedly enjoyed great success at psychically picking winners at the race track. She readily agreed to replicate the experiment with me, though she said ahead of time that she does better when she's personally at the track. Each morning I phoned her at her apartment and got her selections for the nine races that day at Aqueduct Raceway outside New York City.

After a week I concluded that she did no better than the least successful *Racing Form* handicappers, and not quite as well as that publication's sharpest one. Furthermore, if I had bet $2 on each of her horses, I would have had a net loss for the week. (But I would also have lost money betting on the *Racing Form's* picks, too.) Whether she could have done better at the track itself, I cannot say.

The 1992 Baltimore Orioles had finished next to last in '91, but I picked them to win the pennant in '92. Indeed they challenged the Toronto Blue Jays throughout the first half of the season, once getting within one game of tying them for the lead. So I called on a suburban Maryland psychic to help. The first game she worked, the O's lost by

some whopping score, about 15-3. For the next several weeks they played losing ball while I begged the witch to desist. She refused to quit, however, and gamely continued sending her energy while the poor O's slipped further and further behind. They finally dropped to third, where they ended up.

But other trails did lead to apparent success, which only proves, I suppose, that, like everyone else, some psychics are better than others.

♉ You Be the Judge ♉

How does one explain these phenomena? I leave that to each reader to answer for himself. My job is to gather the data. I have tried to check each report as thoroughly as I can. But why these things happened, I don't feel competent to answer with authority, and I welcome your interpretations.

Of course it is possible that nothing "extra-normal" is taking place in many of the following stories. Perhaps the players simply believe in their talismans and get a strong psychological boost from them. But it doesn't matter why the good luck, or bad luck, charms work. If they *do* work, for whatever reason, it's a shortsighted team that would refuse to use them.

I should add, however, that when Laurie Cabot conducted an experiment for me in 1976, sending psychic energy to the New England Patriots, they turned their record around from 3-11 in 1975 to 11-3 in '76. The first game she tried it, the Pats defeated the Oakland Raiders 48-14. That was the only game the Raiders lost all year as they stormed to the Super Bowl. (You can look it up.) The point is that no one else, least of all the Patriots or their opponents, had any idea of what was going on!

It is not my intention to challenge anyone's belief systems. And it makes no difference to me, or to the others in this book, whether a reader believes the stories or not. If reading these pages makes you uncomfortable, please put the book down, and let us remain friends. But if you are comfortable, I hope you'll turn the page and let us together explore a new dimension of baseball that has never been charted before.

I hope you'll enjoy the voyage as much as I have.

PART II

THE BASEBALL ASTROLOGER

In thy breast are the stars of thy fate.

Johann Friedrich von Schiller

I find my zenith doth depend upon
A most auspicious star.

Shakespeare, The Tempest

Chapter 4
Wes Ferrell Sees Stars

FOR FOUR YEARS, 1929-32, Wes Ferrell won 91 games as a temperamental righthander for the Cleveland Indians. In those days, the Indians were a perennial fourth-place club—actually, they were a dismal second-division club without Wes, whose won-lost record for the period was 21-10, 25-13, 22-12, and 23-13.

Ferrell later told sportswriter Shirley Povich of the *Washington Post* that he had had his horoscope read. When he rechecked his day-by-day performances, he discovered that he had won when his stars were favorable and lost when they weren't.

"He makes no bones about his faith in astrology," Povich wrote in 1938 after Wes had joined the Senators. "Astrology rules his life. He is a confirmed disciple and credits astrology with curing the soreness in his arm when all other methods failed, including the ministration of medical and bone specialists, quacks, and voodoo doctors."

Like Nolan Ryan, Ferrell was an Aquarian (mid-winter). His brother Rick, a catcher, was a Libra (early fall). In 1935-36 they formed baseball's greatest-ever brother battery while toiling for the Red Sox. Boston was a lackluster sub-.500 ball club without Wes, who almost single-handedly kept the Sox respectable, running up marks of 25-14 and 20-15.

He told Povich it was no coincidence when Rick broke his finger and manager Joe Cronin was beaned on the same day in 1936. Cronin was also a Libra, and the stars said it was going to be a bad day for Libras.

Did astrology help him? Pitching for a succession of forgettable clubs, Wes ran up 193 victories; that's four more than his contemporary, Lefty Gomez of the Yankees, who is in the Hall of Fame.

> *Like vintage years of wine, we have the qualities of the*
> *year and of the season in which we are born.*
>
> *Carl Jung*

CHAPTER 5
"Oakland's Heavenly Body"

LAURIE BRADY WAS A STUNNING IRISH REDHEAD who went from a convent to a beauty contest, a Hollywood screen test, belly dancing and owning a string of nightclubs, and then to astrologer for the Oakland Athletics in 1976.

She was the first, and so far only, full-time paid astrologer for a major sports team. Sportswriters dubbed her "Oakland's heavenly body."

How did a good-looking girl from Illinois become Charlie O. Finley's official stargazer? To find out, I ascended to her cluttered office-apartment on a sunny summer afternoon while sailboats scudded on blue Lake Michigan far below.

I was skeptical. How can a star—a tiny speck of light—possibly inflence us here on Earth, millions of light years away? And how can a lady who knows nothing of baseball tell a hard-bitten manager he should bench his center fielder next Wednesday?

Brady's sign was Cancer (early summer), a "water" sign along with Scorpio (mid-autumn) and Pisces (late winter). These usually connote psychic ability, she told me, adding that hadn't found many athletes with these signs. Brady believed herself to be psychic, an atavistic power she said she inherited from her grandmother. She said she knew psychically of her brother's death before she heard the actual news.

Once, driving her convertible back from her mother's home, Brady suddenly pulled off the road, "which I had never done, and I could feel the hackles on the back of my neck going up. A streak of lightning zig-zagged down the highway. If I hadn't pulled off...."

Sinking her savings from some Hollywood bit parts into a Chicago nightclub, the Gaslight Club, Laurie was soon opening clubs in Washington, New York, Los Angeles, even Paris. She was a wealthy woman before she was old enough to vote.

Brady became interested in psychiatry. Reading through Carl Jung's works, she found that astrology kept popping up. "He wouldn't even see a patient until he had first made out his horoscope," she said. "At first, I

was skeptical. I was going to write a book to debunk it."

She decided to do charts on 500 complete strangers. She left questionaires in beauty shops and wherever she could. Using them, Brady was able to pick out the days when the subject was divorced, when a parent died, and other moments and events of significance in the subject's life. "That's what hooked me," she said, "because 500-to-one, that's not chance."

In England doing research for a magazine, she attended a swingers' convention with a psychiatrist and got birth data, palm prints, and handwriting samples on 500 people there. "We both came to the same conclusion: All but three of the ladies had the same astrological aspects. The three said later they were there to please their husbands, it wasn't their lifestyle." The psychiatrist shook his head and told her, "Scientists won't believe this; there are never statistics that are this perfect."

At the time we spoke, she was still working with psychiatrists. "Thematic perception tests take many years," she said. "I can come in and in 10 or 15 minutes tell what the problem is." She said she predicted the Liz Taylor-Richard Burton divorce and remarriage, and also claimed to have held some shaky marriages together, but at times would advise a couple that they weren't compatible. They may have ignored her advice, "but they nearly always [called] me on the way to the divorce lawyer," she laughed.

Her business grew rapidly. She wrote for the *National Enquirer*, and appeared on radio and TV talk shows. On one occasion, she said, 76,000 callers to one show jammed the phone lines at Universal City in Hollywood.

In 1970, on assignment for the *Chicago Tribune*, Laurie did horoscopes for the entire Chicago Cubs team and predicted Leo Durocher's departure as manager. She wrote a sports column, "Astro Sports," for the Chicago *Fans* magazine, and started a book on astrology in sports "to see if new babies had any potential." She got as far as page three. "I'm afraid it was too technical," she smiled.

Finley, owner of the Oakland A's, lived in Brady's apartment building on Chicago's Lake Shore. Meeting in the elevator in 1970, Finley asked, "Well, am I going to win the Series this year?" Though the A's were doing

well, Brady told him no. When she turned out to be right, he scratched his chin and shrugged, "Maybe there's something to this, because you were so positive, even when we were on a winning streak."

She did tell Finley his A's were about to win five straight division titles and three world championships. That's just what they did from 1971-75, including World Series rings 1972-74. Finley, who had an eye for the ladies, invited Laurie to his box in Oakland.

At the 1971 World Series, Brady met Roland Hemond, vice-president of the White Sox. "My wife was expecting," Hemond recalled, "and Laurie predicted a son. She said the first year he would have a lot of physical problems and then he'd be fine. And she gave us the personalities of each of our children, whom she had never met. She amazed me with her accuracy." Two years later Brady told Hemond that Sox stars Dick Allen and Ken Henderson would suffer injuries. "They took place just as she said," he said with a shake of his head.

On September 29, 1973, Vice-President Spiro Agnew said he would never resign. The next day, on TV, Brady said he would. Ten days later, he did. In 1972, Laurie says, she had predicted that Richard Nixon would resign. In 1974, he followed Agnew.

Laurie told me she had been asked to predict crops, when to start new corporations, and all manner of things. But she insisted she was not in astrology to make money. "I'm a great believer that a lot of psychics lose their powers when they get greedy. My clients made 500% when I put them in gold in 1973. I didn't even have time to call my broker!" On her TV show, "Astro Business," she predicted three stock market drops in 1974, 1975, and 1976. "I've done better than the economists who study high finance."

Brady once dated Joe DiMaggio and, of course, did his chart. She said she foretold that Chicago Bears running back Gale Sayers would have his career cut short by injury; that coach Don Shula would bring the lowly Miami Dolphins to the Super Bowl; that hockey great Gordie Howe would retire and then make a comeback at the age of 42. "He laughed at me," she said, but she was right.

After Laurie's prediction of five Oakland division titles came true in 1975, Finley asked her to do his personal chart. "I told him the date he'd

go into a hospital, and he went in that day. The doctor said he'd be in traction for a week, but I said, 'You'll be out next Friday,' and he was."

That was enough for Charlie O. He signed her as the A's official stargazer.

Brady hasn't always been right. That winter she cautioned Finley that Reggie Jackson (36 homers) and Ken Holtzman (18-14) would both slump at the end of '76. If he were thinking of trading them, she advised doing it early while their trading value was still high. Whether on her advice or not, Charlie did deal both to Baltimore, where they both did, in fact, start slowly (Jackson .225, Holtzman 5-6 by mid-year). But they finished strong, Jackson adding 50 points to his average and Holtzman going 9-5 over the second half.

Brady told me she could determine what day a player's energy level would be low, what day he would be accident prone or apt to make errors of judgment, when he might get into fights with umpires, what kind of mood he'd be in, or if anything was bothering him. Off-the-field problems, she noted, are as important as on-the-field ones, because a player takes them into the game with him.

Finley asked her to make up astrological charts for all 25 A's players for every day of the 1976 season and mail them to manager Chuck Tanner.

Tanner threw them in the wastebasket. "I think he was skeptical," Laurie smiled in an understatement. But she insisted that he did use her charts, at least at first.

Against the Yankees on May 9, the A's were going against their old teammate, Catfish Hunter, who had beaten them four straight times. Mike Torrez was scheduled to pitch for the A's, but Brady warned against it. "He was low that day," she explained. Tanner, of course, ignored her. Sure enough, Torrez was losing 3-2 after five innings, when Tanner finally yanked him. Oakland won 4-3 in 12.

For *Newsweek,* she predicted that Oakland would beat Boston twice June 15-16. They did, 3-2 and 4-1. On another occasion, she told me they were going to lose "Friday and Saturday, but there's a possibility of winning one game Sunday." But they lost both games Sunday "because [Tanner] didn't use the players I told him to." However, she realized, a

manager couldn't always change his lineup to conform to her charts.

Brady told me she didn't put much stock in the sun signs alone. "Too general," she said. "The inner planets—Mercury, Venus, Mars—are more important."

Now that she had had a good, detailed look at a great many athletes' horoscopes, I asked her if there was anything that stood out as a sure-fire mark of an athlete?

"You have to have a well-aspected Mars," Laurie replied without hesitation. "Mars is the planet of aggressiveness, energy, strength, and stamina. Without it, you don't have the ability to kick or punch. People with a weak Mars tire easily; they're always getting cuts and bruises. Either the sun or moon should be right on top of Mars or 90 degrees or 120 degrees away."

Mars can also mean sexual energy, especially if it's right on top of Venus, the planet of love, Laurie added. The combination produces "such sex appeal that even if you're ugly, this magnetism just radiates." Athletes usually have a powerful Mercury as well, which has to do with speed and the ability to react quickly.

Hitch your wagon to a star.

Ralph Waldo Emerson

CHAPTER 6
Stars of Baseball

BY THE GREAT HEAVENLY STARS! Was Mark McGwire born to hit home runs? You bet your sweet ephemeris he was. And so were Juan Gonzalez, Mickey Mantle, Mike Schmidt, and Jimmie Foxx.

McGwire was born October 1, 1963, an excellent day to be born if you want to grow up to be a big league home run king. For that makes him a Libra (September 23- October 22), and no sign in the zodiac has run off with more home run titles than Libras.

When McGwire and Gonzalez battled it out for the American League title in 1992, they were carrying on a tradition of Libra sluggers going all the way back to 1876. Libras have captured 41 crowns. Since the average is about 20 per sign, Libras have won twice as many as they should have.

By contrast, Geminis (May 21-June 20) have won only seven in 123 years. Three were by Lou Gehrig; the last one by Andres Galarraga, in 1996.

What are the odds on that—41 Libras and only seven Geminis? I asked mathematician Pete Palmer, co-editor of *Total Baseball*. He punched the numbers into his computer and came up with the answer: More than one million to one.

I call it the Gemini Curse.

Other Geminis have been cut down by the Curse. Frank Thomas and Jeff Bagwell both threatened to conquer it in 1995, but perhaps because they blew out their candles on the wrong day, they failed.

I don't know if I believe in astrology. But I can count. And the numbers make me pause and scratch my head.

The chart below shows how signs of the zodiac align themselves with the months of the year. It's followed by a list of home run champs paired to their astrological signs.

SPRING	♈ ♉ ♊
ARIES	Mar 21 - Apr 19
TAURUS	Apr 20 - May 20
GEMINI	May 21 - Jun 20
SUMMER	♋ ♌ ♍
CANCER	Jun 21 - Jul 22
LEO	Jul 23 - Aug 22
VIRGO	Aug 23 - Sep 22
AUTUMN	♎ ♏ ♐
LIBRA	Sep 23 - Oct 22
SCORPIO	Oct 23 - Nov 21
SAGITTARIUS	Nov 22 - Dec 21
WINTER	♑ ♒ ♓
Capricorn	Dec 22- Jan 19
Aquarius	Jan 20- Feb 18
Pisces	Feb 19- Mar 20

HOME RUN STARS

SIGN	TITLES	SOME HOME RUN CHAMPS
Libra	41	Schmidt 8, McGwire 4,* Mantle 4, Foxx 4, Klein 4, Gonzalez 2, Mathews 2
Pisces	29	Ott 6, Rice 3, Murphy 2, Stargell 2, Allen 2,Baker 2, Strawberry, Murray
Sagittarius	29	Kingman 3, Foster 2, DiMaggio 2, Matt Williams
Aquarius	28	Ruth 12, Aaron 4, Banks 2, Oglivie, Larry Walker, Howard Johnson, Bench, Gorman Thomas
Scorpio	22	Kiner 7, Griffey Jr. 4, McGriff 2, Bichette, Dwight Evans
	(20) Average	
Cancer	19	Killebrew 6, Canseco, Armas, Dawson
Virgo	18	Ted Williams 4, Fielder 2, Belle, Sandberg, Cepeda, Snider, Frank Robinson
Taurus	18	Jackson 4, Mays 4, Wilson 4, Hornsby 2
Aries	14	Cravath 6
Capricorn	14	Mize 4, Greenberg 4, McCovey 3, Mitchell
Leo	9	Frank Howard 2, Barry Bonds, Nettles, Yastrzemski
Gemini	7	Gehrig 3, Darrell Evans, Galarraga
	248	

* Does not include McGwire's major-league leading 58 in 1997, which he split between the American and National Leagues.

Odds on this distribution: more than one million to one.

Scorpio Sammy Sosa has the same birthday as I do, November 12. Neither of us has ever won a big league home run title, but astrologers say we are the sexiest men in the zodiac. (Eat your heart out, Mark McGwire.)

Note that almost two out of every three home run champs were born in the autumn (Libra, Scorpio, Sagittarius) and winter (Capricorn,

Aquarius, Pisces). My study of Wimbledon and U.S. Open champs shows that autumn is also the overwhelming season for tennis champions. So if you want your child to grow up to be a big league home run king, you should plan for him to be born after the World Series and before spring training. Warm-weather babies born during baseball season have about half the chance of becoming a home run champ as do the cold-weather kids.

For decades Aquarians—Babe Ruth and Hank Aaron—were the kings, until home-run hitters born under Pisces knocked them from their thrones. Pisces sluggers were later surpassed by Libras.

Ruth and Aaron, incidentally, were born almost exactly 39 years apart, Babe on February 6, 1895, and Aaron on February 5, 1934.

April 6, 1974, was a particularly good day for Aquarians. If Hank had let his eye stray from the sports page, he would have read in Sydney Omarr's horoscope column the following forecast for himself:

"Advancement indicated. Views are vindicated. You receive compliments from professional superior. You make significant gains. Profit potential increases.....Standing in the community is elevated."

That night Hank went out and hit his 715th home run to break Ruth's record.

♌ What Does It Mean? ♌

Palmer warns that one shouldn't count repeat winners. However, to count each winner only once would give Babe Ruth and Dwight Evans equal weight, which is obviously not right either. If we count every *champion* instead of every *championship,* the signs remain pretty much in the same order; however, the odds drop dramatically, because the total number is lower. It is not difficult to throw six heads in 10 tries, but it is infinitely harder to do it 600 times in 1,000 tries.

My feeling is that every Libra must compete against the 11 other signs and he lays his crown on the line every time he starts another season. It's a problem, but statisticians don't have a clear solution to it.

Astronomers scoff that a planet or star billions of miles away exerts an infinitesimal force upon us on earth. But perhaps the stars do not

cause home run champions to be born, but only mark, in some as yet unknown way, *when* they are likely to be born, just as a clock does not cause rush-hour traffic jams at 8 a.m. five days a week.

Not all slices of the zodiacal pie are equal. Cancer has 32 days, Pisces, 29, etc. And births are not distributed equally throughout the year, although authorities disagree on which are the high-birth months and which are low. One says Gemini (late spring) is high and Aquarius (midwinter) low. But another study is just the other way around. At any rate, the differences are not great, about 15% at the most. They hardly explain why Pisces has more than 10 times as many stolen base leaders as Cancer.

I've checked only sun signs because they're readily available, but astrologers say the position of the moon also has a strong bearing on us, especially on our emotions. Other planets also affect us.

Hospitals and police departments report a jump in murders, suicides, hemorrhaging, and births during the full moon. Do batting averages go up then also? What about injuries? Is there any correlation between sunspots and baseball performances?

Relationships like these intrigue me. A stubborn Scorpio, I also checked other categories—U.S. presidents, congressmen, Oscar winners, heavyweight champs, Nobel Prize winners, and astronauts. All showed results well outside the law of averages. If you feel blue because your birthday doesn't hold out hope for becoming a major league champion, you may be cut out for something else. *(See "Other Sports" at the end of this chapter.)*

Palmer was skeptical, so like a good researcher he did some scientific checking. He ran a massive computer study of all 9,366 men who played major league baseball from 1909 to 1981. His readout produced an almost perfect sine curve of births arranged along the calendar year.

The best time for a baseball player to be born is late summer (Virgo), which has produced 921 players, or 18% above average. Worst is early spring (Aries), with only 681 players, or 11% below normal. Virgos lead at every position except shortstop and third base. The chances of this distribution, Palmer reported, are 700 million to one.

Incidentally, this is similar to the result I got in a 1977 study of pro

football players. Virgo was way out in front, Aries next to last.

Oddly, although Virgos stand the best chance of making a big league team, they are not that outstanding after they land a job. They rank about average in combined batting average, home runs, ERA, and won-lost records. Virgos include Ted Williams, Randy Johnson, Frank Robinson, Roger Maris, and Larry "Nap" Lajoie. Virgos are supposed to be painstaking perfectionists. That certainly describes Williams.

It seems unfair that a man's birthday can give him an advantage in hitting home runs or pitching strikeouts. But life is unfair. Athletes are not typical of the rest of us. They're bigger, heavier, faster, with better hand-eye coordination and better muscle tone than most of us. They also differ, I now must add, in their birthdays.

I also did a detailed study of biorhythms and found absolutely no evidence to support that once trendy but now discredited theory. One would think that biorhythm has at least a basis in science and that astrology is sheer superstitious bunk. But I found the opposite to be true. *(See Appendix.)*

Let's check other categories of players—batting champs, pitchers, and base stealers. Do they show the same astrological profiles as home run sluggers?

Aries, the least likely to make the team, are the best hitters once they do sign a contract. According to Palmer, their combined batting average is .267, compared to the average for all signs of .262. (Leo is last with .259.)

In fact, the batting average curve is almost the direct opposite of the total players' curve, with above average totals for babies born from late winter through mid-spring (Pisces through Taurus).

My own study of batting champions tends to confirm Palmer's. Taurus Tony Gwynn was obviously born to hit a baseball. In 1997 he won his eighth batting title, one more than another great Taurian, Rogers Hornsby. Taurians in total are far ahead of any other sign. Ty Cobb's Sagittarians are second. This time winter signs come in last.

BATTING STARS

SIGN	TITLES	SOME BATTING CHAMPS
Taurus	35	Gwynn 8, Hornsby 7, Brett 3, Mattingly, Mays
Sagittarius	27	Cobb 12, DiMaggio 2, Larry Walker 2, Buckner, Kaline, Kuenn
Aries	24	Rose 3, Paul Waner 3, Sisler 2, Appling 2, Puckett
Pisces	22	Wagner 8, Ashburn 2, O'Neill, Reiser
	(19) Average	
Leo	18	Clemente 4, Heilmann 4, Yastrzemski 3, Alex Rodriguez, Garciaparra
Libra	17	Carew 7, Foxx 2, Oliver, Hernandez, Mantle
Virgo	17	Ted Williams 6, Lajoie 3, Frank Robinson, Bernie Williams, Franco
Gemini	17	Boggs 5, Al Simmons 2, Frank Thomas, Galarraga, Gehrig
Cancer	16	Oliva 3, Pendleton, Willie Wilson, Torre, Boudreau
Scorpio	15	Musial 6, McGee 2, Sheffield, Terry
Aquarius	14	Aaron 2, Lansford, Lynn, Ruth, Jackie Robinson
Capricorn	12	Madlock 4, Edgar Martinez 2, Matty Alou, Mize, Flick
	234	

Odds: 50 to one.

Pitchers show a different profile from hitters. Sagittarians like Steve Carlton have the best combined won-lost record and the best ERA. Yet oddly they are down near the bottom in producing individual ERA champs.

Greg Maddux obviously chose his birthday wisely. He's a Pisces like Lefty Grove, Grover Alexander, and Kevin Brown, and they have more ERA titles than any other sign.

Cancers (early summer) are last in won-lost percentage, but average in ERA champs. Geminis and Aquarians are last in ERA leaders.

The two leaders, Pisces and Aries, come next to each other on the calendar, but the other signs swing so wildly that it is obvious that the earth's journey around the sun does not explain the pattern.

ERA STARS

SIGN	TITLES	SOME ERA CHAMPS
Pisces	34	Grove 9, Alexander 5, Maddux 4, Kevin Brown
Aries	29	Joss 2, Saberhagen, C Young, Sutton, Phil Niekro
Leo	27	Clemens 6, Mathewson 5, Wilhelm 2, Pedro Martinez 2, Guzman
Scorpio	23	Walter Johnson 5, Seaver 3, Gibson, Marichal
Libra	21	Palmer 2, Scott, Waddell, Podres, McCormick
Cancer	20	Hubbell 3, Coveleski 2, Magrane, Sutcliffe
	(19) Average	
Capricorn	18	Koufax 4, Appier, Wynn, Lyons, Randy Jones
Virgo	16	Guidry 2, Chandler 2, Randy Johnson 2
Taurus	15	Spahn 3, Smoltz 2, Newhouser 2, Walsh 2
Sagittarius	12	Tiant 2, Gomez 2, Carlton, Burdette, Swan
Gemini	9	Chance, Parnell, Cicotte
Aquarius	9	Ryan 2, Hammaker, Bosman, Reynolds, Ruth
	232	

Odds: 3,000 to one.

Question: Which sign has produced the only man to win crowns in ERA, batting, and homers? The answer is Aquarius and Babe Ruth. Note, however, that Ruth decided to concentrate on home runs, the strong suit

of Aquarians, and not on pitching, where they are weakest.

Power pitchers differ astrologically from finesse pitchers, who are generally the ERA leaders.

Scorpios are far out in front, producing more than one out of every five strikeout champs. Could it just be chance? Yes. Once in about 20 million times.

Aquarians, a distant second, look strong, but that's only because Nolan Ryan is one of them. Without Ryan, they'd be next to last. So Nolan was bucking the odds.

Scorpio is followed by the three winter signs, then by the three spring signs. The other two autumn signs and the three summer signs bring up the rear.

Recent strikeout kings—Randy Johnson, Roger Clemens, Hideo Nomo, and John Smoltz—have not gotten any help from their signs, which are all average or below.

STRIKEOUT STARS

SIGN	TITLES	SOME STRIKEOUT CHAMPS
Scorpio	50	Walter Johnson 11, Feller 7, Waddell 7, Seaver 5, Bunning 3, Vander Meer 3, Randy Jones 3, Schilling 2, Gooden 2, Gibson, Hubbell
Aquarius	22	Ryan 11, Dean 4, Pascual 3, Reynolds 2
Capricorn	19	Carlton 5, Koufax 4, Cone 2, Wynn 2, Bridges 2
Taurus 2,	19	Spahn 4, Walsh 3, Smoltz 2, Newhouser Rijo
	(19)Average	
Pisces	18	Vance 7, Alexander 6, Richard 2, Roe, Hughson
Virgo	18	McDowell 5, Randy Johnson 5, Nomo, Lemon, Lolich
Leo	18	Clemens 5, Langston 3, Drysdale 2, Pedro Martinez, Andy Benes

Gemini	17	Grove 7, Rusie 5, Score 2, Smoltz, Bannister
Aries	15	Young 2, Vaughn 2, Blyleven, Lonborg, Phil Niekro
Sagittarius	12	Gomez 3, Radbourn 2, DeLeon, Jenkins, Grimes
Libra	12	Mathewson 5, Roberts 2, Marquard, Brecheen
Cancer	10	Barker 3, Tanana, Downing, Coveleski
	230	

Odds: 200,000 to one.

Look at the winter babies! However, Satchel Paige, a midsummer Leo, might have moved that sign up a few notches.

↗ **Running With the Stars** ↗

Stolen base champions produce the most amazing odds of all.

Once more, it's cold-weather babies, like Rickey Henderson, who have swiped more titles than anyone else.

Rickey is a Capricorn, born on Christmas Day. Back in 1887 Hugh Nicol, who was born on New Year's Day; set the all-time record of 138 steals in one season. Another Capricorn speedster, Max Carey, led the league in steals 10 times.

Capricorn is closely followed by late-winter Pisces, which has 31 stolen base champs. Pisces is apparently the sign for speed. It's first among astronauts, Indianapolis 500 winners, and NFL running backs. Cool Papa Bell, the Negro leaguer sometimes called the fastest base runner of all time, was a Pisces. How many titles would he have won in the major leagues?

Two sunburn signs, Leo and Cancer, have won a total of only seven titles.

The last Cancer to do it was Willie Wilson in 1979. Now there's a man who outran his stars. (Don't despair, Cancers—you're tops among football linebackers!)

STOLEN BASE STARS

SIGN	TITLES	SOME STOLEN BASE CHAMPS
Capricorn	34	Henderson 12, Carey 10, Taveras, Nicol
Pisces	32	Campaneris 6, Wagner 5, Reiser 2, Hunter, Ashburn
Sagittarius	26	Cobb 6, Minoso 3, Bruton 3, Biggio, Moreno
Taurus	25	Aparicio 9, Mays 4, Lopes 2, Eric Young, North
Virgo	24	Coleman 6, Raines 4, Cuyler 4, Frisch 3
Gemini	21	Brock 8, Lofton 5, Werber 3, Galan
	(18) Average	
Libra	16	Wills 6, Womack 3, Patek, Murtaugh, Crosetti
Aquarius	11	Jackie Robinson 2, Schoendienst
Scorpio	11	Case 6, Stirnweiss 2, Rivers, Tolan
Aries	11	Sisler 4, Grissom 3, Milan 2, Veras, Hunter
Leo	4	Reese, Frey, Isbell
Cancer	3	Willie Wilson, Rivera, Hartsel
	218	

Odds: 10 million to one.

Will the day come when scouts pack an ephemeris, along with a stopwatch and notebook, to look at a budding star? Will managers plan their pitching rotations with horoscopes? It may be in the stars.

♓ **Other Sports** ♓

If you feel blue because your birthday doesn't hold out hope for becoming a major league ballplayer, you may be cut out for something else. Here are leaders in several other fields I studied:

	FIRST	SECOND
Heavyweight champs	Capricorn	Cancer
Tennis champs (men)	Scorpio	Capricorn
Tennis champs (women)	Libra	Sagittarius
Quarterbacks	Leo	Aquarius
Running backs	Pisces	Scorpio
Wide receivers	Capricorn	Libra
Offensive linemen	Leo	Scorpio
Defensive linemen	Virgo	Capricorn
Linebackers	Cancer	Scorpio
Punters	Virgo	Scorpio
Kickers	Aries	Leo
Prize-winning writers	Libra	Taurus
Academy Awards (men)	Aries	Taurus
Academy Awards (women)	Scorpio	Aries
Nobel winner, chemistry	Virgo	Aries
Nobel winner, physics	Sagittarius	Aquarius
Nobel winner, medicine	Gemini	Virgo
Presidential victories	Aquarius	Pisces
Members of Congress	Virgo	Sagittarius
Astronauts, U.S.	Pisces	Scorpio
Astronauts, Russian	Pisces	Sagittarius
Longevity (men)	Taurus	Aries
Longevity (women)	Gemini	Capricorn

I once bet Janet Guthrie, the Indy 500 race driver, that she was a Pisces because she wanted to be an astronaut. "I am," she said "but it's also the top sign in racing. Look it up." I did, and of course she was right.

Capricorn heavyweight champion boxers include Muhammad Ali,

George Foreman, Smokin' Joe Frazier, Floyd Patterson, Jersey Joe Walcott, and Jess Willard. We have never had a Leo champ.

According to tennis writer Tim Joyce, from 1912 to 1999 in the U.S. Open and from 1922 to 1999 at Wimbledon, only a total of three individual cups were won by Aries.

Autumn and early winter are the best season for tennis champs. Scorpio men include Ken Rosewall and Roy Emerson. Libra women are led by Martina Navratilova, Helen Wills Moody, Maria Bueno, Alice Marble, and Pat Hingis. Sagittarians include Billie Jean King, Chris Evert, and Monica Seles.

Joyce predicted an upset in the 1999 U.S. Open, saying, "Keep an eye on seventh-seeded Serena Williams." Indeed, Williams defeated Hingis in an all-Libra final.

In 1985 I did a study of 139 women champions going back to the 1880s. They almost broke my computer! On average, each sign should have won about 11.5 titles. The actual range was 44 Libras, 26 Sagittarians, one Aquarian, and no Aries. According to Tim Joyce's figures, the odds on that distribution are 10 million to one.

When, in 1976, a statement denouncing astrology as a hoax and astrologers as charlatans was published by a group of 185 scientists, I called several, who admitted they had never done any research on the subject and had signed the statement only because they were asked to. So I proposed a bet. I'd pay each of them $100 for every Aries and Aquarian woman who wins a major title, and they'd pay me for every Libra and Sagittarian. They all turned me down. Too bad. Through 1999 I would have made $9,000.

CHAPTER 7
Predicting the Past

IF ASTROLOGY CAN PREDICT THE FUTURE, it should be able to "predict" the past. I gave astrologer Maude Chalfant of Washington, D.C., the birthdays of several athletes and asked her to describe each man, knowing nothing else about him. In five instances, I then asked her what might have happened on a particular day in his career.

The final birthday—April 14, 1941—and event was offered to Laurie Cabot of Salem, Massachusetts. The readings follow. See if you know who the players are. Answers are at the end of this chapter.

≈1. February 6, 1895 ≈

A very emotional chart. He either had an explosive temper or explosive energy, so if he were a baseball player, I would think he was one of your home run hitters, or a heavyweight boxer.

He had sort of a tormented life, lots of problems. There were definitely drinking problems in his natal home. His father or mother sat on him real hard. There was probably quarreling in the home, or a separation or divorce or loss of parent. He was extremely independent and hard to manage.

There's a heavy emphasis in the House of Show Business, and Sports in general. He probably loved kids, and I would imagine he had many love affairs.

Event: October 1, 1932. I'm wondering, was this person having some health problems? It could be a chart where a person was retiring, or the end of his career was coming. It could have been a home run if this was a baseball player.

♍ 2. August 30, 1918 ♍

He is terribly independent, probably was very hard to manage. He might have been frustrated, had to control himself, or was made to control himself. He has a fiery way of thinking, and fire in his hands.

Anything to do with the hands would be good for him. I'm sure he had emotional problems, although I could be very wrong. There's a strong emphasis on his House of Self-Undoing.

♏ 3. October 25, 1923 ♏

A terribly intense person, fixed and stubborn, but very sweet-natured, likeable, and very lucky. He might be a quarterback if he's in football. He would be a power hitter if he's in baseball.

Event: October 5, 1951. I think this event was a very happy one. The moon was touching Venus, meaning that sweet things were coming to him or being stirred up. Jupiter in his House of Work also means good things. Uranus, the planet of Change and Surprise, was exactly over his Pluto (energy). So, whatever this was, it was probably unexpected and very strong and explosive. And very fateful. It's kind of hard to read whether it was pure luck or whether it wasn't.

♉ 4. May 18, 1946 ♉

He's a Taurus, which is a fixed, sort of placid, slow-moving person who is very interested in money. He's very lucky with money. He might be a little erratic with it, but i think he will make good money.

He probably has tremendous energy and heavy hands.

I'm sure he's very charming. Probably women like him. He could be flirtatious and have lot of affairs.

I suspect he's a little hard to handle because of that stubborn Taurus sun: "Don't tell me what to do." He probably loses his temper very easily. He might have a tendency to flare up and speak more angrily than he means to. He's probably very impulsive and quarrelsome.

Event: October 18, 1977. A terrific massing of planets in his House of Work. The north node of the moon—the lucky part—the moon itself, the sun, Pluto, and Venus, which usually means nice things and gifts, are all in his House of Work. This was just a fantastic day with all those planets—half of all his planets are all in one place. On the whole, I would think this was a fortunate event.

♐ 5. November 22, 1950 ♐

I'd say he's a sweet person, perhaps idealistic. He probably likes to talk a lot, is jovial, likes people. He could be a good storyteller. Women like him.

A lot of energy. And he has the Saturn-Mars square found in a lot of boxers, so I would say he has power also.

Event: September 23, 1978. This is so complicated, I can't make a flat statement whether it was good or bad. But it was of great significance, because there were aspects after aspects [of the stars] hitting his chart that day. There could be something very surprising about this event.

Saturn is right on the edge of his House of Career. Saturn is the planet of the ending of things, so this was very significant in his career and life.

Was he hurt, or could there have been anything involving a hospital in this situation?

There was something mysterious, something about this whole thing. It may be that he had a sense of mysterious things happening around him that he felt very strongly. I sort of lean to something very disappointing, but I can't quite back it up.

But there is a strong emphasis on hospitals and health.

♈ 6. April 14, 1941 ♈

This is a strong, strong person. Super strong. A lot of self-confidence. Even before he opened his eyes, he knew what he wanted. He's aggressive. And stubborn. He wanted what he wanted when he wanted it. He rushes into things, just shoots out and does what he thinks he has to do. When he's playing, he's totally into it. His whole being—his brain, his body—all are working for one thing.

He's got tons of physical energy. His friends would think he's courageous. His enemies would consider him pushy.

Sometimes he can be very strong-willed, rebellious, anti-social when Mars hits him. All of a sudden he can turn into a really raging per-

son. These are tendencies from birth; he may have mellowed since then.

I would think he's extremely dexterous. His timing is excellent. He moves like a panther. He moves beautifully.

He's got a quick mind, like a hair-trigger. Really, really fast mental chemistry. He's quarrelsome and independent. He needs power, he likes to be on top.

He would also have to learn the value of sexuality. I think when he was younger he would rush into love affair, but I think he's outgrown that. He's very charming and attractive. He may not be beautiful, but he's bewitching. I see a little gleam in his eye.

He's dominating and attracts people who have a lot of needs, especially females, very sexual, who want a lot and are very demanding. I like him, whoever he is. I would want to stay away from him with a 10-foot pole, as a female. But I think he's dynamite.

Event: August 1, 1978. I get the feeling there has been a lot of strife going on. He may have been very aggressive in the few days just before this. He's so damn strong, you'd think he could overcome almost anything that goes wrong. But he may have been a little disappointed. Things may not have turned out the way he wanted them to.

♉ Answers: ♉

1. Babe Ruth's "called shot" home run.
2. Ted Williams.
3. Bobby Thomson's "shot heard 'round the world" that beat the Dodgers for the pennant.
4. Reggie Jackson's three World Series home runs.
5. Lyman Bostock is shot to death.
6. Pete Rose's hitting streak ends.

Part III

Psychic Baseball

The unthinkable phenomena of parapsychology appear somewhat less preposterous in the light of unthinkable propositions of modern quantum physics.

Arthur Koestler

*Ask and it shall be given you, seek and ye shall find,
knock and it shall be opened unto you.*

Matthew 7:5

CHAPTER 8
Connie Johnson's Wish

"I NEVER INTENDED TO PLAY BASEBALL, never thought about playing professional ball," said Connie Johnson, who pitched for the Kansas City Monarchs, Chicago White Sox, and Baltimore Orioles from 1940-58. "It happened something like a dream, a miracle that God did to get me what I wanted. The strangest thing I ever heard in my life.

"See, I used to pray. I was born in Stone Mountain, Georgia, in 1922. I worked with my father in a quarry. I knew a chauffeur who would come back from a trip and tell me about all the places he had been—New York, Chicago, New Orleans, California—and I would sit there and just see them in my mind. So I started praying; I said, 'God, let me see them.'

"Then I forgot about it."

Johnson had been a softball player when he was shoved, against his will, into pitching on a baseball team against the Toledo Crawfords, a professional black team. "I struck out so many people, they just stopped playing ball and stood in a line to see how many I could strike out."

Then Connie went back to work at the quarry. "I was sitting there thinking about travel, but I didn't have but $14. I said, 'Man, I've got to go. I don't know how, but I've got to go.' I threw down my hammer and started over the hill. I said, 'I can't tell my mother, I'll run away.'

"Then something said, 'Turn around.' I looked and saw a big black LaSalle car. It was six or seven blocks away, but for some reason I knew who it was, I knew it was someone coming for me to play ball. I said, 'Now first it's going to stop in the blacksmith, the blacksmith's going to show him to my daddy, then they're going to look for me.' And it was just like I said it would be. My daddy said, 'They want you to play ball with them,' and he introduced me to Jesse Owens, the owner, and Oscar Charleston, the manager."

They told Connie to put on his best black suit and come with them. They gave him a uniform several sizes too large—he had to roll the pants and sleeves up and pin his hat so it wouldn't fall off. The crowd thought he must be a clown.

When they told him to "warm up," he asked, "Warm up what?" The

fans were laughing their heads off. But about the fifth inning "they stopped laughing and started applauding, because I was striking out everyone."

After the game a happy Charleston asked him if he wanted a chicken. Thinking that was his pay for the day, Connie told him, "Give me a whole one," ate it all, and stood up to go home.

"Where you going?" Charleston demanded. "We want you to play with us. You know who you played today? The Kansas City Monarchs, the best team in the league! Man, you were great out there, you shut them out."

Johnson started thinking: "Where you going?" he asked.

"Oh, different places."

"Well, you'll have to ask my mother."

"There's no use asking me does he want to go," Mrs. Johnson said. "I know he wants to go." Charleston promised to take good care of him. "O.K.," she said, "then you can go."

They drove to Texas, where, as Connie recalls, "I saw some beautiful sights!" He sat and looked up at "the prettiest moon I ever saw."

Connie woke his roommate at three o'clock in the morning. "Hey, man, what's wrong?" the startled player mumbled.

"Do we go to Chicago?"

"Do we *what*?"

"Do we go to Chicago?"

"Yeah, we go to Chicago."

"Do we go to New York?"

"Yeah."

"What about California?"

"No, we don't go to California."

"What about New Orleans?"

"Yeah, we go to New Orleans."

Connie sat down and wrote his mother: "This is what I want to be."

His long journey took him to the Monarchs in 1940, Europe in '43, the White Sox in '53 and the Orioles in '56, when he had his best season, 14-11.

"After I started playing ball, I realized that was what I wanted, but I

never planned on it," Johnson said. "It was just like I was supposed to do it, and that was it. The strange thing—the thing that got me—was when I saw that car and I said, 'They're going to stop there, then they're going to stop there....' At first I didn't understand it. Now I realize I had prayed to go, and it happened. It all came true."

*I can't exactly describe it, but as I looked at the putt,
the hole looked as big as a wash tub. I suddenly
became convinced I couldn't miss.*

*Jack Fleck, amateur golfer,
on defeating Ben Hogan in the 1955 U.S. Open*

CHAPTER 9

Called Shots

I REMEMBER IN 1946 WATCHING HANK GREENBERG, the major league home-run champ that year, stepping into the batter's box in Yankee Stadium. Perhaps it was just youthful fantasizing, but somehow I could just "see" a home run in his bat. Yes, a moment later Hank did pull a line drive into the left field seats. I've tried to do that again on occasion, but I've never been successful.

That is, not until Lenny Dykstra of the Phils gritted his teeth in Game 4 of the 1993 World Series and banged one over the fence. Anyone who saw that game on TV with the closeups of Dykstra's jaws tightened and his eyes narrowed in intense concentration, must have also felt that Lenny was going to do it.

Calling home runs is apparently a pastime in many a major league dugout.

Ω **Babe Ruth** Ω

The most famous call of all, of course, was Babe Ruth's legendary pointing to center field against Cubs pitcher Charlie Root in the 1932 World Series. Babe hit 43 homers in 472 at bats that year, including the Series, so if he did call his shot, the odds against delivering on the audacious gesture were about 11-1.

Did he call it, or didn't he? The debate raged for half a century, the Yankees generally swearing that he did, and the Cubs generally sneering that he didn't. Was Babe pointing to the bleachers or just pointing to Root? (And which finger did he use?)

Then, in the 1980s, a home movie of the historic game was discovered in a Chicago fan's attic, where it had lain for half a century. It showed the Babe clearly cocking his finger like a pistol and snapping off three "shots"—pow, pow, pow—just before Charlie delivered. My own impression after seeing the film is that Babe was pointing, not to center field, but to the Cubs' third-base dugout, where the players were giving

him a good old-fashioned "riding."

There's better evidence to support the legend of Babe and little Johnny Sylvester in the '26 Series. The day before the fourth game Ruth visited the boy in the hospital and promised to hit a homer if Johnny got well. Babe not only hit one homer, he hit three. And Johnny did get well.

♍ Oscar Charleston ♍

Some authorities call Oscar Charleston the best black player of his day, 1915-35. John McGraw called him the best player, period. Charleston played center field like Willie Mays, slid into bases like Ty Cobb, hit like Ted Williams and blasted more balls over the fence than any Negro Leaguers except Josh Gibson and Mule Suttles.

At some time—no box score has yet been found—Charleston and the legendary pitcher, Smokey Joe Williams, teamed up in a game against the great Walter Johnson. According to legend, Johnson struck Charleston out three times while battling Williams to a 0-0 draw. On his fourth at bat Charleston reportedly said, "You done struck me out three times, this time I'm going to hit you out of here." Then he hit a home run to win the game 1-0.

Ted Williams heard the story as a youngster from an old man in Connecticut. When Ted got to the big leagues, he met Johnson and asked him if the story was true.

"He just nodded his head," said Ted. "He just nodded his head."

♉ Red Fields ♉

Negro Leaguer Wilmer "Red" Fields of the Homestead Grays remembered calling "about four of them." "I could usually tell my wife whether I was going to do good or bad that night," he told me. One called shot came against the New York Black Yankees. Two came in Brantford, Ontario after the Negro Leagues folded, and the fourth was in Venezuela in 1952 against Johnny Hetke of the St. Louis Browns.

♈ **Hack Wilson** ♈

In 1930, his 56-homer year, the Cubs' Hack Wilson booted a ball in center field to let in a run against his pal, pitcher Pat Malone. Hack felt so bad about it, he promised to get the run back "this very inning"—and did, with home run number 52.

≋ **Superman Pennington** ≋

In 1946 Art Pennington, outfielder for the Negro League Chicago American Giants, joined an exodus to Mexico of many of America's best players, black and white, lured by *muchos pesos* waved by millionaire promoter Jorge Pasquel. One of the pitchers Art faced there was Sal "the Barber" Maglie, who would go on to the New York Giants and Brooklyn Dodgers.

As Pennington told Brent Kelley in *Voices From the Negro Leagues*, his wife was in the hospital on the Fourth of July. He told her to be sure to listen on the radio, because "I'm gonna hit you a home run today." While she tuned in, "Maglie threw me his curveball, and I hit him over the Fourth of July sign in Puebla."

≋ **Tom Lasorda** ≋

Dodger manager Tommy Lasorda tells the story of managing a team in Venezuela when Dodger shortstop Bill Russell (lifetime 46 home runs) asked in English at a clubhouse meeting what time Lasorda planned to leave after the game.

Tom liberally translated the question into Spanish for the other players: "He said, 'Milt Wilcox [the opposing pitcher] isn't going to last an inning and that he personally is going to hit a three-run homer off him.'" Russell turned white as a ghost, Lasorda laughs.

The prediction proved to be inaccurate, however. Bill didn't hit the three-run homer off Wilcox until the fifth inning.

⨯ Hank Aaron ⨯

On August 31, 1957, Hank Aaron belted several drives out of Cincinnati's Crosley Field during batting practice. "How did you like those?" he asked Milwaukee pitcher Lew Burdette.

"O.K.," shrugged Burdette. "But sock one at 10 minutes after eight."

The game began at eight, and Aaron hit a first-inning homer. The clock on the scoreboard registered 8:10.

⚎ Bob Aspromonte ⚎

Bob Aspromonte, a .252 hitter with only 60 lifetime homers, called three of them!

Bob had hit a total of exactly one in his life when he joined the expansion Houston Astros in 1962. He called the first one that year when young Billy Bradley, who had been hit by lightning and temporarily blinded, visited the Astros locker room. Billy was going in for surgery in the morning and asked Aspro to hit a homer for him. "How about a bunch of base hits?" replied Bob, who had hit only one in his life. Billy looked downcast. "O.K.," Bob said, "I'll try."

After three failures, Bob got the homer. He hit only 10 more the rest of the year.

The operation was a success, but two more were needed. The next year Billy was back in the locker room before his second operation. "I'll do my best," Bob promised. After four hitless trips, he came up in the 10th and blasted a grand slam.

Six weeks later Billy was back for his final operation and a final plea. "I don't hit many homers," Aspro said, "but with you here, I really believe I'm going to hit one." In the first inning against the Mets, the bases were loaded again, and Bob unloaded again for another grand slam. He hit eight homers that season, two of them for Billy.

Bob averaged a homer every 59 at bats that season, so the odds against calling one of them was 59-1. The odds on calling two were 59 x 59 or 3,481 to one. The odds on all three are 3,481 x 59 or 170,5690 to one.

Eleven years later Aspromonte himself was blinded when a car

battery exploded in his face. He went to Billy's former surgeon, who restored his vision 40 percent.

♎ Ed Hobaugh's Last and Only ♎

On September 2, 1963, Washington pitcher Ed Hobaugh (lifetime average .127) "had a very strong feeling that I was going to hit the ball out of the park." He did. It was the only big league home run Hobaugh ever hit and came in his last at bat in the majors.

Bill Deane, former research associate at the Hall of Fame, says only 34 other men have ever gone out with *sayonara* homers.

♍ Graig Nettles ♍

In the Yankees big comeback of 1978, Graig Nettles led the league with 32 homers (one per 18 at bats). He called two of them in two days, relief ace Sparky Lyle reports in his book, *The Bronx Zoo*. According to Lyle, fans draped a banner, "Albany Loves Nettles," over the upper right field railing. Before the game on August 26, Graig announced, "I'm going to hit one right over that sign," and, says Lyle, "son of a bitch, he hit it right where the sign was."

The next day Nettles hit another homer. "Well," he told outfielder Paul Blair, "only one more to go."

"What do you mean?" Blair blinked.

"I decided I'm going to hit two today," Nettles said.

"And son of a bitch, he did."

The odds against Nettles coming through were 18 x 18 x 18, or 1:5,832.

♌ Johnny Bench ♌

In the final game of the 1972 National League Championship Series between the Reds and Pirates, Pittsburgh took a 3-2 lead after six innings.

In the seventh Cincinnati's Johnny Bench, the NL home run king

with 40, struck out with the tying run on base. He stomped back to the dugout and told teammate Pete Rose, "I hope somebody's on base when I come up next time, because I'm going to get somebody."

Bench led off the ninth against righthander Dave Giusti, who had whiffed John back in the ninth inning of Game 3 to save a 3-2 win. "I couldn't hit him with a boat oar," Bench admitted. Nevertheless, "I wasn't up there for a triple," he told himself. As John tossed his extra bats away, he turned to hear his mother in a box seat calling, "Hit one, John!"

He did hit one, into the right field seats of Three Rivers Stadium, only his second home run of the year to the opposite field, throwing the game into a 3-3 tie. The Reds went on to win the pennant on a wild pitch.

♓ Bob Gibson ♓

Pitcher Bob Gibson hit 24 homers in his career. The next-to-last one came June 21, 1973. He told Cardinals batting coach Harry Walker before the game against Expos pitcher Bill Stoneman, "if he throws me that big curve, I'll hit one out of here." Stoneman did, and Gibson did.

♊ Darrell Evans ♊

Darrell Evans was making his debut with the Tigers on Opening Day 1984 against Dave Stewart. His wife LaDonna had been teasing him all morning. "She kept saying, 'You're gonna hit a homer the first time up. I know it.'"

Stewart "threw his best pitch. I knew it would be a fastball." Darrell smashed it into the upper deck.

♍ The Twilight Zone ♍

On August 8, 1986, Thomas Boswell of the *Washington Post* told what he called this "Twilight Zone tale":

A week earlier Baltimore pitcher Mike Boddicker caught two liners back to the mound, prompting pitcher Brad Havens to remark on the bench, "I've never caught a liner in my life." Mike Flanagan and two

other Orioles heard the remark. An inning later Havens caught a liner.

On August 6 the Orioles' Larry Sheets hit a grand slam, and Jim Dwyer, who had hit 50 home runs in his career at that point, said idly, "I've never hit a grand slam in my life." The same three Orioles heard that remark too.

"We looked at each other funny," Flanagan said. "We have a game where we call homers in advance. In eight years I've never joined in. But when Dwyer came up—with the bases loaded—all three of us were putting in a call."

Yep. Grand slam.

♍ **Devon White** ♍

Devon White says he called two. The first was called in honor of his new son in a game in Chicago in 1987, his best home run year with 24.

Four years later, May 13, 1991, White was with Toronto when teammate Kelly Gruber decided to hit a homer for his own newborn daughter, Cassie. He did.

So White, in an 0-for-11 slump, declared that he would also hit one for his daughter's first birthday and delivered a two-run shot that won the game.

♈ **Joe Carter** ♈

When Toronto's Joe Carter kissed his wife goodbye and left home for Game 6 of the 1993 World Series, he told her something special was going to happen that night. "I'm either going to catch the last out or drive in the winning run." A few hours later his ninth-inning home run off Philadelphia's Mitch Williams won the game and the Series for Toronto.

♐ **Ted Williams** ♐

The all-time leader in called-shot home runs, Williams apparently called six of his own, plus one by Arky Vaughn. "I get funny hunches that way," Ted told me, "but sure as I say something about them, they don't come true."

Once in Washington, Williams recalled, he promised a boy in a hospital he'd hit a homer for him. "And I happened to to hit one over the lights that night." He doesn't remember the date.

In his rookie season, 1939, Ted arrived in Detroit's Briggs (late Tiger) Stadium, which had received a new roof two years earlier. Ted unloaded one into the stands in his first at bat, against righthander Bob Harris (4-13 that year). "I hope that guy is still pitching when I come up next time," Ted told catcher Rudy York as he crossed home plate. "I'll knock it clear over the roof."

The next time up the count ran to 3-0. "You're not hitting, are you, Kid?" York asked.

"Yes, I am," Ted answered. A fat "cripple" came in and Ted smashed it into the upper deck, foul. "I'm still hitting," he warned York, then blasted the next pitch over the roof, the first man ever to do it. (It would be 18 years before Mickey Mantle duplicated the feat.)

"You weren't kidding, were you, Kid?" York said as Ted crossed home plate.

In his book, *My Turn At Bat,* Williams tells of facing Hal Newhouser, probably on June 17, 1946. Hal struck him out on three pitches, and back on the bench Ted growled, "Five bucks says if he throws that same pitch to me again, I'm gonna ride it out of here."

Wrote Ted laconically: "He did, and I did."

In his great .406 season of 1941, Williams called four homers, three of them his own.

On Labor Day in Fenway Park, he socked two "tremendous drives" 420 feet, over the bullpen. Between innings of the second game, Ted told the boy in the left field scoreboard, "I think I've got another one coming. Watch me next time up." In the sixth he unloaded one clear over the right field roof, which is at least 400 feet away and 60 feet high. It was the first ball ever hit out of the park to right, and only one man, Carl Yastrzemski, has done it since. But the ball was ruled foul. So Ted stepped in again and drove the next pitch far over the bullpen into the stands.

Williams hit 37 homers that year. It should have been 38. He hit Lefty Gomez of the Yankees like his proverbial "cousin," but by September 7 he hadn't hit a homer in Yankee Stadium all year. He promised to hit one

against Lefty that afternoon.

In those days parks had just a thin foul pole, and in his first time up Williams smashed one down the right field line that struck the pole, glancing off into foul territory. Although foul poles are actually in fair territory, the Stadium's crazy ground rules said a ball bouncing fair was a homer, one bouncing foul was a double. So Ted actually hit the homer, though he didn't get credit for it. (Give him 522 for his career, not the "official" 521.)

Williams' most famous home run was his shot to win the 1941 All Star Game in Detroit.

It was Ted's second All-Star Game. He had gone 0-for-2 in the 1940 classic, and he'd been telling his teammate, Jimmie Foxx, for weeks that he was looking forward to doing something big in this one.

When the National League came up in the seventh, Arky Vaughan, who had hit only four home runs so far that year, lined one into the upper deck to put the Nationals ahead.

In the American League half, Williams faced Cubs righthander Claude Passeau. Passeau was one of the first men to pitch the now common slider, which sailed into lefthanded batters on the thin parts of their bats. Ted would later indict the slider as one reason no one hits .400 any more. Passeau got two strikes on Williams, then threw a slider low. Umpire Babe Pinelli's thumb went up in the air, and Ted walked away, muttering about low National League strikes.

The A.L. was losing by two runs with one inning left to go. There seemed almost no chance Ted would get another time at bat. Yet "I had this funny feeling that I was going to get up there at least one more time and hit one," he told me later.

Ted had another premonition as well. Vaughan came up again in the ninth, and Ted says he had a feeling that Arky might park it again, and he did, to lengthen the Nationals' lead to 5-2. "Something seemed to tell me he was going to do that. Well, I figured I was going to get up there again, too."

In the Americans' do-or-die ninth, Passeau got the first out, and the fans began filing out of the exits as pinch hitter Ken Keltner legged out a lucky hit. Instead of two outs and the bases empty, Passeau now had one

out and a man on first. Joe Gordon singled Keltner to third, and the fans stopped to watch. Cecil Travis walked, loading the bases, bringing the great DiMaggio up, with Williams on deck.

Joe, who had just hit in his 46th straight game, hit a double-play grounder to short. Eddie Miller's toss to second got one out. A 90-foot throw from future Hall of Famer Billy Herman would end the game before Ted got up again. But Herman "fancy-danned" it, in his own words, and threw wild. First baseman Frank McCormick made a great stop to save one run, but Keltner scored to make it 5-4. Passeau should have had four outs by now. Instead he still had only two outs and two on as Williams stepped into the box and pumped his bat.

If Herman's throw had gone into the stands, DiMaggio would have been awarded second, and Passeau could have put Williams on. National League manager Bill McKechnie could still walk Ted to load the bases and take a chance on Dom DiMaggio. Or he could yank Passeau and put in lefty Carl Hubbell, whom Williams had never faced before. But, impressed with Passeau's strikeout of Ted on the previous at-bat, McKechnie decided to leave him in.

With a 2-1 count, Passeau threw another slider, the same pitch Ted had struck out on in the eighth. "I said to myself, 'This is it,'" Williams recalled saying to himself. "I shut my eyes and swung."

The ball climbed into a stiff crosswind as the partisan fans gasped, fearing it would be blown foul. Right fielder Enos Slaughter turned his back, hands on hips, craned his neck, and watched the ball smack the front of the roof, hang there for an instant, and fall back onto the field.

Williams leaped into the air, clapping his hands, and set off galloping and romping around the bases, frolicking, frisking, gamboling.

What are the odds on calling four home runs (his own, plus Vaughn's)? The odds are 12 x 12 x 12 x 47, or 81,216 to one.

The things that one can do when he is sincere and when his spirit and body are one is astonishing. The cornered rat has been known to turn on the cat and down him.... Women have been known to lift automobiles to drag children out from under them.

Koichi Tohei, aikido master

CHAPTER 10
Sadaharu Oh: The Zen Way of Baseball

IN 1962 HIROSHI ARAKAWA CALLED not one, but 676 home runs.

As batting coach for the Tokyo Giants, he was given a tough case—an ex-high school star who was spending his nights drinking on the Ginza and was about to be cut loose. The kid's name was Sadaharu Oh. Oh had a bad hitch in his swing and couldn't get his bat around fast enough. As a rookie in 1959, he hit .161 with seven homers. Oh means "king" in Japanese, and the fans were taunting him with the nickname, "Strikeout Oh."

Looking back on that period, Oh wrote in his book, *The Zen Way of Baseball,* that fortune is "as real as the ground you walk on." And his good fortune was Arakawa.

The first thing the coach said was, "You will do exactly as I say for three years."

Sighed Oh, "My drinking days were over."

Oh and the Giants visited the Dodgers' training camp in Florida and watched Frank Howard, with his enormous size, attack the ball. Obviously Oh couldn't do that. The solution, Arakawa decided, was to apply the Japanese psyche to an American game.

Arakawa was a devotee of aikido, "the Way of spirit harmony." He took Oh to see Ueshiba (pronounced *Way-shiba)* Sensei, or Master, the founder of aikido. As they watched, Ueshiba, in his 80s, five feet tall with snow-white beard, bushy eyebrows, and a flowing black kimono, defended against hefty wrestlers who rushed at him from all directions. With the flick of a hand, he sent them all tumbling. In Tokyo's leading judo center, I've seen an identical demonstration by an elderly master on one knee, who simply cupped his hand behind each attacker's neck as he rushed forward.

Both sensei were using *ki*, the life force that extends from below the navel and out through the fingertips. The kung fu film star Bruce Lee could reportedly knock a man down simply by pointing at him. Ueshiba used his opponents' force to double his own by drawing the other's ki to himself. "A child might do it easily," Oh writes.

The master held a wooden pole in front of him in a swordsman's ready position while Arakawa hit it as hard as he could with a bat. The pole didn't budge. "You have seen the focusing of energy," Arakawa said.

That fall an American All-Star team visited Japan—Pete Rose, Rod Carew, Mike Schmidt, and others. Arakawa held out his arms and invited the Phillies' 220-pound Greg "the Bull" Luzinski to bend them. "What if I break your arm?" Luzinski asked.

"Let's worry about that later," Arakawa replied.

Greg strained, his face turning red, but Arakawa's arms didn't move. "Luzinski used strength, but Arakawa used ki," Oh writes. "If you are dubious, this is an exercise you can try yourself. Ask a friend to hold out his arms. Unless he's very much stronger than you, you can bend them. Tell him to do it again, but instead of contracting his muscles, tell him to imagine that power flows from below his navel in a direct line to his shoulder and then through his arm, beaming outward through his fingertips through the walls of the room. He must keep his hands open, think about not using his strength to resist, and see what happens."

Meanwhile, however, Oh still couldn't hit an inside pitch. His baseball dreams seemed over.

"How can we get rid of that goddam hitch?" Arakawa growled. "We are going to have to be a little extreme." He picked up a bat and took a one-legged stance. Now if you hitch, he told Oh, you'll topple over. "And thus," Oh writes, "began the biggest gamble of my life."

Without aikido, Oh would not have learned to stand on one foot. Aikido requires balance and agility, impossible if one is not perfectly centered at the "one point," the energy center two fingers below the navel. If it was too high, in his chest, for example, he became top-heavy.

An elderly geisha, who had spent her life performing classical dances, gave Oh another valuable pointer. In dance the center of balance is the big toe, she said, rolling down her sock to reveal a toe gnarled and callused. Oh imagined "a thick iron bar" running through his kneecap and big toe to the center of the earth. What was the bar anchored to at the top? The bat, of course. By turning the barrel toward the pitcher, he was in perfect balance, like a tightrope walker with a pole.

Oh practiced hour after hour until his hands became blistered, and

the blisters became calluses that cut his face when he washed. Eventually he was able to stand "coiled and comfortable" for three minutes.

Aikido teaches the concept of *ma,* the space between two opponents. One must eliminate ma, make the opponent one's own, absorb his thinking, and become one with him. Tom Seaver and other Americans later recalled how unnerving it was to look in and see Oh standing there like a stork, calmly looking at them.

Finally Oh tried it in a game. The crowd laughed as he stepped to the plate and began their chant, "Oh, Oh, Strikeout Oh!" But he flicked out his bat and singled to center. The next swing was a low line drive that just got over the right field fence. It was home run number 40 in his career.

"Well, what do you say?" Arakawa beamed. "Shall we try beating Babe Ruth?" Oh was 685 behind the Babe, but, he writes, Arakawa "planted a goal that I might not have striven for on my own." Oh finished the 1962 season with 38 homers.

Next it was time to learn kendo, the "Way of the Sword." For three solid months that winter, Oh and Arakawa left home at 5 a.m., drove through cold, deserted streets, and worked far into the night before driving home to grab a few hours of sleep. In spare seconds, Oh read *Zen and the Art of Archery*.

The sword is held with a tight grip but loose thumb and forefinger, just as in batting. Drawing the sword from the sash requires a twisting motion of the torso, much as a batter cocks his hips before swinging. And the down stroke was the shortest, fastest path to the ball. (Here Oh disagrees with Ted Williams, who preaches the uppercut.) The focus must be where the power is to be concentrated, just in front of the plate. "Teach him to wait," Ueshiba counseled. By waiting, Oh found he could move the point of contact back, giving him an extra split second. (This sounds like a paragraph from Williams' book, *The Art of Hitting*). Then when Oh finally planted his foot, "power exploded in that instant." By the end of the winter, he could make contact harder and more precisely than he ever had before.

"Set your mind on Babe Ruth," Arakawa repeated. "You are going to beat him."

Arakawa still had other lessons to teach. "The enlightened one merges with the universe," he said. "He loses all sense of struggle." How could a professional athlete give up all desire to win? Oh wondered. But eventually he would feel that at bat the world became "a noiseless, colorless, heatless void, in which the pitcher and I together enacted our certain, pre-ordained ritual of the home run." The result was 40 home runs in 1963 and 55 the next year, a Japanese record.

Foes pulled a Williams shift on Oh, and pitchers walked him more than once a game. (He eventually passed both Ruth and Williams for most walks in a career.) Japanese teams played 130-140 games a year, and Oh never came to bat 500 times officially in any season. If he had come up 550 times, a big league average, he would have hit 60 homers several times and a McGwire-esque 70 twice.

Seaver said Oh could have hit 35 homers a year in the U.S. From 1966-74 visiting big leaguers walked him 80 times in 89 games, but he hit 22 homers in 286 at bats against them. That's 42 per 550 at bats. Ruth averaged 48; Aaron, 30.

Oh would retire with 868, or 51 per 550. If he had as many at bats as Aaron, he would have hit 1,254. How many men in Cooperstown could hit that many in any league?

Aaron came to Tokyo in 1974, leading Oh 733 to 634. Hank won a homer-hitting contest, 12-11, but Oh already knew that "I would probably surpass him."

"Oh fever" hit Japan in 1975 as he closed in on Ruth's 714 and passed it on the final day. Still ahead: Aaron, who had retired with 755.

By August 31, 1977, Oh pulled even. On the night of September 3 his mother suddenly appeared in the clubhouse with a gift of apples for everyone. "Her eyes spoke so much to me—certainty that I would make it that very night. When I left the locker room, I could feel in my bones that this indeed was the night."

In all, Oh hit 868 homers. As number 756 sailed into the bleachers, passing Aaron, Oh's first thought was to call Arakawa, because "without him, there would have been no record."

*The ball kept sailing. It goes over! I was so damned
shocked. Bucky Dent! How do you explain that?*

Mike Torrez, Red Sox pitcher

CHAPTER 11

Bucky Dent and Mind Control

SURELY THE MOST FAMOUS HOME RUN in the last 25 years was the one the
Yankees' Bucky Dent hit in the 1978 AL East playoff to beat the Red Sox.
Dent (.243) had hit only four homers all year when he stepped to bat with
two men on and the Yankees losing 2-0 and lifted a fly just over the
Green Monster at Fenway Park. The Yankees, once 14½ games behind,
won the pennant in one of the greatest comebacks in baseball history.

Dent told me the home run may actually have been born several
weeks earlier on the sands of a Florida beach. The Yankees had suffered
a disastrous series of injuries early that year, and Dent himself spent a
month on the disabled list. He spent it lying on the beach, "visualizing"
with chin on his fists. "You program," said Dent. "You think of what you
want to do, visualize yourself hitting or fielding. You can do it in basketball—practice shooting foul shots in your mind." He told of experiments
in which one group practiced on the court while another didn't touch the
ball but mentally visualized it going through the hoop. When the two
groups were re-tested, he says, the second improved more than the first.

Michael Murphy, in his delightful book, *Golf in the Kingdom,* speaks
of visualizing the flight of the ball before swinging. The ball, he says, will
then follow the "lines of force" mentally drawn for it.

Bucky's programing was not so specific as a game-winning home
run in the playoffs. He couldn't foresee the details. But he knew what he
wanted to happen, and, on the beach in Fort Lauderdale, he began seeing the thought become real.

But the story of the home run goes back even three years earlier
than that. If the battle of Waterloo was won on the playing fields of Eton,
was the 1978 American League pennant won in a classroom in Florida
in the spring of 1975?

That's where two White Sox rookies, Dent and pitcher Rich "Goose"
Gossage, along with 23 other nervous rookies, filed into classes in Sylva
Mind Control as part of an experiment by Sox general manager Roland
Hemond.

Mind control can help an athlete handle pressure, said Rich Herro,

the Chicago businessman who taught the White Sox class. "Until I became involved with the White Sox, I had never realized the tremendous pressure these young kids are under—kids, 18-19 years olds, in a highly competitive arena, for big money, fame, and glory. One out of 10 makes it. Tremendous psychological pressure. No wonder they have so many injuries. They're not taught to deal with pressure, and that's one thing we're trying to do with Sylva Mind Control.

"The athlete in camp who is the easygoing kind, nothing bothers him, has a better chance of making it," Herro continued. "The very serious, intent guy who always tries to excel can buckle under pressure. Learning to relax mentally but be alert physically is hard."

Herro noted there were many different "mind sciences"—mind control, hypnosis, Scientology, psycho-cybernetics, and Transcendental Meditation, for example. Both outfielder Roy White and catcher Thurman Munson of the Yankees were among the many big leaguers into TM.

"Some approaches are more meditative, but all deal with altering the state of consciousness," Herro told me. "It's a real thing. You can hook people up to an encephalograph and see the brain frequencies go down. TM is more relaxation, it's passive, an attempt to contact the inner self and inner feelings. Sylva is a more active meditation. It's motivational; it relies on concentration and focusing attention on something, or on nothingness. You try to discover where the problems are and the solutions. It utilizes physical actions as well as concentration and meditation to achieve something. It should be called 'Dynamic Meditation.'"

One thing Dent and Gossage learned is that failure communicates failure. According to Herro: "If a pitcher is afraid someone will let him down, that fear appears to be transmitted and is picked up by the other players. They subconsciously respond to it and do, in fact, fail and become part of the overall failure pattern."

"It helps off the field, too," said Gossage. The White Sox course covered 48 hours, but only eight were devoted to athletic skills.

"A ballplayer only plays ball for three hours a day," Herro said, "but off the field he has problems and worries. He's got a business, he may have had a fight with his wife. When he goes on the field, that carries

over." That's why wives were encouraged to take the course, too.

Herro felt his program could also cut down on injuries, many of which are subconsciously invited by the athlete himself, he said. "They're good excuses: 'I could have made it, but I had such-and-such happen to me.' Take a businessman whose business failed because he was in the hospital with a heart attack—he allowed the attack to take place. That was once a radical view, but it's becoming a more conservative view as we understand more about the body."

Former quarterback John Brodie, a devotee of Scientology, has written that good teams don't have injuries, bad teams do. Although an auto accident almost ended his own career, Brodie wrote that he was convinced he subconsciously brought the accident on himself because he feared advancing age and the competition of a hot rookie. Once he understood that, the pain in his shoulder disappeared and he resumed setting records.

Herro kept files on the players who took his course, and additional files on a control group of rookies who didn't. The 10 pitchers who enrolled were already a cut above the others. Their combined ERA for 1974 was 3.28, lumping all records together, major league and minor. This compared to 3.76 for the control group.

The Sylva students improved more than the non-students. Most moved up a step in '75, from the low minors to the high, or from the minors to the majors. Yet their ERA's remained about the same, 3.33. The other rookies went to 4.13.

One graduate, Ken Kravec, took one full run off his ERA, dropping from 3.41 at Knoxville to 2.41 with the same team in '75. In '77 he was 11-8 with the White Sox, and in '79 had his best season: 15-13, 2.74.

Another Sylva student, David Frost, stayed with Knoxville several years before reaching the California Angels in 1979, when his 16-10 record helped the Angels win the division crown.

But the shining stars of the course were Dent and Gossage.

Herro introduced his teen-aged daughter to Bucky, whose poster soon became a favorite among nubile girls all over America, "and it was the thrill of her life." Mind control didn't help Bucky's batting average, which in fact dropped from .274 to .264. But he did develop into a Gold

Glove shortstop, and, said Herro, "impressively overrode the sophomore jinx."

Gossage had had two previous trials with the White Sox. In 1973 his record was 0-4 with a horrendous ERA of 7.38. In '74 it was 4-6, 4.15. After Sylva Mind Control, Goose cut his ERA to 1.82, best in either league.

"Gossage was totally receptive to the training," Herro said. "He's the kind of person who is willing to look into anything new. Some people will not."

The following year Hemond planned to do another course for the regulars, but the players' strike and lockout ended those plans. In '76 Herro was occupied with his own business and couldn't do it. In addition, Bill Veeck, the new White Sox owner, may have been a little dubious, Herro thought.

"I've always felt frustrated that I didn't have time to pursue it further," Herro admitted. "I did it to show what could be done and hoped others would follow up."

Dent was traded to the Yankees in 1977, and Gossage was dealt to Pittsburgh, where he had 26 saves and cut his ERA to 1.62, making him one of the best relief pitchers in baseball. That winter Goose signed a multi-million-dollar contract with the Yankees, where he was reunited with his old classmate, Bucky.

♉ The Fateful Game ♉

Early in 1978 the Yankees were hit with injuries to key players and a bitter personality clash between manager Billy Martin and several of his stars. The Red Sox shot out to a 14½-game lead.

In midseason Bob Lemon replaced Martin in the dugout, and the injured returned to duty. Meanwhile, the Red Sox were suddenly hit with a rash of injuries and lost their lead in the biggest fold in baseball history.

The two clubs finished in a dead heat. They met in Fenway Park for a rare one-game playoff, New York ace Ron Guidry (25-3) against Boston's Mike Torrez (16-13), a former Yankee.

The Red Sox's Carl Yastrzemski homered just inside the foul pole to give Boston a 2-0 lead.

In the seventh, the tiring Torrez gave up singles to Chris Chambliss and Roy White. That brought up Dent, the weakest hitter in the lineup. It was a perfect spot for a pinch hitter, but the Yankees had no one left to bat for him.

Bucky may have brought something besides mind control lessons to the plate with him. After Dent hit himself on the foot with a foul and hopped around in pain, Mickey Rivers, in the on-deck circle, shoved a new bat into his hands and told him to "go hit a home run."

Years later Rivers told Torrez that the bat was corked, making it lighter and with more bat speed. Still later, Rivers denied that he was serious. We'll never know.

Just as fatal as the bat was Torrez's behavior. For several minutes while Dent held up the game, he stood on the mound, watching, without taking a few tosses to keep his arm warm.

Earlier, Dent had swung at a slider. In his book, *The Bronx Zoo*, bullpen ace Sparky Lyle says Bucky told third base coach Dick Howser, "If that son of a bitch comes in there again with that pitch, I'm going to take him into the net."

Torrez did, and, says Lyle, "Bang, there it went." Bucky put his head down and streaked toward first without even watching the ball. It sailed up into left field while everyone waited for it to come down for an out. Instead it just kept sailing over the short wall.

The game had been completely turned around; the Yankees now led 3-2.

Then it was Reggie Jackson's turn. Reggie also practiced visualizing. "When I want to turn it on," he told me on one occasion, "I get away from the plate. I stretch, control my breathing, and slow up my heart rate. I remind myself to see the pitcher's release and the spin on the ball. I imagine myself putting the 'sweet spot' of the bat in the hitting area just as the ball is getting there. I see a line drive going to center field. I don't want to try too hard or tense up. I mumble, 'All right, Reggie, just let it happen, let it flow. *Now*, let it happen!"

Jackson lifted his 27th homer into the right field bleachers to make it

4-2. Munson doubled in another run to make it 5-2. Gossage was waved in to protect the lead. "I'm a fastball pitcher," he told me, "they're a fast-ball-hitting club. It was them against me in the biggest game of my life."

In the bottom of the seventh, the Red Sox desperately needed a left-handed pinch hitter like Bernie Carbo, who they had traded to Cleveland. Red Sox skipper Don Zimmer had to call on righthanded Bob Bailey (.191). Gossage fanned him on three called strikes. It was Bailey's last at bat in baseball.

In the eighth, Goose gave up a double to Jerry Remy. He got Jim Rice, but Yastrzemski, Carlton Fisk and Fred Lynn all singled to make the score 5-4. With the tying run just 90 feet away and the Boston crowd howling, Butch Hobson stepped into the box, and Goose stepped off the rubber. He exhaled and let his mind visualize the Rocky Mountain peaks back home in Colorado.

"If you keep a level head instead of getting all excited, you're going to be better off," Gossage told me when we talked about Sylva Mind Control. "The mind functions best at low frequency. If you're upset, you might do something dumb in a tight situation. Now if I give up a hit in a crucial situation, I don't feel it's the end of the world. I feel I'll 'come down to my level,' as the saying goes. That's where mind control really helped me."

Then he stepped back on the mound and got Hobson on a high fast-ball for the second out. George Scott also went out on the same pitch, and the danger was over.

In the bottom of the ninth, with one out, Gossage walked Burleson. Remy hit a line drive to right that Lou Piniella lost in the sun, but he decoyed Burleson into stopping at second, and a lucky bounce landed the ball right in Pinella's glove.

That brought up the best hitter in baseball, Rice, who was having an amazing year with 444 total bases, to be followed by Yastrzemski, with the flag in center field blowing briskly away from the plate. "Lord," thought Graig Nettles at third, "all I could think of was Bobby Thomson and that '51 playoff home run!"

Rice hit a fly ball deep enough to score Remy if he had not held up at second. The Red Sox had one out remaining—the lefthanded Yaz, the

best clutch hitter on the club. "He's the greatest player I ever played against," Gossage says. "I just told myself that I wasn't going to let him beat me with a bad pitch. I wasn't going to throw him a lousy breaking ball. My fastball got me this far, and I was going with it."

Once again, Goose let his mind turn to the mountains. In a tight spot, "I just step off the mound and tell myself that, no matter what happens—even if it's the worst that happens—I'll be going home and enjoying myself pretty soon." Yaz, meanwhile, had spotted a hole at first base and concentrated on the pitch he wanted to hit there.

Then Gossage wound up and pitched. It was a fastball, low and inside, Yaz recalled. "I started swinging, and all of a sudden the ball jumped in on me. Goose has that kind of fastball. It has a lot of movement on it. I tried to hold up, and if I had, we might still be playing. But Gossage made a hell of a pitch, and I popped it up."

The greatest pennant race in a quarter of a century was over.

The universe is not only queerer than we suppose. It is queerer than we can suppose.

J.B.S. Haldane,
Nobel laureate, physics.

CHAPTER 12
Darrell Evans' Close Encounter

DARRELL EVANS IS NOT A FLAKE. He was active in the Baseball Chapel Movement. From his father, who worked on casings for the space shuttle at the jet propulsion lab in Pasadena, he developed "a sense of wonder. My dad loved to read, and so do I." He read the encyclopedia "by the hour" and began looking through telescopes when he was 12. "I used to wonder what it must have been like for Columbus and Magellan sailing across a world they were told was flat. The human spirit is amazing."

In 1973 Darrell, by then the first baseman for the Atlanta Braves, batted .281 and hit 41 homers, one more than his illustrious teammate, Hank Aaron. But by '81 Evans had been traded to San Francisco, his homer total had sunk to 12 and his batting average to .258. On June 10, 1982, the 35-year-old Evans was at the lowest period of his career. He was batting .216 with only five home runs. The Giants were 13½ games behind, and manager Frank Robinson benched him. It looked like the end of the road.

After the game that night, Darrell drove to his home at Pleasanton, outside San Francisco, on a steep hill not far from the Livermore airport. On the deck of the house he slumped into a seat overlooking the canyon and the lights of the airport. The moon was out, the night was clear and warm.

He blinked. There, about 100 yards away, he and his wife LaDonna saw something hanging in the sky. "It was triangle-shaped with a wingspan of about 30 feet. Like a flying wing," Darrell recalled. "It had a line of red and green lights, and it had a bank of white lights in the back. The fuselage was an opalescent charcoal-gray. It looked like steel and sloped down to a dome that had no windows."

At first they thought it must be an experimental plane from the airport. But the object hadn't come from that direction, and "the lights were bright and white, not at all like the lights on an aircraft." The craft made no sound at all; even the Evans' two dogs watched without barking. "I think we knew from the start what it was. I'm sure it was a UFO."

LaDonna whispered to him to get a camera, but Darrell just wanted

to watch. For several minutes the Evanses and the object watched each other. "It definitely wanted us to notice it." When it dipped its wings as if to say, "O.K., you see us," Darrell went up to take a closer look.

But as soon as he did, it flew away, making "funny turns." "It seemed to say, `You've seen us, but you're not going to take our picture,'" Darrell recalled. The craft flew off over the house "about a million miles an hour."

For several days the Evanses watched the newspapers and TV, but no one else reported seeing a strange object. "It was almost as if they had singled us out," Darrell recalled. The Evanses assumed people would think they were crazy, so they didn't mention what they had seen. (They were in good company, however—former president Jimmy Carter also claims to have seen a UFO.)

Injuries on the Giants put Darrell back in the lineup. For the second half of the season he batted .267, and the Giants suddenly awoke; for the rest of the year the team played the hottest baseball in either league. By season's end the Giants were battling the Braves and Dodgers for the division title and ended up only two games behind Atlanta. Darrell and the team both showed a marked difference before and after:

	EVANS				GIANTS		
	AB	H	AVG	HR	W	L	PCT
Before June 10	165	39	.216	5	26	32	.448
After June 10	300	80	.267	12	61	43	.586
Total	465	119	.258	17	87	75	.537

"The whole thing has been incredible," Evans declared. "We smile all the time now. Nothing can be bad any more."

In '83 Darrell had his best season in 10 years. He batted .277, almost doubled his home runs with 30, and was voted to the All-Star team. But the Giants were going for youth, and at season's end they let him go. Who else would want a 36-year-old who was coming to the end of his career?

The answer was 18 other teams. He chose the Detroit Tigers and signed a $2.25 million contract.

By May 21 the Tigers had a 32-5 record and, though Darrell's stats for the year were down (.232, 16 homers), Detroit won the World Series.

The next year, 1985, the 38-year-old Evans slugged 40 homers, making him the oldest man ever to do that and the oldest ever to lead the league. Seemingly ageless, he followed that with seasons of 29, 34, then 22 home runs at the age of 41.

His final total, 11 in 1989, brought Evans to 414 lifetime—more than 150 of them after his brush with the UFO at the "washed up" age of 35. In the first 14 years of his career, Darrell averaged a homer every 7.5 games. In the seven years after his brush with the UFO, he hit them at the pace of one every five games.

As for the experience that night on the hill, he told me, "I guess I'd always hoped there'd be something like this, something that would come in peace. The craft seemed to be saying, 'We're here, and maybe because you believe, we're showing you.' Maybe it means they've gotten through the times we're going through now, that what we're going through doesn't matter."

What would he have done if he had been given the opportunity to board a UFO, as the character played by Richard Dreyfuss did in "Close Encounters of the Third Kind"? "It'd be a tough decision to leave your family," he said, "but...."

They say there's divinity in odd numbers,
either in nativity, chance, or death.

Shakespeare,
Merry Wives of Windsor

CHAPTER 13

The Book of Numbers

≈ Mort Cooper Wins Number 20 ≈

FOR THREE YEARS BIG MORT COOPER of the Cardinals had been trying to win 13 ball games. But the number 13 he wore on his back seemed to be a jinx. As a rookie in 1939 he went 12-6; in 1940 he was 11-12.

Finally, in 1941 Coop was rolling, with a 13-9 record in August, when bone chips in his elbow ended his season as the Cards lost the pennant to the Dodgers.

In '42 the Birds and Bums were in another pennant fight, Cooper was back on the mound and had run his win total to 13 again. Twice he tried for number 14, and twice he failed.

So he took off his jersey and borrowed number 14 from catcher Gus Mancuso. Since Coop stood 6'2" and weighed 210, compared to 6' and 185 for Mancuso, it must have been a tight fit. One can imagine buttons popping as big Coop went into a windup. But it worked: He won the game.

On his next start Mort borrowed brother Walker Cooper's number 15 and got his 15th win with ease.

When Brooklyn arrived for its final series in St. Louis, Mort sucked in his gut again and squeezed into Ken O'Dea's number 16 (O'Dea weighed in at 180). Mort battled Brooklyn ace Whitlow Wyatt for 10 innings to win, 2-1.

Coop kept changing and winning. No one on the roster wore number 17, so Mort had the numerals sewn onto his uniform and won again. Ditto number 18. He borrowed Harry Gumbert's number 19 for his 19th win, Coker Triplett's number 20 to win his 20th, and Johnny Beazley's number 21 for still another win, his ninth in a row. Mort's 22nd and final victory came with Murray Dickson's number 22, though it must have fit like a straitjacket—Dickson weighed 157.

The Cards ran out of games before Cooper ran out of uniform numbers. They won the pennant over the Dodgers by two games, thanks to Mort's 22-8 record and 1.78 ERA.

Inexplicably, Cooper went back to number 13 for the World Series against the Yanks, who batted him out of the box in the first game, 7-4.

Four days later they knocked him out again with six runs in five innings. The Cards recovered, however, and went on to win the game and the Series, four games to one. Their only loss was by Cooper, wearing his jinxed uniform.

≈ The Tigers' Jinx ≈

For three Detroit players, uniform number 15 was apparently a jinx.

Pitcher Johnny Gorsica was the first to meet the hex. After seven years with the Tigers and a 2-0 record in 1947, John put on number 15 in the spring of 1948, developed arm trouble, and never pitched another game in the major leagues.

Pitcher Art Houtteman was next to wear number 15. He was coming off a 7-2 season in 1947 but lost his first eight games in '48, many of them by one run. He ended with a record of 2-16.

Art begged his roommate, George Kell, to trade numbers. Kell agreed, scoffing, "I don't believe in all that stuff."

Houtteman went on to win 15 and lose 10 in '49.

Kell broke his arm.

)(The Miracle of Coogan's Bluff)(

In 1951 the New York Giants were breaking camp to start the season when manager Leo Durocher's wife, Laraine Day, dragged him and coach Freddie Fitzsimmons to a numerologist in the hotel lobby. "Laraine took that kind of thing very seriously," Leo winked.

In his book, *Nice Guys Finish Last,* Leo reported that the lady told Fred to change his uniform number from 6 to 5. Then, turning to Durocher, she said he was going to get off to the worst start he'd ever had, but by the time his birthday came around on July 27, things would change, "and I would go on to have the greatest season of my life and end up winning everything." And, "she was right."

The Giants lost their first game, and continued losing until they'd

lost 11 straight. On August 13 they were 13½ games behind the Dodgers, but made one of the greatest comebacks in history to beat Brooklyn in the last game of the playoffs on Bobby Thomson's fabled home run.

♈ Number 21 ♈

Roger Clemens had always worn number 21. In 15 years with Boston and Toronto, it brought him 233 wins and four Cy Young awards. Then in 1999 he moved to the New York Yankees, whose first baseman, Tino Martinez, wore number 21. So Clemens shrugged and accepted 22. He won 14 and lost 10, his worst season since 1985.

God heals; the physician takes the fee.

Ben Franklin

CHAPTER 14
Healers

♊ **Babe Ruth** ♊

ONE OF THE BEST-LOVED STORIES of Babe Ruth is the tale of saving the life of Johnny Sylvester during the 1926 World Series. Amazingly, Johnny's fever broke and his recovery began. According to *The New York Times*, the boy's father and doctors attributed it to messages from the Babe and other stars.

Less well known is another incident witnessed by writer Fred Lieb during spring training in Tampa, Florida. As Ruth trotted off the field, he waved to a paralyzed boy in a parked car and called his usual greeting, "Hello, Kid." The boy was so thrilled that he half-stood. "Tears were streaming down the face of the boy's father, and he had difficulty in controlling to his emotions. 'He stood up! He stood up!' repeated the father. 'It's the first time in two years. If he has stood up once, he can do it again!'"

Lieb never saw the boy again and didn't know how the story came out. But these and similar tales made him wonder if there was more to these miracle cures than just an inspirational word from a charismatic athlete. Perhaps, Lieb wondered, Babe was a "healer," one of those reportedly gifted people who can impart healing energy just by the laying on of hands.

♍ **Tito Fuentes** ♍

They called Fuentes a "hot dog"—a show-off who made easy plays look hard and played with that extra panache that made him the center of attention. When the Giants' shortstop stepped up to bat, he retraced his steps of the previous at bat—that is, if he had gotten a hit. He tapped his bat handle on the plate, gave it a flip and caught it in mid-air. If he swung and missed, he spun completely around, flipping his bat like a baton. He wore a ring on every finger and jewelry around his neck, one dedicated to Santo Barbara, his protector.

Tito is not Catholic. His faith comes from Africa, by way of Haiti, and

then to Cuba, where Fuentes was born. Africans in the New World often gave to Christian saints the attributes of the gods they had worshipped in Africa. In *Shango in the New World,* William Bascom says Santo Barbara is identified with Shango, the Nigerian Yoruba god of thunder.

"I don't believe in many things," Fuentes told Jim Hawkins of *The Sporting News.* "You have to prove things to me. I don't believe in Gypsies or people reading cards of telling fortunes or things like that." But he believed in witch doctors, he said, "because I know it worked for me."

When Tito started with the San Francisco Giants in 1966, the flashy second baseman injured his left shoulder. "Every 10 days it would pop out. The Giants told me I had to get an operation. But the doctor said there was no guarantee."

Giants outfielder Matty Alou, a native of the Dominican Republic, offered help. "He suggested I see this guy in the Dominican Republic who had cured him. I didn't believe it was going to work, but I went to see him anyway. I figured, what did I have to lose?

"He put a few leaves on my shoulder, he touched me and prayed. And my shoulder never popped out again. I hate to talk about it because I know it's hard to believe. But believe me, it works."

Eight years later Fuentes developed a problem with his back. "I went to see all the different doctors in San Francisco and during spring training, and they all said something different. They put me in the hospital in traction for 25 days, but the minute I went back on the field, it hurt again. The pain was so bad, I couldn't sit. So the Giants said I had to go to the knife. Hey, no knife for me!" Tito said.

"My housekeeper told me about a guy in San Salvador who had cured her son who was born deformed," he continued. "I couldn't believe it when she told me what he had done. But I wrote him a letter anyway and told him what was wrong with me.

"He sent me some leaves to use to make tea and some stuff, like cocoa butter, to put in a single line down my spine. He said to use it every day for 15 days, but he didn't guarantee anything until the 21st day. He said, 'Don't start celebrating until then.'

"Again I didn't believe it. But I figured, why not take a chance and

see if it works? If it didn't, I could still have the operation. After 21 days I went to the Giants and said, 'I'm cured.' They said, 'Come on, you haven't even been to see the doctor.' But I missed only one game the second half of the season."

The first witch doctor charged $10 to fix the shoulder. The second bill came to $37 to cure the back.

"The doctors in San Francisco all got mad at me when I told people that," Tito said. "But I just said, 'Hey, man, I gave you guys first shot.'"

♎ Luis Tiant ♎

The Red Sox ace with the herky-jerky windup, *El Tiante* was both a pious Roman Catholic and a follower of Santo Barbara. He wore all white off the field, including shoes and hats, and devoted his off-field time to thanking God for the good things life had brought him. He ate his meals alone on the road and worshiped at a private shrine in his home. Controlling one's mind, he explained, is as important as controlling one's pitches.

In 1975 Tiant developed a sore back, perhaps a result of his distinctive windup. Reporters kept harping on his age, 34, and said he had lost his effectiveness.

A neighbor, June Elam, was a practitioner of acupuncture and Shiatsu massage. "We don't believe in filling up bodies with pills and medicines," she told Ed Fitzgerald in his book, *El Tiante*. "We study the diets used by the Zen Buddhist monks, who were known for their long life spans.... It sounds like a lot of witchcraft, but we're really not crazy. We're simply trying to get back to a tradition that people had thousands of years ago in the Orient, when they were very spiritual and liked to live in harmony with the universe."

Elam suggested massaging Tiant's back according to the Chinese clock, that is, at one o'clock in the morning. "If you massage at the right time, it gives the whole body a boost." She also prescribed ginger root compresses. "You grate enough ginger root to make a pile the size of a golf ball. Then you wrap it in cheesecloth and dip it into a pot of water with the exact temperature of 158 degrees.... Then you just dip towels

into the water and press them against the sore area. This gets the circulation going."

Finally, June put Luis on a regimen of Bancha tea, the only tea, she said, that doesn't contain carcinogenic dyes. If someone at dinner opened a wine bottle, she gently took Tiant's glass away and pushed a cup of tea forward instead.

Meanwhile, Dr. Nathan Shapiro was also taking x-rays, prescribing exercise, and giving Luis ultrasonic treatments.

Between the two of them, Tiant was back in action on September 11. He pitched a no-hitter against the Tigers for 8⅔ innings before a scratch hit broke it up.

♎ Darryl Strawberry ♎

Saying he had been born again, the perennial bad boy credited his pastor and prayer for healing a separated left shoulder after he slammed into an outfield wall on June 15, 1991. "I couldn't sleep," he had told reporters. "My shoulder was throbbing all night. It kept waking me up. It's destroyed my whole swing. It's one of the hardest things I've been put through as a player; I'm practically crying about it."

The doctor told Straw the only cure was rest, and the team put him on the disabled list. Then, as Darryl told *Sports Illustrated*, "my pastor prayed for me all night and the next morning. He calls me up and tells me that if I come in to Bible study that day, the Lord was going to heal my shoulder. He laid hands on me and prayed for me, and before I knew it, I took off my sling and had no pain."

The doctor pronounced him ready to play against the Mets that night. However, Strawberry sat out the 15-day disabled period. On his second night back, July 4, he homered his first time up and went on to hit .289 for the rest of the year. "The shoulder is *there!*" he exulted.

Darryl's stats, before and after:

	AB	H	HR	AVG
Before 7/3	183	41	7	.224
After 7/3	322	134	21	.289
Total	505	175	28	.265

PART IV

LUCKY CHARMS

*If a man look sharply and attentively, he shall see Fortune;
for though blind, she is not invisible.*

Francis Bacon

TESSIE,
You Are The Only, Only, Only.

Words and Music by Will R. Anderson.

Moderato con moto.

Piano.

Tes - sie is a maid - en with a spark - ling eye,
Tes - sie has a par - rot that she loves quite well,

Tes - sie is a maid - en with a laugh, _____
Pol - ly's just a learn - ing how to woo, _____

5139-4

Who is there that, in logical words,
can express the effect music has on us?

Thomas Carlyle

CHAPTER 15
"Tessie" Conquers All"

CAN A SONG PSYCH A TEAM to the championship? Boston fans think "Tessie," a hit Broadway waltz, did that for the Red Sox and Braves six times between 1903 and 1916. When Boston fans lustily bellowed "Tessie" at the top of their lungs in the postseason, their teams were unbeatable.

Some pundits blame the Red Sox's troubles after 1918 on the "Curse of the Bambino," which they ascribe to punishment for selling Babe Ruth to the New York Yankees. It could just as well be argued that the team's curse began after the fans mysteriously stopped singing "Tessie." The lilting, albeit at times cacaphonous rendition of the once-popular love ballad hasn't been heard in a Beantown ballpark since 1916, and Boston hasn't won a World Series since 1918.

There are other instances of teams psyching themselves with music—most notably, perhaps, the story of Kate Smith singing "God Bless America" at Philadelphia Flyers' hockey games. In 1974 her recording was played before 40 Flyers games; Philly won 37 of them. In the Stanley Cup finals, the Flyers were leading the Boston Bruins three games to two when they asked Kate to sing in person before Game 6. She did, to the greatest ovation of her career, and the Flyers left the ice with a 1-0 victory and their first Stanley Cup.

In '75 Smith gave a repeat performance before the seventh game of the Cup semifinals against the New York Islanders. The Flyers won again, and went on to their second Stanley Cup

There is another parallel to "Tessie"—the 1986 National League playoff and World Series. Though millions watching on TV were unaware of it (because it came during commercial breaks), the Shea Stadium PA system blared Frank Sinatra singing "New York, New York" 18 or 20 times at every home game against the Astros and Red Sox. I, a Boston fan, became sick of hearing Old Blue Eyes. I don't believe that Bill Buckner's fateful error in the last inning of Game 6 was entirely unconnected with the maddening song. Others may scoff, but they'll never convince me.

Were the effects of Kate's and Frank's singing simply coincidence or luck? Or can music actually effect the outcome of a game?

These stories might also be examples of what students of the psychic call Tibetan "Tantric" magic, in which one person can draw on energy from others. It's the principle of Dracula, for instance, who imbibed his victims' life force along with their blood.

We all believe that 50,000 howling fans can give a charge of energy to athletes on the field. It's called the "home field advantage," and it is real—the home team does win some 55% of the time in the major leagues, which is a pretty good betting edge.

In the early days of this century, when great-great-grandpa was wearing knickers and rolling hoops, fans were much more a part of the game than they are today. The energy with which they zapped their favorite athletes was almost palpable. And in no city was this more true than Boston, with its screaming, adoring fans known as the Royal Rooters.

Baseball was different in another sense back then, 80 or 90 years ago. A day at the park was mostly, though not entirely, a male activity—with spitting, cigar smoke, and probably a lot more cussing than is heard in the grandstand today. Above all, most of the fun of going to a game came from the chance to bet. Back then "sportsmen," as they were known, laid wagers on almost every inning, or even every pitch, and the Royal Rooters were probably the most famous such "sportsmen" in America.

They were a colorful, gregarious bunch. Their leader was Mike "Nuf Ced" McGreevey (sometimes spelled McGreavey or Greevey), who owned a saloon near the third base entrance to the old Huntington Avenue Grounds. He got his nickname because he ended all baseball debates with an imperious "'Nough said." Alongside him were Johnny "Jack" Keenan and the city's leading politician—pudgy, diminutive John "Honey Fitz" Fitzgerald, grandfather of President John Fitzgerald Kennedy.

Music hath charms to soothe the savage breast,
To soften rocks or bend a knotted oak.

William Congreve

♎ The Royal Rooters ♎

The first mention of the Royal Rooters was in the Temple Cup Series of 1897, forerunner of today's World Series. Although Fitz, McGreevey and the rest of the Rooters demonstrated great lung power and enthusiasm, the Baltimore Orioles defeated the Boston Beaneaters in five games.

It would be six years before the Rooters got another chance; indeed, it would be six years before baseball saw another postseason series. But by 1903 a new Boston team, the Pilgrims, won the flag in the new American League.

The Bostons had the AL's home run champ—Buck Freeman, who clubbed 13 taters, most of them over the 280-foot right field porch in Boston. (Center field, however, was an unreachable 635 feet.) The Pilgrims' pitching aces were Cy Young (28-9) and Bill Dinneen (21-13).

The National League kings, the mighty Pittsburgh Pirates, had won their third flag in a row, led by batting champ Honus Wagner (.355), probably the best player in the game. They, too, boasted two fine pitchers, Sam Leever (25-7) and Deacon Philippe (24-7). Although Wagner and Leever were playing hurt, the new American League was considered no match for the National, which challenged the Pilgrims to a best-of-nine series.

"That was probably the wildest World Series ever played," Pirates outfielder Tommy Leach told Lawrence Ritter some 60 years later in *The Glory of Their Times.* "Arguing all the time between the teams, between the players and the umpires, and especially between the players and the fans. The fans were *part* of the game in those days. They'd pour right out onto the field and argue with the players and the umpires. Was sort of hard to keep the game going sometimes."

The Rooters turned out in force again to cheer their team. But this time they had a new and potent secret weapon—"Tessie." Will R. Anderson had written the tune that summer, and singer Joseph Welsh had made it a hit in the Broadway musical, "The Silver Slipper":

One can imagine our great-grandpas and great-grandmas "spooning" on front porch swings while the tinkling notes of player pianos in the

parlor floated through curtained windows all over America. In the fall, when the chill harvest moon rose, the *belles* and their *beaux* took their flirting indoors, and the Pirates arrived in Beantown for the historic first Series game.

Pirates president Barney Dreyfuss came to town with a $30,000 bankroll, and many of his players also expected to augment their meager pay by making bets with the local suckers. Pittsburgh manager Fred Clarke, however, worried that it would affect their play. Eager Boston fans covered all the Pittsburgh bets, so that at game time the teams took the field at even money.

The game took place on Huntington Avenue next to the New Haven and Hartford Railroad tracks, where Northeastern University's Cabot Athletic Center now stands. A standing-room crowd of more than 16,000 packed the grounds, craning to see the players, as well as former heavyweight champion Jim Corbett, who sat with the Pittsburghs. Other fans perched perilously on the top of the fences, threatening to topple onto the people below.

The two aces, Philippe and Young, faced each other. Boston catcher Lou Criger had a miserable first inning, making two errors and allowing two key steals as the Pirates won 7-3. Although they lost a pile of money, the crowd was well behaved—"probably the most impartial baseball people in the country," said the *Pittsburgh Post*.

The Rooters got their money back in Game 2 as Dinneen won 3-0 over the sore-armed Leever.

That Saturday carpenters worked all morning building 2,000 "circus seats" for what was expected to be "the biggest crowd that ever saw a baseball game." Indeed, 18,000 people, a Boston record, swarmed to the park, hanging out of streetcars, for Game 3. Ten thousand had to be turned away. Surrounding housetops were thick with people, and the men on the fence were squeezed elbow-to-elbow. Even the roof of the Boston dugout was covered with fans, and the players had almost no room for the game until 100 extra cops were called in to push people back. Ropes restrained the masses standing in the spacious outfield.

Philippe, back after only one day's rest, faced Boston's Tom Hughes (20-7). The unlucky Hughes gave up three fly balls that fell into the

center field crowd for ground-rule doubles and a quick 3-0 Pittsburgh lead, and Boston skipper Jimmy Collins waved Young in from the bullpen.

The fans remained good-natured and cheered good plays by both sides, especially a great catch behind second by Wagner, who lunged 20 feet for the ball and threw the runner out with his left hand. The fans on the fences risked bodily injury by waving their caps and beating the fence with their feet. The crowd especially cheered the Pirates' Kitty Bransfield and Jimmy Sebring, two Massachusetts boys. The iron man, Philippe, won 4-2, and the visitors entrained for home, "howling with joy" and taking thousands of Boston dollars with them.

Honey Fitz, McGreevey, Keenan, and a band of Royal Rooters pursued the foe on their own train. In the Smoky City, the Rooters checked into the Monongahela Hotel, where their heroes were staying. There was no game on Sunday, and Monday was raining, giving Philippe two days to rest his throbbing arm.

The skies were still dripping and the field was soggy for Game 4 in Exposition Park, Philippe against Dinneen. The Rooters hired a local band to march ahead of them in a parade of carriages to the park, where they marched beneath red parasols to their seats behind third base. They deposited their Negro mascot on the roof of the Boston dugout, then rose and gave a cheer for each Boston player as he took the field. Then they rose again and cheered each Pittsburgh player.

The Pirates scored in the first, and "8,000 people went bughouse," the *Pittsburgh Dispatch* reported. The Rooters came to life in the third, when Dinneen whiffed Bransfield with two outs and two on. Their band struck up a hit tune, "Mr. Dooley." "Beans promote hilarity," the *Dispatch* wrote, referring to Boston's favorite Saturday night dish.

Half an inning later, when Criger knocked in the tying run, McGreevey whipped up a new round of cheers from the Rooters and a chorus of "In the Good Old Summertime" from the band. Alas, the Pirates went on to win 5-4, Philippe's third straight complete game. Pittsburgh now had to win only two of the last five games.

But the Rooters kept up their sunny spirits, rushing the Boston dugout to pose with seven Pilgrims players, the only ones who had not

escaped into the clubhouse. "The Boston rooters were the feature of the game," the *Dispatch* said.

For Game 5, the odds against Boston had fallen to 10-6. It would be Young against Pittsburgh's veteran Brickyard Kennedy (9-6). A special section in right was set up for Ohio fans, who had flocked to see their native son, Young. The Bostonians had to let the band go because they had lost so much money they couldn't afford it.

For five innings, Kennedy matched the great Young 0-0, leaving the bases loaded in the first. Then, groaned Tommy Leach, the "invaders" from Boston suddenly started singing "that damn 'Tessie' song. You could hardly play ball they were singing 'Tessie' so damn loud." It was "a real humdinger" of a song, Tommy admitted, "but it sort of got on your nerves after a while."

In the sixth Clarke and Wagner let a fly ball fall between them, Freeman singled, and Wagner dropped a throw, loading the bases. Brickyard walked Candy La Chance for one run. Wagner made another error, letting in two more runs. Then Young and Pat Dougherty (.331) both tripled to score three more, and the welkin rang with the Rooters' new song.

As the Red Sox came to bat, the lyrics were changed to "Freeman, you know I love you madly," or to suit whichever batter was up. When the Pirates were up, the words became "Honus, at bat you look so sadly." The target of the satire, Wagner, tapped a grounder to shortstop, and the Beaneaters went on to win, 11-2.

The Bostonians were flush again and hired another band for Game 6. When it struck up "Tessie," the Rooters rose and waved their miniature parasols, opening and shutting them in time to the music. The Pittsburgh rooters also had a band near the right field bleachers, and also kept up "an incessant noise."

Dinneen faced Leever. As usual the Rooters applauded both sides impartially. When Pirates outfielder Ginger Beaumont ran down Freeman's long drive, the Bostonians rose "and compelled him to doff his cap."

Losing 6-3 in the seventh, Pittsburgh loaded the bases with Claude Ritchey up. He tapped a grounder to second to end the threat as the

Rooters waved their parasols wildly and their band played lustily. The Series was tied.

After the desperate Pirates called a day off for "cold weather" to rest Philippe for one more Herculean start, the Pittsburgh rooters paraded in carriages, wearing badges of red and navy blue and the word *Pittsburgh* in white to serenade their gallant ace. The stands were "slopping over with people" to watch the two aces, Young and Phillippe, do battle in Game 7. The hometown fans played a "cowbell chorus"; both bands played patriotic airs, as well as "Tessie," "Mr. Dooley," and other popular tunes.

But after the second batter, Collins, drove a triple to right, the Pittsburgh band grew quiet, while the Boston tooters erupted with "Tessie." Then the Rooters struck up "My Country, 'Tis of Thee" and the crowd stood, whipped off their hats, and joined in. The local band picked up verse two, then the rival bands alternated "Yankee Doodle," "Dixie," and "Marching Through Georgia" as the stands reverberated.

Phillipe pitched heroically, his fourth complete game of the Series, but Young beat him 7-3. That put Boston ahead for the first time, four games to three, and on Cy's final at bat, the Rooters broke into "Tessie" until their hero tipped his cap.

The Pilgrims players left the park perched on coaches, followed by the Rooters marching four abreast through streets jammed with cheering, smiling Pittsburghers. The parade made one brief, hurried stop, while a Rooter jumped from his carriage and dashed into a shop to collect on a bet.

The teams and the Rooters climbed back onto their trains to return to Boston. The Rooters would be missed, the *Dispatch* admitted. Under a headline blaring, "ROOTERS HELPED BOSTON TO WIN," the paper declared: "Their daily parades through downtown streets and their impartial but enthusiastic cheering at the games have won the hearts of the Pittsburgh people, and a delegation of Smoky City fans has promised them a real sendoff this evening.

"Had it not been for the Boston rooters," the article continued, "this series would now have been over, and it would not have been necessary to go to Boston. The little band of loyal rooters who wiggled over from

the Hub gave the visitors heart all the way. What other city in the country would have sent out a band of 200 rooters to fuss for what looked like a lost cause?

"Pittsburgh had beaten Boston twice in sight of her friends and was bringing them over here to kill them in a four-game series at Exposition Park. Did the Boston rooters quit? No! No! They dove for their grips [suitcases] and came over... to see that the boys didn't lose, and their purpose was served.

"That loyal little bunch of rooters in Section J during the past four games did more to win for Boston than did the pitching of Cy Young or Dinneen. They put heart in the boys. They dug in their socks [for money] and hired bands. They danced, screamed, shouted, and sang by turns, always with eyes of love turned on their own.

"Bravo, Boston rooters!"

Three days later, in Game 8, Philippe pitched his fifth complete game in 13 days, holding Boston to three runs. But Dinneen trumped him with a shutout, "and before we knew what had happened," the shell-shocked Leach moaned, "we had lost the World Series."

"Boston tonight is a town gone mad," the *Dispatch* marveled. "Frenzy and insanity of joy spilled out of the stand and onto the field."

The Pilgrims had lost three of the first four games. After the Rooters had raised their voices in "Tessie," they swept the next four in a row.

Moaned Leach a half-century later: "I think those Boston fans actually won that Series for the Red Sox."

⚔ 1904 ⚔

Although hardly anyone today recalls it, the 1904 American League pennant race between the Bostons and the Greater New Yorks, or Highlanders, was one of the hottest of all time. If today's fans don't remember it, their great-great-grandfathers could never forget it. It set the stage for the long Red Sox-Yankees rivalry that endures to this day.

The Bostons had the best pitching staff in the league, led once again by Young (26-16) and Dinneen (23-14). But the Highlanders had the best single pitcher in the league, the iron-man spitballer, Happy Jack Chesbro

(pronounced CHEESE-bro), who was 40-10 going into the final week. Their top batter, Willie Keeler, batted .343.

On October 7 the New Yorks were half a game behind when Chesbro beat Boston for his 41st win and put the Highlanders half a game in front. The Pilgrims won a doubleheader the next day. Dineen whipped Chesbro 13-2, and Young beat Jake Powell, 1-0. That put the Bostons back in first by a game and a half with a final doubleheader in New York October 10.

The Highlanders had to win both games. They pinned their hopes in the first game on Chesbro, pitching for the third time in four days. Boston countered with the hero of the '03 Series, Dinneen.

Some 300 Royal Rooters entrained for Gotham ahead of the team. They were bedecked in red badges reading "World Champs" and blue badges with pictures of all the Boston players. For good luck they carried the same satchels they had taken to Pittsburgh the year before. As the train pulled out of Boston's Back Bay station, the Rooters lifted their voices in speeches and songs. Their favorite tune, of course, was "Tessie":

Tessie, you make me feel so badly,
Why don't you turn around,
Tessie, you know I love you madly,
Babe, my heart weighs about a pound;
Don't blame me if I ever doubt you,
You know I wouldn't live without you,
Tessie, you are the only, only, only.

The fanatics filled five cars on the train and passed the hat for $100 to hire a band when they arrived. Although the Red Sox offered to pay the cost, the Rooters wouldn't hear of it, but they roundly cheered the team for the offer. The merriment soon degenerated into fans battling each other with rolled up newspapers. Someone tried to steal an overcoat from the rack; he was beaten up and thrown out of the car. At New Haven the Rooters made a rush for the lunch car, which was soon swept clean. At New York local fans welcomed the merrymakers, who checked

into the Marlborough Hotel, where their heroes would also be staying.

The next morning, carrying "Boston Rooters" signs, they hurriedly hired a minstrel band, which, unfortunately, didn't know how to play "Tessie." Nevertheless, they all climbed into electric cars for the trip uptown to Hilltop Park at Broadway and 165th Street, not far from the present Yankee Stadium. Alighting, they formed into a march unit for the final assault. At their head walked their mascot, an elderly black man just five feet tall with a gray beard, carrying a long pole with a Boston bean pot on top.

The players were warming up when they heard the cacophonous strains of "Tessie" wafting from the street, and soon the Rooters were romping through the gates, singing and cheering. They marched to their reserved seats behind the Boston bench. Cheerleaders with mega-phones strode back and forth on the dugout roof, shaking wooden rat-tles, banging brass cymbals, and whipping up a yawp of yelling. They finally quieted down so Chesbro could be presented with a sealskin coat by his fans, and the game got under way.

In the third, Happy Jack himself lashed a three-base hit with one out, but, egged on by the Rooters, Dinneen whiffed the next two batters, including the pesky Keeler.

In the fifth New York scored twice, and "from this moment on," the *Boston Globe* reported, the Rooters "yelled and sang themselves hoarse down to the very finish."

In the seventh Candy LaChance got a hit, and the Rooters rose to their feet. Hobe Ferris followed with a fierce grounder between the sec-ond baseman's legs as the cheerleaders exhorted the crowd to even greater noise. Lou Criger sacrificed Candy to third, and the cheering redoubled. Dinneen hit a hopper to shortstop, and LaChance dived into home; when the ball slipped away from catcher Mike Kleinow, Ferris came home as well, just beating the throw. The game was tied.

The Rooters jumped onto their seats, threw everything they could into the air, and bellowed at the tops of their voices. The band struck up "Tessie," though no two musicians played it alike.

In the ninth came one of the most notorious plays of all time. Criger got a scratch hit and took third on a sacrifice and infield out. With the

JOHN B. HOLWAY

yelling about to burst his eardrums, little Freddy Parent stood in to bat. On a 2-1 count, Chesbro took his stretch and pitched. The ball, possibly a spitter, sailed outside and high, so high, in fact, that it flew over Kleinow's head as Criger streaked home with the winning run. It was probably the most famous wild pitch in baseball history.

The Boston fans broke into a pandemonium, dancing, throwing their hats in the air, and singing so loud they even drowned out the band. The ancient mascot did a buck and wing atop the dugout, and the Rooters swarmed out of their seats and onto the field. After the meaningless second game, the Rooters raised one last, wild chorus of "Tessie" and marched jauntily out of the park.

Sit down before fact as a child, be prepared to give up every preconceived notion, follow humbly wherever nature leads, or you will learn nothing.

Thomas Huxley

  CHAPTER 16
Connie Mack and Little Van

CHEERING PHILADELPHIA FANS opened a gauntlet at the station on October 24, 1910, to let their victorious Athletics pass through as the band struck up "Hail the Conquering Heroes Come." The A's had just arrived from Chicago, where they had whipped the Cubs four games to one to win the championship of the world.

At the head of the players marched lanky, kindly Connie Mack, in his black derby hat and starched collar. Beside him, barely reaching to Connie's belt buckle, limped hunchbacked Louis Van Zelst. It was Mack's first world championship, and, wrote the *Philadelphia Inquirer,* "Little did [the fans] know that away down in that corner where superstition is safely locked up, many of the players felt that the diminutive chap who walked beside the great Connie Mack had a lot to do with the humbling of the Cubs. Connie himself thinks so."

As every baseball fan knew, rubbing a hunchback's hump was the best luck in the world for a ballplayer. The tradition apparently goes back a long way, but the first recorded case I've been able to find was little Joe Magore with the Cubs in 1907. Presumably he was with them when they beat Ty Cobb and the Tigers that October, and perhaps again in 1908 when they defeated the Giants after the disputed "Merkle boner."

Was Van Zelst true to the tradition? "Indeed he was," wrote sportswriter Fred Lieb emphatically. "Nothing but good luck followed in his wake."

Louis had been born in 1895 and received his hunchback at the age of eight, according to his younger brother, T.P. Van Zelst, a retired beer distributor. Louis had hitched a ride on a wagon and fell off, collapsing a lung and almost killing himself. He remained a tiny, stunted boy with a twisted torso much too short for his legs. Yet his happy smile "seemed to light up one's heart, no matter how trouble or defeat pressed on it," as one sportswriter later put it. He was "an exceptionally bright chap, winsome and clever," another commented.

Today Mack's visage smiles down from a bronze plaque at Cooperstown, a baseball immortal considered one of the great

managers of all time. But until Mack met Louie in 1908, his managerial career had been spotty. In 12 years, including three at Pittsburgh in the 1890s, he had finished seventh twice, sixth twice, fifth once, fourth twice, second three times, and first twice—1902 and 1905. There was no World Series in '02, and in '05 he was whipped by the New York Giants. Connie vowed to get revenge.

By 1908 the A's had plummeted to sixth place. Their best batsman, Danny Murphy, hit only .265. Connie had to put pitcher Colby Jack Coombs (.255) in the outfield. On the mound Coombs was 7-5. Chief Bender, a Chippewa from Minnesota, was 8-9. Lefty Eddie Plank was 14-16, and rookie Rube Vickers 18-19.

In 1909 Connie brought up four key rookies from the minors. Frank Baker played third, Jack Barry short, and lefty Larry Krause pitched. Mack's prize catch was Eddie "Cocky" Collins at second base. In spite of his degree from Columbia, Collins had his superstitions. He believed that chewing gum would help get a hit after two strikes, so he always carried a wad on the button of his cap and picked it off and chewed furiously whenever needed. (Teammates delighted in sprinkling pepper on it when he wasn't looking.)

By September 1 the A's were four games behind Ty Cobb's Tigers as the two teams opened a four-game series at brand new Shibe Park (later Connie Mack Stadium). It would be the best-attended four games in Philadelphia history to that time, with 120,000 fans rushing the gates. Tempers were high. Cobb was leading the league in everything, including dirty slides. Earlier that year he had spiked Baker, and death threats were waiting for Cobb in the mail. Police were out in strength.

One can imagine 14-year-old Louis hustling to the park on Friday for the big opening game to watch Plank face Cobb and Wahoo Sam Crawford. Eddie struck out Ty in the first inning and did it again in the third with the bases loaded. The A's won 2-1 to move to three games behind.

But the Tigers beat Krause the next day, and after an off day Sunday, little Van hobbled to join the crowd as soon as school was out. The game had been sold out for two hours, but Louis had struck up a friendship with center fielder Rube Oldring, and, lacking a ticket, flashed a picture

of Rube taken from a cigarette pack. An indulgent ticket-taker smilingly waved him in.

Mack spotted the kid and called to him, "How'd you like to be bat boy?" How would he *like* it? Louis hurried over to take up his duties.

The A's got a lucky break in the fourth when Collins was caught off third but boldly dashed home with a run. They got another gift in the eighth. With two out and one on, Collins was safe on a close play at first as the runner broke for home. Detroit's Bill Donovan, thinking Collins was out, didn't even throw the ball, and the A's won, 2-0. They were three games behind again. "Come around tomorrow," Connie told Louis. "We'll need you again."

The next day Plank took a 4-3 lead into the ninth, but it looked like trouble when Cobb led off with a single. Fortunately, he was wiped out in a double play as the A's pulled to two games behind.

With Louis on the job, Philadelphia won four of their next five games. But they couldn't catch the Tigers, who won three straight to clinch the flag.

℣ 1910 ℣

That spring Connie signed Louie Van Zelst to a full-time contract. He wore a regular A's uniform and made all the road trips. Barry and Coombs acted as his guardians and made sure he went to Mass every Sunday. Travel was an ordeal, though. Behind his cheerful smile, Louis was subject to spasms of pain. But he never complained. "He had the courage of a Spartan," a reporter wrote.

"Louie's lovable disposition won the hearts of our players," Mack said. All the A's adopted him. When Collins got married, Louis was invited to the wedding, naturally.

Oldring and Louie made it a ritual to toss the ball to each other before every game. Once Rube forgot and warmed up with someone else. He later found Van in the dugout, crying.

Fans in every city, and even the other players, also took Louie to their hearts. He was a special favorite of Chicago pitcher Big Ed Walsh, Cleveland manager Larry Lajoie, and even Cobb, who didn't make many

friends. Louie told Walsh confidently the Macks would win the pennant.

Van was also a good comic. Detroit manager Hughie Jennings had once dived into an empty pool, and Louis made the skipper hopping mad with his imitation of a swan dive. Mack sent Van to the coach's box to do his act, although the ump ordered him back.

Van had lucky holes in the turf. He dug his spikes into them and carefully stepped in the same places thereafter for luck. If a hitter was in a slump, Lou said, in his weak, quavering voice, "Better rub me for a hit this time." It must have worked. Danny Murphy raised his average 19 points to an even .300. Barry improved 44 points to .259. Oldring jumped 78 to .308. And Collins, .322, beat out Cobb in stolen bases.

The pitchers, meanwhile, cut their team earned run average to an amazing 1.79 a game. Bender was 23-5, the first 20-win year of his life, and Coombs was 31-9 In all, the A's won 102 games, then a record in the young American League, and trotted to the pennant.

But their World Series foes, the Cubs, had done even better, with 104 victories to win their third flag in four years. When Plank reported a sore arm and Oldring broke his leg, the Athletics went into the Series as distinct underdogs. But they laughed at the odds.

In Game 1 Bender pitched a three-hitter to win, 4-1.

Next Coombs faced Chicago ace Mordecai "Three Finger" Brown (25-13), who had lost a finger in a threshing machine as a kid and claimed the stump gave him a better curveball. Brown was holding a 3-2 lead in the last of the seventh, but the A's must have rubbed Louie's hump furiously, bcecause they erupted for six runs and went ahead two games to one.

Moving to Chicago, Mack called on Coombs with one day's rest, and the big Down East pitcher coasted to a 12-5 victory.

After the Cubs won the fourth game, Coombs came back to pitch his third complete game in five days and won it, 7-2.

In the Series Collins hit .429, Baker .409. As a team they hit .316, a record that would stand for 50 years until broken by the 1960 Yankees of Mickey Mantle and Yogi Berra. Mack had won his first world championship; his dream had come true right on schedule. No wonder he shared his position at the victory parade with little Louie Van Zelst.

A really true, on-the-level, honest-to-jiminy jinx can do all sorts of mean things to a professional ball player. I have seen it make... a Kansas farmer with two or three screws rattling loose...[travel] the circuit [saying] he was accompanied by Miss Fickle Fortune.

Christy Mathewson

CHAPTER 17
"My Middle Name Is Victory"

FEW PENNANT DRIVES HAVE EQUALED that of the 1911 New York Giants and their grinning, comical good-luck mascot, the Kansas hayseed, Charles Victory Faust.

Back in 1911 the world was filled with unseen forces for good and evil, as real to great-great-grandfather as the buggy or the outhouse, no less palpable for being invisible as, say, the modern atom or cathode ray. No less than the uneducated ruffians, even college men like Giants pitcher Christy Mathewson, a graduate of Bucknell University, knew these forces were real. College men "fall hardest for jinxes," Matty admitted.

Hitters felt that bats had only so many hits in them and discarded perfectly good lumber when the hits were used up. They also had "lucky bats," which could be deprogrammed by a photographer. Honus Wagner, who hit .300 or better 13 years in a row, once threw his now-worthless bat at a newsman who had clicked a surreptitious picture. Ballplayers considered crossed bats the worst kind of jinx. On the other hand, rubbing a Negro's head was considered as lucky as rubbing a hunchback's hump.

Giant third baseman Art Devlin couldn't abide anyone humming on the bench. "He nearly beat a youngster to death" for humming, Matty reported. Devlin's worst phobia was crossed eyes. Matty himself fervently believed they were a sure hex. The only antidote was to spit quickly into one's hat, and he himself had ruined many a good hat that way. One wall-eyed lady was so enamored of Devlin that she took to sitting behind third at every game, sending him into the worst slump of his career. Art considered poisoning her, and manager John McGraw cried that he couldn't go on losing ball games "because you are such a Romeo, Arthur." Luckily, the lady learned of the crisis she was causing and graciously stayed away. "With this weight off his shoulder," Mathewson wrote, "Arthur went back into the game and played like mad."

Seeing a load of empty barrels was a good omen. According to Matty, the Giants were in a protracted slump when catcher Frank

Bowerman spotted such a load. Sure enough, Frank slapped four hits in five at bats. The next day three other players spotted some empty barrels, and they also hit the ball hard. Soon the whole team was seeing empty barrels and hitting like Ty Cobb. Only later did McGraw admit that he had hired a wagon to drive around the park with a load of barrels every day. "That," wrote Mathewson admiringly, "is why I maintain that he is the greatest manager of them all."

McGraw had his own jinx-killer: He always slept in a stateroom while traveling by train. (Cubs manager Frank Chance slept in a lower-13 berth.)

As Mathewson wrote, "Luck is a combination of confidence and getting the breaks. Ballplayers get no breaks without confidence in themselves, and lucky omens inspire this confidence. On the other hand, unlucky signs take it away."

♐ McGraw and Faust ♐

Like Connie Mack, John "Muggsy" McGraw, the truculent bantam Irishman, is today in the Hall of Fame, venerated as one of the top baseball geniuses of all time. But in 1911 his career, like Mack's in 1910, had not yet approached geniushood. With Baltimore in 1899 and 1901, McGraw had finished fourth and fifth. Moving to New York in 1902, he came in last. In 1903 future immortal Christy Mathewson joined the team, won 29 games, and the Giants jumped to second. Matty won 34 in 1904, and the Giants beat the Cubs by 13 games.

In 1905 Matty won 32, young Red Ames won 22, outfielder "Turkey" Mike Donlin hit .356, and the Giants won again. They went on to beat Mack's A's in the World Series four games to one as Mathewson hurled a record three shutouts.

But in 1906 Donlin broke his leg—the bats were crossed when he slid into third, Mathewson noted—and the Giants fell to second, 20 games behind the Cubs. The year after that they dropped to fourth.

In 1908 the Giants lost a one-game playoff to the Cubs, a game neccessitated by Fred Merkle's failure to touch second base on September 23, which cost New York a game it should have won. The next year they were third.

The 1910 season also started ominously. Dogged by bad luck, Ames had a reputation as a hoodoo, or bad luck, pitcher; no matter how well he pitched, the Giants made errors or couldn't score. On opening day he pitched a no-hitter and lost it in the 13th. The Giants finished second, again 13 games behind the Cubs. Thus, in his first 11 years, McGraw had won only two pennants.

The league traditionally opened on Thursday, but in 1911 that day fell on the 13th. The next day, Friday, was also considered unlucky. To avoid both "hoodoos," says historian Gabe Schechter, the league owners agreed to start April 14. On the following Friday, the Polo Grounds— the Giants' beautifully rebuilt park—mysteriously burned to the ground.

By late July the Giants were in third place, 4½ games behind the Cubs. Only Matty (18-7) and rookie Rube Marquard (12-5) were keeping them in the race. Dumbo-eared Otis "Doc" Crandall, 18-4 a year earlier, was 6-4. Lefty "Hooks" Wiltse was 2-5. Pitcher Arthur "Bugs" Raymond had succumbed to alcoholism and had been released.

Ames was still snake-bit. On his daily trip to the park, Red had to pass the home of a one-eyed man, and though he detoured several blocks, he still bumped into the Jonah. "Although Ames did his duty by his hat, and got several small boys to help him out," as Matty euphemistically described his teammate's spitting, Red was blasted from the mound in two innings. By late July his record was 4-8.

The hitters were in a slump. Josh Devore was down 24 points from 1910, and Fred Snodgrass had plummeted 51 points, from .321 to .270.

A brain-frying heat wave blanketed the nation from New England to Kansas. Hundreds died, and insane asylum admissions soared. On the sizzling night of July 27 the third-place Giants arrived in St. Louis. Against the second-division Cardinals the next day, Matty was beaten, 5-2.

The following afternoon, July 29, during batting practice, Fate walked out of the grandstand, gave a loud whoop of a hog call, loped over to the Giants' bench, and stuck his hand out to McGraw.

Fate was 30 years old. He wore a little black derby hat, the sleeves of his suit barely reached his elbows, his vest didn't reach his belt, and his trousers were several inches above his high-top shoes. Various

accounts describe what happened next. This is how Snodgrass remembered it in Lawrence Ritter's *The Glory of Their Times:*

"Mr. McGraw, my name is Charles *Wictory* Faust," Fate announced in a heavy German accent. "I live over in Kansas, and a few weeks ago I had a dream that I would pitch the Giants to the pennant. I went to a fortuneteller, who told me that if I would join the Giants and pitch for them, the dream would come true. So here I am."

There are many versions of the Faust legend. One, unconfirmed, says Charlie had actually received a telegram from McGraw, offering him a tryout, and ran leaping to the train station like a prairie jackrabbit, while some anonymous jokester snickered at the gag.

The following account, based on research by Gabe Schechter and myself, sticks as close as possible to contemporary newspaper stories.

Perhaps winking at the others, McGraw tossed Faust a mitt and told him to throw a few. Charlie went into a double windmill windup and fired a fastball that, Snodgrass estimated, might have broken a pane of glass. Next the candidate was given a bat and told to hit a few. He tapped a grounder to shortstop and lit out for first. "You could have timed him with a calendar," one player said. The infielders, catching the spirit, deliberately kicked the ball and threw it wild while Charlie chugged to first, slid into second in his Sunday suit, slid into third, and slid home.

Everyone, except poor, trusting Charlie, had a good laugh. But the Giants won the game 8-0 behind Marquard, his 13th victory of the season.

The next afternoon McGraw gave Faust another workout—and won that game, too, 6-0 on a two-hitter by Wiltse.

A big crowd was on hand for the third game—word of the Kansan's antics had gotten around. Marquard came back with one day's rest and won 3-2 behind 12 hits. That lifted them into second place, 1½ games behind the Cubs.

The next stop was Pittsburgh. According to Snodgrass, McGraw informed the surprised players, "We're taking Charlie along to help us win the pennant."

The Pirates and Wagner boasted a nine-game winning streak. Pitching in near gale-force winds, Mathewson gave up 15 hits but won, 8-1.

The Giants lost the next two games and entrained for Chicago and three games against the Cubs. Charlie arrived at the station along with the other players, but McGraw was getting tired of the Kansan. He slapped his forehead in mock dismay. "I left your contract back at the hotel," he said. "If you hurry, you can go back and get it before the train leaves." Charlie dashed back to the hotel, as McGraw, nudging the players and winking, boarded the train without him.

Mathewson opened the Chicago series, and on the first play of the game, Devore was beaned and carried off the field. Meanwhile, Matty's personal nemesis, Cubs shortstop Joe Tinker banged two singles, a double, and a triple, and stole home, to beat Matty 8-6.

Wiltse lost the next game 3-1 on an error, and the Giants fell to three games behind. But Marquard salvaged the final game 16-5, and the Giants headed back to New York 2½ games behind the Pirates.

When they arrived, Faust was waiting at the players' entrance, caked with mud from his trip on a freight train but eager to play.

Workmen were still putting the upper deck and roof onto the Polo Grounds' new grandstand as Mathewson warmed up amid whispers that the old man was washed up. "I can pitch as well as ever," Matty insisted, "but luck has been breaking against me." This time he shut out the Phillies, 6-0.

The next day a big crowd in the lower stands and beyond the outfield ropes gave a hearty laugh at "Rube" Faust cutting capers in his new Giants uniform. He butted into the Phils' batting practice, stealing first, second, and third as the Phillies joined in the laughter. Wrote reporter Damon Runyon: "He runs like an ice wagon and slides as if he had stepped off a moving trolley car backwards." *The New York Herald* sniffed that Faust was "the biggest boob that ever came out of Boobville."

But others saw him differently. Later that season the *Cincinnati Enquirer,* for instance, described him as "a big, quiet, good-natured fellow... a little simple but not a fool by any means."

In the game, Ames pitched a two-hitter, but again he was notoriously unlucky. Two runs scored on him without a hit as a result of errors, and Red lost 2-0. "Gee," he said afterwards, "if it was raining

soup, I'd be caught with a fork."

Next the Giants faced two games against the Phils and their sensational rookie, Grover Alexander (28-13 for the year), and Earl Moore (15-19), who held a hex over them that season. New York's own rookie phenom, Marquard, battled Alex for 12 innings to win 3-2. Then Wiltse ended Moore's jinx, 5-4.

Despite the wins, McGraw ordered Faust out of the clubhouse. Charlie broke down and cried, but he wouldn't give up and talked his way back onto the team.

Cincinnati followed the Phillies into town. Matty whipped them 6-1 on a two-hitter. "HAVE GIANTS CHANCE TO WIN PENNANT?" the *New York Herald* wondered. If Marquard could stay hot, if Matty could pitch like his old self, and if Ames could shake his hoodoo, they had a chance, the paper concluded hopefully.

"Me and McGraw and the Giants are gonna win this pennant," Charlie assured the writers. The newsmen and the players chuckled when he predicted New York victories, but they had to admit he was usually right. Charlie was great for morale. Fans loved his windmill windup and his imitations of Mathewson and other stars.

Faust didn't have a contract. McGraw slipped him spending money and let him wear a uniform and sit on the bench, though he begged for a chance to pitch. Charlie religiously warmed up before each game to be ready, just in case the Giants needed him. They never did.

On August 17 the Giants beat the Reds twice. Ames finally got some batting support to win 10-4, and the Giants won the second game 15-2 to move back into second place, two games behind.

Runyon commented on "the wonderful improvement" of Snodgrass, Devore and Beals Becker in the outfield. "Snodgrass' work of late in fielding, hitting and base running makes him look like a different player entirely."

Faust put on his act for the crowd on the 18th. Warming up Marquard, a fastball got through his mitt and hit him in the eye. When he came to, he circled the bases on a bunt.

The next day Mathewson tried the iron-man feat of winning two games in one day. He won the first but lost the second, 7-4.

There was no game on Sunday, while the New Yorkers braced for an invasion by the Cubs. Chicago had suffered two pieces of ill luck. Their sparkplug second baseman, Johnny Evers, was lost for half the season, the result of a nervous breakdown after an auto accident, and their first baseman/manager, Frank Chance, had been beaned and was out of the lineup.

At this critical moment Charlie became a holdout. He reportedly wanted $10,000, or $1,000 more than Mathewson was making. "If I don't sign today," he said before the series opened, "I leave the team flat." The Giants didn't make a move, and Charlie caught a subway for Brooklyn to offer his arm to the Dodgers.

Without Faust, Marquard battled Chicago 2-2 for nine innings before the Giants got two scratch hits in the 10th to win and pull into a virtual tie for the lead.

The next afternoon, August 22, with Faust still absent, New York won 6-5 in the 10th and moved into first place.

The next day, the *Herald* reported, Charlie "was in Frank Chance's company." Chicago beat Wiltse 6-2, and the Giants dropped back to second. Wiltse may have injured his hip; he wouldn't pitch again for three weeks. With Ames also out since the Cincinnati series, McGraw was forced to go with a three-man staff—Marquard, Mathewson, and Crandall.

Apparently rebuffed by both the Dodgers and Cubs, "Looney Faust" had a long salary talk with Giants president John T. Brush, who reported that "a slight difference of $10,000" still separated them. Nonetheless, Charlie decided to rejoin his teammates. He apparently had some property in Kansas, which allowed him to support himself. His major expenses reportedly were massages and "electric treatments" for his pitching arm.

Pittsburgh was next to arrive for two games on the 24th. The press recognized the new star by putting Charlie's picture in the paper. In the two games that day, the Giants pitched their two stars, Matty and Marquard. Matty lost 3-1, but Marquard won, 2-1.

The third game was played in a downpour as Charlie demonstrated his speed on the bases, and everyone laughed as he slid into the

muck at second base. New York won 3-2 behind Crandall.

On August 26 the brass band from the Catholic Protectory Orphanage was on hand to play some waltzes, and Charlie grabbed a baton and began waving it. "He did that just about as well as he plays ball," the *Times* commented. Fans in the new upper tier whistled and threw their cushions, bowling several women over and knocking off their hats.

Thus inspired, Matty beat the Pirates 6-2 to give New York a 1½-game lead. On August 28, Marquard whipped the Cardinals 2-0 on a one-hitter. The next day Crandall beat them 7-5 to lengthen New York's lead to 2½ games.

Moving to Philadelphia September 1, the Giants swept the Phillies three straight. Mathewson and Marquard joined in a doubleheader victory, 3-2 and 2-0. It was Rube's second one-hitter in a row. "Well," said Charlie, mopping his brow, "I certainly did my share."

The next day Marquard came back in the ninth inning with one out and two on and saved the victory, 7-6.

The Giants returned to New York on Labor Day for two games against the last-place Boston Braves. Charlie, however, wasn't with them. Schechter reports that the Kansas Cyclone had received an offer, reportedly for $200, to take his act on the vaudeville stage, doing his hog calls, his windup, and his imitations of Mathewson, Wagner, and other stars. He also demonstrated the fine points of his new slide, "the fall-apart," which he had learned from a book.

Ames, pitching for the first time in four weeks, won the first game 6-4, but Marquard lost the second, 8-7. It was the first time Rube had been defeated since Charlie joined the team.

Seventh-place Brooklyn arrived next and shocked Mathewson with a 4-3 defeat, the first time he had lost to them in years. Several errors did him in.

Since Charlie had taken up his theatrical career, the Giants had lost two out of three games to the two weakest teams in the league, and the Cubs were now only one game behind. Wrote Heyward Broun of the *Globe:* "It is certain that the defeats would not have happened if Charlie had been within call."

On September 8 Marquard faced Brooklyn's ace, Nap Rucker (22-18), and dueled 0-0 for two innings. Meanwhile, at the Manhattan Theater downtown, Faust was fidgeting. He grabbed a subway and sped to the ballpark, arriving with Billy Gane, the theater manager, in tow, as the Giants came to bat in the third. Doyle promptly walked, Snodgrass and Merkle singled, and an outfield error let all three score as Rucker was driven from the box.

Meanwhile "the time for the next show at the Manhattan was approaching, but Gane found that the call of art was drowned by the call of the ballfield. Marquard was going great guns, but Faust was anxious to warm up to be ready in case an unexpected break should come."

Marquard set the Brooklyns down for six innings before Gane at last dragged his star away. No sooner had Charlie left, Broun reported, "than the tide of battle turned. The Giants made not another run or hit, and Brooklyn, in a hard finish, came very near victory." Two doubles and a single scored two runs and left a man on second with two out, but Bill Bergen "lined a steamer over first," where Merkle leaped and gloved it.

Marquard was lucky to win, Broun wrote. "The real reason for the Giants' success lay not in the staunch arm of Marquard, nor the ready bat of Fred Merkle, but in the presence of Charlie Faust.... In the future McGraw plans to rig up an emergency call from the bench to the stage of the Manhattan."

That same afternoon the *New York Globe* carried an interview with Charlie by Sid Mercer, saying he wanted to retire from his stage career. "There is more money in this acting game," he said, "but I don't want to be an actor. I am keeping in good condition doing my famous windup and slides, but I'll quit any time McGraw gives the word. McGraw needs all us good pitchers." The Giants were leaving on a 23-game road trip Saturday night. Charlie said he'd better accompany them "now that the fight for the pennant is going to be so close."

The next day, as Snodgrass recalled, Charlie returned to the Giants' dressing room. "Charlie, what are you doing here?" the players asked. "What about your theatrical contract?"

"Oh," he replied, "I've got to pitch today. You fellows need me."

The two teams played to a 4-4 tie, and the players grabbed their suitcases to catch the train to Boston.

Ames meanwhile was filled with self-doubts. "I don't see any use in taking me along, Mac," he told McGraw. "The club can't win with me pitching if the other guys don't even get a foul." However, with Wiltse still injured, the skipper couldn't spare him.

As the train pulled out of Grand Central Station, a vaudeville agent was left standing on the platform, vainly waving a $500 contract.

The Giants called Charlie into the smoking lounge to do his vaudeville routine and greeted it with shouts of applause and demands for an encore. Even the sourpuss umpire, Hank O'Day, broke into a grin. As the laughing players climbed into their berths, a helpful teammate told Faust that he should rest his pitching arm in the little hammock provided for clothes. Charlie awoke in the morning shivering, and with an aching pitching arm.

The players meanwhile had stuffed several pounds of pig iron into his satchel, and tittered as he gamely lugged it to the hotel. Faust kept the whole team in high spirits, Matty wrote, "and the feeling prevailed that we couldn't lose with him along."

At Boston, Ames found a surprise waiting. A famous actress had sent him a four-leaf clover and a necktie, a garish cloth of clashing colors that Matty said "would have done for a headlight." Ames was told to wear both at all times, on and off the field. He could hide the tie beneath his uniform, but he had to wear it, she stressed.

Mathewson beat Cy Young, then 44, by a score of 11-2.

Ames took the mound the following day. Red pitched a three-hitter for a 4-1 victory. He'd wear the tie until he lost, he vowed. He even slept with it.

When the team gathered for a group photo the next day, there was Charlie with the rest of the squad, in his Giants uniform. He predicted they would win the pennant by five games. Commented Runyon: "So superstitious have the players become that they believe it. They say that he can always call the turn on a hit while on the bench during a game. If he should quit the team now it would never win the pennant. The players believe in him absolutely."

McGraw often called Faust to his hotel room and asked him to go through his repertoire. Charlie also let out a whoop or two in the middle of the game, to the great delight of the fans. Sometimes he let one out in the middle of the night as well, startling the players and half the hotel guests out of a sound sleep.

Charlie had two idiosyncrasies. One was eating pie three meals a day, plus another one at bedtime. The other was his love of manicures and facial massages. Some writers kidded him that Broadway had brought out a streak of vanity, but Matty said Faust had manicures the way other men had drinks, for sociability. Whenever a player went into a barber shop, Charlie climbed into an adjoining chair. In St. Louis, McGraw marveled, Charlie set a world record with five massages in one day.

"I always like to talk to the boys while they're getting a shave," Charlie explained. "When a man is getting shaved, he ain't thinking about much of anything. I'd tell 'em that if this happened or that happened, he'd get a hit that afternoon. They listened and didn't kid me so much. I'd always see that what I suggested happened. Lots of times I had to get in a barber chair three or four times a morning so I could talk to a number of the boys. It always worked."

Wiltse started the final game in Boston and was hit hard but managed to win, 13-9.

That night the team headed west, luckily missing their regular train, which was later involved in an accident near Albany.

At Pittsburgh, where the Pirates were still in the race, a huge crowd turned out. Faust declared confidently that he knew how to strike out Honus Wagner, the batting champ at .334—he had read of Wagner's weakness out in Kansas while studying pitching by correspondence school. A *mano a mano* duel was arranged before the game, and sure enough, Wagner swung mightily at three Faust pitches, missing each by a foot. Charlie strode triumphantly off the mound as the big crowd clapped and cheered. (Schechter notes that in Goethe's poem, Faust's assistant was named Wagner.)

The Giants beat the Pirates three straight. Ames won the final game 3-1 as the Giants stole eight bases—they would set an all-time record for

steals that year. "I am glad Faust is going to stick," Red told the press, "because he has certainly brought good luck to us all.... If he should quit us now, we would never win the pennant, but if he sticks, it's ours."

"The Giants and McGraw are goin' to win," Faust declared, and McGraw happily agreed that he didn't see how they could lose now. "Get out of the way," *The New York Times* told its readers, "the steamroller is running away." As the team rolled on to St. Louis, a jubilant president Brush wired the skipper, "May good luck and Charlie Faust stay with you."

The *St. Louis Post-Dispatch* devoted almost a full page to a feature on Charlie, accompanied by a cartoon of him on the bench "thinking the Giants to the pennant."

Luckily, Ames was hot, because Wiltse was still limping. The doctors didn't seem able to help. Mathewson suggested that McGraw see what Charlie could do. According to one report, Wiltse was moaning in pain when Charlie walked in and touched his hip. "Shucks," the Kansan said, "there ain't a thing the matter with you."

Hooks swung his legs off the bed and stood up. "The minute Charlie touched me," he said, "the pain left. I felt fine. There isn't a damn thing wrong with the hip now." Whether true or not, two days later Wiltse beat the Cardinals 3-2, the Giants' 10th straight victory since Charlie had rejoined the team.

In the second game of the doubleheader, some writers thought it would be a lark to kidnap Charlie and sit him on the Cardinal bench. That's right: New York lost, 8-7.

The next day, September 22, Ames was carrying a 3-0 lead into the eighth inning and then blew up. He uncorked two wild pitches, yielded a run and loaded the bases when McGraw yanked him and put in Marquard. The Rube promptly gave up a double to tie the score, but the Giants scored in the 10th on an error. If Marquard could hold them in the last of the 10th, the game was theirs.

Instead, Devore and shortstop Art Fletcher ran into each other chasing a pop fly, then Rube walked the bases full, and McGraw waved to the bullpen for Wiltse. The cry went up: "Where's Charlie?" "Stop the game!" Mathewson shouted, "stop it any way you can until we find

Charlie!" Then, instead of Wiltse, Faust jumped up from the bullpen and loped across the outfield to the pitcher's mound, as the Giants rushed to greet him. "Stop right there," McGraw ordered. "Just stand there and let the boys see you." With a cheer the players ran back to their positions, Marquard smiled and waved at Faust, then got the next two batters out.

Mathewson was a nervous wreck. He said he never gained back the weight he lost that day. "It was as nice a piece of pinch-mascoting as I ever saw," he wrote.

Two days later Charlie was unable to find a restaurant serving apple pie for breakfast. Without his "matutinal bracer," Runyon wrote, "the jinxing power of Charles Victory is almost nil." Faust left the hotel to scour the city for a slice, and while he was gone, Marquard let in four runs, one on a wild pitch, and was yanked in the fourth with the bases full. The Reds went on to win, 6-5. Marquard "feels a little bitter toward Faust tonight," Runyon reported.

With a seven-game lead the papers speculated that Charles Victory would finally be allowed to pitch a game in Chicago. The city greeted him with a huge banner welcoming "the Kansas Cyclone," and the fans called on him to perform his comedy act each day.

But Charlie had also received a letter presumably from the notorious "Black Hand," a sort of early Mafia, threatening a dire fate in the Windy City. Indeed, Runyon reported rumors of "a foul plot afoot" to lure McGraw's court jester to a remote section of the city and tie him up until the Giants left town. McGraw placed a Pinkerton detective at Charlie's side day and night.

The Cubs also tried a jinx of their own, listing Charlie on their score-cards as number 13. He was "flustered," Runyon wrote. "He fears that someone has put a 'thought' on him." For whatever reason, Charlie's powers suddenly left him. Marquard was knocked out of the box, 8-0, and Mathewson went down to defeat 2-1 as his old nemesis, Tinker, drove in the winning run.

After two losses, McGraw withdrew Charlie's name as a starting pitcher. Instead, Ames took the mound against the great Brown for the third game of the series. With his necktie frayed but still knotted around his neck, Red outpitched the Cubs' ace 3-1 for his fifth victory in a row. It

virtually knocked the Cubs out of the race and sent the Giants on another 10-game win streak.

Marquard shut out the Cubs. Wiltse two-hit the Phils, winning on a fly ball by Merkle that fell into the temporary seats to break up a 0-0 tie. Crandall crushed Philadelphia 12-3, and the Giants headed home with a record of 17-3 on the long road trip. They needed only one more victory to clinch the pennant.

A wild crowd welcomed the team to Pennsylvania Station. McGraw declared that he had fielded other teams with more ability, but never one with the will to win of the 1911 squad. "My friends," Charlie told the fans, "far be it from me to boast about myself, but you can plainly see what is what."

That afternoon at Brooklyn, Mathewson blanked the Dodgers and Rucker 2-0, and the pennant was theirs.

The last eight games on the schedule didn't matter, and McGraw rested his regulars. The Giants split the eight, with Ames taking on the great Alexander in one of them, beating him 10-5 as the team scored nine runs in the last two innings. Red took a lot of kidding, but he just grinned. He'd won four straight games since putting on his tie.

≈ Now Pitching: Charlie Faust ≈

The next day, October 7, was a memorable day in New York base-ball history. That was the day Charles Victory Faust pitched his first major league game.

The Giants were losing 5-2 to Boston. In the ninth, rain clouds were threatening, and most of the fans had aleady filed out, when McGraw crooked his right arm and beckoned Charlie to the mound. At last, "the sunflower phenom" would fulfill the fortuneteller's prediction. The thousand or so patrons who were still on hand bellowed applause.

As Charlie rushed to the mound on ungainly legs, shouting, "My moment has come!" another figure leaped over a railing and rushed onto the diamond, waving his arms angrily. This was Charlie's agent, cussing McGraw for not having tipped him off so he could have one of those new-fangled motion picture cameras ready to

record the historic event.

But McGraw refused to postpone it. "This guy [Faust] has been a thorn in my side for months," he said, adding, "Lately he's become a cactus." He hastily scribbled a contract on an old-fashioned collar, making Charlie's appearance legal. With a flourish, Charlie signed "Charles V Faust." "What does the V stand for?" McGraw asked quizzically. Charlie pulled himself up to his full height. "Wictory," he replied in his heavy German accent, "is my middle name."

The agent walked away muttering dejectedly, "Some days some people don't have any luck."

Faust lifted his cap and gave a sweeping bow to left and right, much like Ichabod Crane asking Katrina Van Tassel to dance. Then his eagle eye spotted a speck of dirt on the rubber, and he carefully brushed it away.

Charlie took his warm-up throws with a windup that looked like two or three men pitching at the same time, the *Brooklyn Eagle* declared. He twirled around in the air like a pretzel, then released the ball like a mainspring that had just gone "sponnggg." Bill Rariden stepped in to start the inning, and Charlie "wound up like a worm that had been cut in three pieces and uncoiled." As one paper put it, batters didn't know if he was pitching or waving to friends in the stands.

"Strike!" the umpire bawled.

Most of Charlie's face disappeared behind his grin, and the fans howled.

"Look out for his fast one," the Giants' rookie catcher, Grover Hartley, warned as the next pitch slowly floated over the plate.

"I want [Chief] Meyers to catch me," Faust shouted at McGraw. "I'm afraid this youngster can't hold my 'up-in.'" But Hartley squatted back down, and Faust flashed his own sign, the big closed fist, the signal for the dreaded "up-in."

Rariden walloped it over George Burns' head in center field, though if Burns had been playing his regular depth, he would have caught it. Burns fired to second in time to catch Rariden, but Art Fletcher dropped the throw.

Next Boston pitcher George "Lefty" Tyler bunted toward Faust, who

made a good play and threw Tyler out, Rariden taking third. Then Bill Sweeney hit a long fly, and Rariden scored.

Finally the dangerous Turkey Mike Donlin (.314) "nearly broke his bat reaching for one of Charlie's slow balls" and walloped a weak one to Fletcher, and the side was retired. "Charlie didn't have enough on the ball to hit it," chuckled Snodgrass.

Faust would be the sixth man up in the last of the ninth. The first two men flied out, but a double and a hit batsman raised hopes that Faust might indeed get a chance to bat as well as pitch. If the weak-hitting Hartley could get on, Faust would be the next man up. But Grover lifted a soft fly for the third out.

"But what are three outs to Faust?" Runyon asked. "He strode to the plate, and the Boston fans fell for him, as everyone does. He swung his bat as though he were driving spikes for the circus and rolled an easy one to the pitcher." The infielders deliberately kicked the ball, dropped it, and threw wildly, making him slide into every base. His final slide into home came in the midst of a dozen fans who had rushed to greet him. Charlie whooped all the way to the dugout. "Mac," he hollered, "I want to pitch the first game against the Athletics [in the World Series]."

"You're fired," McGraw shot back, "for letting Boston score. I thought you said you were ready." Everybody laughed.

At last the Giants were down to their final two games, against Brooklyn. Ames lost the first game and at last threw away his frazzled necktie.

The Giants were losing the second game 5-2, and Faust "wore a path between the outfield and the pitcher's box trying to horn in," Runyon wrote. Three times he tried to reach the mound, but each time second baseman Larry Doyle intercepted him and sent him back to warm up some more. At last in the ninth McGraw relented and waved Charlie in as the New York crowd roared its thanks.

The first batter, Zach Wheat, bunted to Faust, who pegged him out at first, though Runyon thought umpire Bill Klem missed the play by several feet.

Next Jake Daubert almost drove a pitch into the Harlem River, but Snodgrass pulled it down. Jud Daley was on by an error, and Charlie lost

his hitless inning when Dolly Stark singled to left. Faust then ended the inning, getting rookie Bob Higgins on a grounder.

Once again Charlie got to bat, though not officially; they let him hit after the Giants went down in the ninth. His stance resembled "an untamed demon," the *New York Sun* wrote, causing the pitcher to "plunk the terrifying figure at the plate in the ribs."

Faust trotted to first and summoned batter Buck Herzog for a conference. "I'm going to steal second and third," he whispered to the grinning batter, "and I want you to sacrifice me home." And that's what he did, probably with the amused connivance of the Brooklyn fielders. Herzog dutifully bunted, and Charlie barreled through several fans who had rushed onto the field, then slid home in a beautiful spread eagle.

⫼ Did Charlie Make a Difference? ⫼

The wonderful season was over, and the Giants finished 7½ games ahead of the Cubs. But there were really two Giants teams that year, one before Charlie, and one after.

Prior to Charlie, the Giants were a respectable 54-36 (.600). But once Charlie joined the team, the Giants had played some of the hottest ball in history, winning 41 and losing only 14 for a .745 percentage. More dramatic was the performance of the pitchers: Marquard (13-2), Ames (6-1), Wiltse (7-4) and Crandall (8-1) all showed significant improvement. Only Mathewson (18-8 before Charlie, 8-5 after) experienced a letdown.

The Giants hitters also fattened on Charlie's presence. Art Devlin's average climbed 100 points after Charlie joined the team; Josh Devore improved 97 points. Meyers ended at .332 for the year, only two points—just one hit—behind Wagner, the league leader. If Charlie had arrived just a week sooner, would Meyers have been champ?

The ungrateful Giants, however, refused to vote Charlie a share of the World Series money. Of course he forgave them. He appeared in white tie and tails at a banquet honoring the team on the eve of the Series against the A's and predicted a New York victory.

The winner of this game has already been decided, but we don't know which team yet.

Dizzy Dean

CHAPTER 18
Van vs. Faust

LOUIS VAN ZELST AND THE A'S repeated as American League champs in 1911, beating Detroit by 13½ games as Jack Coombs led the league with 28 victories. The World Series would pit little Louie against Charlie Faust—the game's number-one jinx vs. its number-one jinx-killer.

The opener, scheduled for October 13, a Friday, was postponed, naturally, to Saturday. Christy Mathewson (26-13) would go against Chief Bender (17-5) in New York.

The Giants surprised everyone by marching onto the field in black uniforms, replicas of the ones they had worn to beat the A's in 1905. Van's luck seemed bad as the A's first baseman, Stuffy McInnis (.332), injured his hand and had to be replaced by aging Harry Davis (.197). But it turned out to be a break as Davis got them off to a 1-0 lead when he singled Frank Baker home from third.

However, Mathewson thought there was something wrong with that hit—Davis seemed to step into the pitch as if he knew what was coming. From then on, Matty flashed his own signs to catcher Chief Meyers.

Faust's Giants tied it in the fourth when Bender hit Fred Snodgrass, who scored on an error. New York almost scored again in the sixth, but Van's A's stopped them when Snodgrass was out trying to steal home.

The Giants finally went ahead in the seventh on a double by Meyers and a single by Josh Devore, giving Faust the victory, 2-1.

Moving to Philadelphia two days later, New York rookie Rube Marquard (24-7) faced Gettysburg lefty Eddie Plank (23-8).

The A's had a little surprise. The Giants had just set a record for stolen bases, but A's manager Connie Mack soaked the infield to stop their running game.

Meanwhile the Giants had figured out how the A's were stealing their signs—"the little hunchback" is the culprit, Marquard wrote in The *New York Times*. The Giants changed all their signs; this plus a case of nerves by Marquard led to a quick Philadelphia run. With a man on third on an error, Meyers called for a high fastball; Marquard, confused

THE BASEBALL ASTROLOGER   125

momentarily, tried to change in mid-pitch and uncorked a wild pitch.

Twice Rube got the dangerous Baker, the American League home run king with 11, out on curves. But in the sixth, Marquard decided to "cross" him with a fastball—just the pitch Baker loved. Frank lined "a tremendous clout over the right field fence" to give Van a 3-1 victory. Baker "outguessed Marquard very cleverly," Mathewson wrote the next morning in his column in the *New York Herald*.

In Game 3, Matty, pitching on two days rest in a New York drizzle, dueled Coombs, who hurled a masterful three-hitter.

In the second Matty pitched out of trouble with a man on second, getting Jack Lapp to line into a double play. In the eighth, leading 1-0, he was in trouble again with men on first and third, but got Coombs on a grounder to shortstop Art Fletcher, who kicked it away, but got the runner at home.

By the ninth the fans were beginning to file out, and Mathewson "lorded it haughtily" over the A's. He got Eddie Collins (.365) on an easy grounder for the first out, with Baker up next. The superstitious A's engaged in one of their favorite rituals, tossing their bats and jumping in the air to change their luck. Shortstop Jack Barry got so carried away, he hit his head on the concrete dugout ceiling and knocked himself out.

Mathewson threw the still-hitless Baker a slow fadeaway (screwball), then a sharp curve on the inside, and a slow curve on the outside. Then, like Marquard, Matty decided he, too, would "cross" Baker with a fastball. "Baker eats this kind," Marquard winced knowingly. Sure enough, Frank slugged it into the stands to tie the game and win himself his immortal nickname, "Home Run."

The Giants knew they were beaten, Marquard wrote, and the exhausted Mathewson admitted that he staggered through the rest of the ninth and the 10th "with very little on the ball." However, the Faustmen almost won it in the 10th. Snodgrass reached second, but when the catcher, Lapp, dropped a pitch, Snodgrass raced to third and was out by several feet. Score one for Van Zelst.

In the 11th Collins singled, and Baker sent a hard hopper to third baseman Buck Herzog, who threw wildly, putting men on second and third. Danny Murphy then grounded to shortstop Fletcher, who fumbled

as one run scored; Davis sent a whistling line drive to right as another run came in. It looked as if Faust and the Giants had been KO'd.

They weren't through yet, however. In their half of the inning, they put a man on third with two out, and Beals Becker hit a ground ball that Collins fumbled to make the score 4-3. The Giants' last slim hope was to get Becker home. But that hope ended when Beals unaccountably lit out for second on a steal and was caught at the bag. Little Louie's A's had opened up a one-game lead.

After a one-week rain delay, Mathewson took the mound again, though he said he didn't feel in his best form.

The Giants got two lucky runs when Philadelphia's Rube Oldring slipped on the wet grass and misplayed a fly by Larry Doyle into a triple.

Matty struck out Baker in the first on a curve. But in the fourth, Frank slapped a low fly into a mud puddle for two bases. Murphy and Davis also doubled to tie the game, and the A's went on to win 4-2 and take the lead three games to one.

The next day Marquard carried the Giants' last hopes against Coombs. Faust entertained the pregame Polo Grounds crowd by leading the band. The attempt was not too successful, however, the musicians finding it hard to laugh and play at the same time.

Rube whiffed Baker in the first. In the third, the Athletics got a break when Doyle muffed a grounder, putting two men on base. Bris Lord flied out for what should have been the third out, bringing up Oldring, who had hit only three homers all year. He slugged a home run for a 3-0 lead, as the boos crashed around Doyle.

Fighting mad, Larry stormed into the dugout and whipped the Giants into a fighting pitch, and McGraw pulled Marquard from the hill. As the *Times* wrote: "When the situation looked darkest and hope was waning with the dying day," Leon Ames "took the task on his shoulders and measured up heroically." He and Otis Crandall held the Athletics scoreless the rest of the game.

In the ninth, with Charlie's Giants losing 3-1, Herzog grounded out, but Fletcher got a hit and stretched it into two bases. Meyers also grounded out, leaving New York with just one out left, and Crandall at bat. The pitcher smote one over Oldring's head for one run,

and Devore singled in another to tie the game 3-3.

The Giants received a series of lucky breaks in the 10th. Coombs pulled a groin muscle, and the lefty, Plank, was rushed in to pitch to the lefthanded Doyle, who had three straight hits since the booing. Larry swung late on a curve and lined a drive to left for two bases. Snodgrass bunted, and Plank threw to third to catch Doyle, who went in with a beautiful hook slide; Baker, thinking it was a force play, forgot to tag him.

Then came the third, and most fateful, break of the afternoon. Merkle hit a fly down the line that Danny Murphy should have let fall for a foul. Instead, he caught it, and Larry streaked for home, sliding across the plate—but not touching it. As the New York fans poured onto the field, umpire Bill Klem waited for the A's to protest, but Mack didn't make a move. Realizing he had a potential riot on his hands, Klem said nothing and quietly walked away.

Plank's bad luck continued for another game, and the Giants had pulled to within a game of the Athletics.

Could the Faust miracle continue? McGraw sent Ames to the mound against Bender for Game 6. But Red should have kept his lucky necktie. The A's drove him off the mound in the fourth and crushed the Giants, 12-3.

It was the second straight world championship for Mack and his diminutive good luck charm. Van Zelst "outjinxed our champion jinx-killer," Mathewson wrote simply. The A's voted Louie a half share of the Series money. "Lots of players will tell you he deserved it, because he has won two pennants for them."

As for Faust, Mathewson wrote severely that winter, "A jinx-killer never comes back. He is gone. And his expansive smile and bump-the-bumps slide are gone with him.... But he was a wonder while he was at it. And he did a great deal toward giving the players confidence. With him on the bench, they thought they couldn't lose, and they couldn't."

You were a stranger to sorrow; therefore Fate has cursed you.

Euripedes

CHAPTER 19
The Kansas Curse

ALL OTHER STORIES OF CHARLES VICTORY FAUST end there. The press tired of him, the historians forgot him. But one reporter and one historian were not content to let the story die there. Eighty years later Gabe Schechter scoured every 1912 newspaper in New York until he found one man, Sid Mercer of the *Globe*, who continued reporting the exploits of Charlie Faust. The story of Faust in 1912 is even more fascinating than his better-known exploits of 1911.

In November 1911 Faust was back on the boards of Broadway. He sang the "Star Spangled Banner," recited a poem about a mule, cavorted about the stage in imitation of a train and a cow, and of course demonstrated how to bat, pitch, and slide. So many customers walked out that the acts following Charlie demanded he be fired.

In March Charlie wrote to McGraw that he had been working on two new skills, which would double or quadruple his value. First, he could now pitch with either hand. Second, he could catch as well as pitch. When Mac showed no enthusiasm for either skill, Charlie hopped a train to Brooklyn's training camp at Hot Springs, where the Superbas let him pitch a game. He lost 4-1. They offered him no contract.

Charlie showed up next at the Giants' camp in Texas. He confided that he had received offers from the Phillies, Pirates, and Red Sox but assured McGraw that "I'm going to stick with you." He promised to hit .300 and steal "about 70 bases" or "you don't owe me a cent." He reminded the skipper that the team could have won the Series if they'd only put him in to pitch. With a sigh, McGraw tried to option his jinx to George Stallings, the superstitious manager of Buffalo in the International League. Stallings promised "to get back to him."

Charlie followed the team to Hot Springs, where the Red Sox were training. There he met none other than Mike "Nuf Ced" McGreevey, who, as he did every spring, had journeyed to be with his favorite team at his private "fantasy camp." As usual, he sent each player a St. Patricks's Day card, and, always a physical fitness nut, he stayed in shape by running 15 miles in three hours through the Arkansas hills. Black waiters at one

of the resort hotels planned a cakewalk to entertain the guests and approached the visiting sportswriters to be judges. The writers turned them down, so they asked Mike and Charlie to do the honors, along with millionaires Jay Gould and Andrew Carnegie. And so Fate brought together these two merry mascots, McGreevey and Faust, in a meeting that was almost ignored by the rest of the world, which remained unaware of the psychic, not to say cosmic, conjunction.

In April in the North Atlantic, the Titanic struck an iceberg and went down. In the Polo Grounds Charlie Faust tried to buttonhole Giants owner John Brush in his limousine about a job, but got brushed off. A week later Charlie attended the home opener, wearing a derby hat as he delivered a pregame oration. Thereafter he "wandered through the Polo Grounds," enviously watching, as Bob Uecker one day would, from "a high perch" in the grandstand.

On April 21 the Giants and Yankees played a benefit game for survivors of the Titanic, and Charlie demonstrated his lefthanded pitching skills before the game. But the press had lost interest in him; Runyon dismissed him as "squirrel fodder."

The Giants got off to an excellent 11-5 start. On a western road trip, they won 11 and lost two, giving them a 21-7 record. Rube Marquard especially started strong, with eight straight victories.

Oddly, through a quirk of scheduling, plus some rainouts, only seven of the Giants' games had been at home, where they were only 4-3. Thus, their fast start was obviously not due to any whammies Charlie was putting on the opposition.

The Giants caught the subway to Brooklyn for two games against the Superbas and won them both, including Rube's ninth straight. Did Charlie go with them? It is not clear.

It began to dawn on him that he was never going to pitch again for McGraw, who was "discriminating" against him in favor of Marquard and Mathewson. So Charlie sadly left the Giants, lugging his satchel to the train station to join the Cubs. "Chance needs pitching," he said. But the Cubs apparently didn't need pitching as much as Charlie had thought, and he probably returned to New York for the Giants' long homestand, when they won 10 and lost five. That gave them a record of

38-11 and a huge lead of 11 games—and it was still only the middle of June.

Three of the wins were by Marquard. Number 13 was lucky; Rube left after eight innings with the score 2-1 against him. The Giants won it in the ninth, but Rube got credit for the victory under the rules of the day, on the principle that he had pitched better than his reliever, Hooks Wiltse, and deserved it more. Number 14, an 11-inning win over Pittsburgh, tied the modern record for consecutive wins set by Jack Chesbro in 1904 and equaled by Ed Reulbach in '08.

On June 19 Faust traveled to Chicago, still pursuing Frank Chance for a job. The Republicans were also in town, locked in a convention battle between President Taft and ex-President Theodore Roosevelt. If the Cubs rebuffed Faust, Mercer suggested, he could become a compromise candidate for the GOP. But Mercer tipped his hat to the departed Kansas Cyclone, who, he wrote, had remained with the Giants long enough to insure another championship.

The Giants also caught a train, to Boston, where Rube won his record-breaking 15th and 16th straight, and the Giants swept five games against the last-place Braves. We don't know where Charlie was at this time.

The New Yorkers came back home and won 11 more in a row, making 16 in all, the last one coming against Brooklyn, thanks to a passed ball; it put the Giants a whopping 16½ games ahead of the second-place Cubs. Marquard won three more to run his consecutive win streak to 19. He was lucky to win the last one. In Brooklyn the Dodgers' Nap Rucker outpitched him, and twice Rube loaded the bases with no outs and escaped without a run.

McGraw's men split a doubleheader against Brooklyn amid a ceremony laying the cornerstone for Ebbets Field. Then they boarded their Pullman to invade the West, beginning with Chicago.

Charlie had already left for Cincinnati, where he appealed to Garry Herrmann, the equivalent of the commissioner, for back pay he claimed the Giants owed him. Herrmann rejected his claim. Bitter, Faust bought a ticket to the Windy City. He arrived just as the Giants hit town and predicted that, in spite of their prohibitive lead, they would not win the pennant.

This was the first time since his arrival a year earlier that Faust had predicted defeat instead of victory for the Giants. It seems to have shaken the players up. Larry Doyle, batting .360, and utility infielder Tillie Shafer both reported sick with ptomaine poisoning.

Marquard took the mound, seeking his 20th win in a row. In the first, New York substitute Heinie Groh messed up a double play, letting two runs in. Chicago scored two more in the fourth on a walk, a sacrifice, and two errors. Meanwhile Rube was battered for six runs in six innings, breaking his winning streak. Worse, three more Giants infielders were knocked out of the game with injuries—Art Wilson, Art Fletcher, and Groh. Outfielder Fred Snodgrass and even pitcher Otis Crandall had to be rushed in to plug the holes.

The next day Matty was rocked for 12 hits, though he won his game 5-2 over Mordecai Brown. Then Ames was shut out, 3-0.

Faust gloated that the Giants' bad luck was the result of the way they had treated him. He claimed to have put a jinx on them "and is mighty unpopular with them now," wrote Mercer. "Faust must be a vindictive cuss if he won't even allow a team to score a run."

The Giants dropped the fourth game of the series, 11-7.

Charlie followed the team to St. Louis, where the bad luck continued against the sixth-place Cardinals. Matty won the opening game, though again he was pounded for 12 hits. Then, Mercer wrote, "Faust got in his deadly work." Marquard tried an iron-man feat, two games in one day, and lost them both, making three losses in a row since Faust had laid his curse. (One of the defeats would be a "no decision" today, since the Giants tied the game after he left before going on to lose it.) The Giants also lost the fourth game, 10-6.

The crestfallen champions returned to Chicago for a single game and lost it 3-1, cutting their lead to nine games. They had now won two, both by Mathewson, and lost seven in their western trip. Their fielding was awful, Mercer wrote, and as for their pitching, "Any time our boys can knock out eight or ten runs, they can make the game close."

The Giants begged Charlie to go back home to Kansas or go down to the minors and work his way up. Charlie haughtily refused. He also demanded back wages for all his work in 1911. "The poor deluded

Jayhawker's case is pathetic," Mercer wrote. "The Giants get nervous now when he hangs around, as they fear he may become violent."

In Pittsburgh, the next stop, Mathewson was beaten 6-2. "The Giants believe Faust put the Kansas Curse on them," Sid said. "Faust is no longer a mascot, he's a menace."

Then Faust mysteriously disappeared, and the Giants won three from fourth-place Cincinnati to end the road trip.

But even back home, New York lost three more to the Cubs, two of them on late-inning errors. The team snapped back to beat the Reds four times, but lost three out of four to the Pirates. They "just haven't been able to get the breaks," Mercer declared. In one loss their fielders booted three balls good for four Pittsburgh runs. Meanwhile their "impotent hitters" left 12 men on base; Red Murray came up with the bases loaded and struck out on a pitch over his head. The Giants' lead dwindled to 7½ games. "It looks as if Charlie Faust will have to be recalled," Mercer advised.

The Cardinals beat Wiltse 4-2, then KO'd Ames after two innings as the team showed "a great lack of pepper." The Giants' margin had plummeted to 6½.

It was one of their worst homestands ever, 6-8. On August 14 the nervous players piled into their Pullman berths to return to Chicago, where Marquard was pounded 5-1 to cut the lead to five games. The players even talked about hiring Charlie back to lift "the Gypsy curse." Perhaps, Mercer agreed, "a little pinch-mascoting might do a lot of good."

On August 19 McGraw got a letter from Marion, Kansas. Charlie Faust would join the team in St. Louis, it read. However, Charlie didn't show up, and no one ever found out why. Freed at last from his baleful influence, the Giants played .600 ball the rest of the season and slowly built their lead back to finish 10 games in front of the Pirates.

We may divide New York's season into three periods: before, during, and after the Kansas Curse:

Before (April 11-July 6)	54-14	.794
During (July 8-August 18)	19-18	.514
After (August 19- end)	30-16	.652
Total	103-48	.682
Second-place Pirates	93-58	.616

More than any other player, Marquard's success seemed to rise and fall with Charlie. Before the curse, Rube was 19-0. During the curse, he was 4-6. After the curse, he was 1-1, to finish the season at 24-7.

Ahead lay the World Series. The Giants would go into it without either the benediction or the malediction of "the world's most famous adult mascot," Charles Victory Faust.

Boston runs to brains as well as to beans and brown
bread. But she's cursed with an army of cranks whom
nothing short of a straightjacket or a swamp elm club
will ever control.

William Cowper Brann

CHAPTER 20
The Royal Rooters' Revenge

WHILE THE RED SOX were in eclipse after the 1904 season, "Nuf Ced" McGreevey had been keeping busy. He did some work as a boxing commentator, and competed for the New England handball championship. He posed for newspaper pictures taking a dip through the ice in midwinter, showing off his figure-skating form and doing handstands in the snow in his bathing suit.

Mike was also attending the Red Sox's spring training camp at Hot Springs religiously. He beat Sox manager Fred Lake in bowling, and prowled the hotel lobby looking for players to shake hands with. On the field he stationed himself at the first base railing and shook hands with each Boston player who went past, then moved to third base and glad-handed the opposition, too. He shook so enthusiastically that he once fell over the railing onto his head.

Meanwhile, the Red Sox slipped to fifth in 1911. In the spring of 1912, the team put a sign in Mike's honor on the right field fence, and Red Sox president John Taylor made him an honorary team member, noting that "ordinarily he is a quiet and law-abiding citizen."

That season the Sox had a new manager, Jake Stahl, and a new park, Fenway. Smokey Joe Wood won 34 games, 16 of them in a row; Tris Speaker batted .388 and anchored one of the best defensive outfields ever with Harry Hooper and Duffy Lewis. Boston jumped all the way to first, 14 games ahead of Washington.

Louie Van Zelst's A's dropped to third.

So when the World Series opened against the Giants, Nuf Ced, Boston liquor store owner Bill Pink, and "Honey Fitz" Fitzgerald, who was now mayor of Boston, once again led led 300 Rooters in a special train, following their team to New York. The good old days were back. The "migration," as Hugh Fullerton of *The New York Times* called it, lasted all night, ending with a torchlight parade through Gotham's streets. With his diminutive honor, Fitzgerald, in silk top hat, silk tie, and frock coat, singing in an Irish tenor, the Rooters bellowed "Tessie" and waved dollar bills at the eager New Yorkers.

Prior to Game 1, the players were throwing warmup tosses when "suddenly the blare of music attracted every eye to the Eighth Avenue gateway as it swung open to admit Nuf Ced McGreevey and his 300 Rooters, and a 30-piece brass band." Each Rooter wore a hatband proclaiming "Oh you Red Sox" and sashes of red socks knitted together around their waists. Above them floated a banner: "Red Sox, World Champs." They marched across the field and took their seats in section 23, the "skidoo" section. Fitz and New York mayor Gaynor were given seats of honor next to the press box.

Immediately the New York rooters raised a cheer for "Tammany," whereupon, the two cheering sections opened a good-natured duel, answering each other cheer for cheer. Honey Fitz couldn't restrain himself, and the pudgy mayor raced across the field, silk hat in hand and coattails flying, to the Rooters' section, where he seized a megaphone and shouted to the loyal visitors to root until the end. McGreevey grabbed Fitz and insisted that he lead a chorus of "Tessie." Then hizzoner doffed his silk hat to the cheers of the New York fans, and everyone settled down to see Wood battle big Jeff Tesreau.

The Giants took a 2-0 lead in the third. In the sixth Speaker drove the ball to left-center, where Josh Devore called to make the catch, but the crowd's yelling was so loud that center fielder Fred Snodgrass couldn't hear Josh and cut in front of him as the ball fell for a triple. Speaker then scored on a groundout. In the seventh, with two men on, Wood hit a double-play ball to Larry Doyle that should have ended the inning, but the Giants could get only one runner and the Sox scored three runs for a 4-3 victory.

The teams caught the overnight train to Boston. So did the Rooters. (It was a joke to label their cars "sleeping cars," Fullerton noted.) Ever the politician, Honey Fitz declared a citywide holiday. Some 30,000 people jammed Fenway, and Fitz rode grandly into the stadium to present Stahl with a big new roadster—red, of course. The Rooters took the seats reserved for them in temporary bleachers in front of the left field wall.

Mathewson and Boston's Ray Collins staggered through a ragged game. With the game tied in the 10th, the Giants scored on a long triple by Merkle. But Speaker hit a triple of his own and kept racing around

third and headed home, where substitute catcher Art Wilson dropped the relay, putting the teams back in a tie. That was how it ended an inning later, when darkness fell.

The make-up game was scheduled for Fenway the next day. Marquard, who had won only one game since Charlie Faust disappeared, won 2-1. Once again the Rooters were praised for their "orderliness and good sportsmanship." They applauded good plays with impartiality, McGraw declared.

Fitzgerald asked for 600 tickets for the Rooters in New York. The Giants agreed on condition that the Rooters would "make it lively and noisy" for the customers before the game. (Were they kidding?) Honey Fitz's office took charge of selling the tickets for $15 each, which included train ticket and sightseeing autos to and from the ballpark. The game opened under dull, dark skies, which made Wood's fastball look even faster. Smokey Joe won, 3-1.

In Boston the next day—Columbus Day, another holiday—the city celebrated with a dozen parades in the morning. In the afternoon, Mathewson faced rookie Hugh Bedient (20-9). Matty retired 17 men in a row. But Hooper's hit rolled into a little opening in the fence to cost New York one run. Doyle's error let in another, and the Giants got only three hits as Matty lost a tough one, 2-1. The Red Sox now had a commanding three-to-one lead, and the Rooters rushed onto the field, singing, shouting, roaring, clanging cowbells, and blowing horns.

The teams took Sunday off. On Monday ex-President Teddy Roosevelt, "the Bull Moose," was shot in the chest as he campaigned for re-election. (He finished the speech.) Meanwhile, Marquard beat the Red Sox, 5-2.

Back in Boston, a northeast gale whipped up swirls of dust, and Wood, winner of two games so far, was set to wrap the Series up. However, McGraw was about to get the break he had been waiting for.

The Rooters, as ebullient as ever and charged up for victory, marched in, in perfect lockstep order, waving miniature red stockings and singing "Tessie." But when they arrived at their seats, they found them already taken by New Yorkers. Just as Wood was stepping into the box to start the game, the angry Rooters took their tubas and trombones,

leaped over the low fence, swept aside the police, and stampeded onto the field. Mounted policemen galloped in from right field and drove them back into the bleachers. But a second rush pushed the fence down like paper, and the Rooters spilled onto the field again. They hurled peanuts, canes, and anything else they could at the cops, who galloped back and forth, charging the maddened fans. The umpires threatened to forfeit the game, and the Boston players pleaded with the fans.

Slowly, sullenly the now disloyal Rooters dispersed into the stands to squeeze into standing room wherever they could. Some stomped over to Red Sox secretary Rob McRoy, who tried to explain that the rain-out and makeup game earlier in the Series had caused confusion as to which tickets would be honored on which days. McRoy said he had hundreds of requests for those seats and had agreed to hold them until 9 a.m., then finally opened the section to other fans. That didn't mollify the Rooters, however. Fitz demanded that McRoy be fired, and his name would be a cuss word in Boston until he fled the city a year or two later.

There would be few cheers for the Red Sox that afternoon. Nor could any chorus of "Tessie" be heard throughout the strangely quiet grandstand. Meanwhile, Wood's arm had gotten cold, and he was shelled for six runs in the first inning as the Giants won, 11-4. The Series was all tied up.

After the final, out, there was no usual rush for the gates and the el trains. The crowd of almost 33,000 waited tensely to see what the Rooters would do. Emerging one by one from the stands, they formed up as the band played a mournful "Tessie." They stopped at the Red Sox bench, where their leaders lifted their megaphones to give three loud boos for McRoy, then three loud cheers for New York.

The final game would be in Boston on a cold, bleak afternoon. There was no rush for the ticket windows. "For the first time," Fullerton wrote, "the Boston fans had apparently quit." At game time the stands were half empty—only 17,000 people showed up. The Red Sox distributed noisemakers, which helped a little, as clicking could be heard throughout the game.

Bedient and Matty dueled brilliantly under the leaden atmosphere. By the time Bedient retired for a pinch hitter in the seventh, the score

was 1-1. It was a game that cried out for Charlie Faust to waken his heroes or for "Tessie" to lift the hearts of her boys. But on this gray afternoon the players were on their own. Wood, who had hardly broken a sweat the day before, relieved Bedient in the eighth, and he and Matty dueled into the fateful 10th, one of the most famous innings in baseball history.

The Giants scored on a double and a single as the usually sure-handed Speaker juggled the ball in the outfield. But Wood stopped further danger with a strikeout and a groundout. In Boston's half, Snodgrass made one of the most famous muffs in World Series annals, when he dropped an easy fly ball by Clyde Engle (.234). He promptly atoned with a great catch to rob Hooper of a sure hit, but then Speaker lifted an easy foul that fell among Matty, Meyers, and Merkle (Matty should have called the play). Revivified, Tris lined the game-tying single, and Larry Gardner drove in the run that won the game and Series.

But there was little joy in Boston. At a Fanueil Hall gathering the following day, Fitz paid tribute to McGreevey, Keenan, and the other Rooters, and the fans gave a loud cheer at Nuf Ced's name. Keenan thanked New York for its courteous treatment throughout the Series. As for the Red Sox, he said, "We'll pay McRoy the last cent for those tickets. I'll never attend another ball game as long as he's the secretary of the club."

One wonders with what mixed emotions, back in Marion, Kansas, Charlie Faust must have read the news. The final seventh game had been the perfect opportunity for him to spook his team to victory.

Why had McGraw so adamantly given Faust the cold shoulder? In a superstitious age, McGraw, the master of psychology, was not above rigging good luck charms to inspire his players. Charlie certainly kept the team loose, and the men believed in him; they clearly played better ball when he was there. And the team must have made more money at the box office with the Kansas Cyclone doing his antics before the game. It would have cost the Giants only a few dollars to keep Faust on the bench. Then why didn't they?

Schechter's theory is that McGraw was jealous. The papers made it appear that it was Faust, not McGraw, who was responsible for the

Giants' winning. (Indeed, this jealous reaction is what latter-day witches would receive from managers for the pains they took in psyching modern teams to win.).

Could Charlie Faust have made even a small difference in the World Series? Would Speaker's foul, for instance, have been caught with Charlie on the job?

We'll never know. History does not disclose its alternatives.

God: I'll just r'ar back and pass a miracle.

Marcus Cook Connelly,
GREEN PASTURES

CHAPTER 21
Annus Mirabilis

THE GIANTS PROVED THEY COULD WIN without Charlie. In 1913 they won 101 games and finished 12½ ahead of the Phils. Christy Mathewson was 25-11, Rube Marquard 23-10, and sophomore Jeff Tesreau 22-13. Red Ames was traded to seventh-place Cincinnati, where he lost 13 and won 11.

Meanwhile, in the American League, Jack Coombs of the A's was stricken ill and won only one game. While Louis Van Zelst went faithfully to the hospital, talking and reading to big Jack by the hour, the other pitchers took up the slack. Chief Bender was 21-10, Eddie Plank 18-10, and newcomer Bullet Joe Bush 14-6. Stuffy McInnis, Eddie Collins, and Home Run Baker all hit better than .300, and Baker led the league in homers and RBIs as the A's won the pennant. Then they beat the Giants four to one in the World Series. It was Van's third world championship in four years.

In 1914 the A's added lefty Herb Pennock (11-4) and Rube Bressler (10-4) to help veterans Bender (17-3), Bush (16-12), and Plank (15-7). They got .300 seasons from McInnis, Collins, and Baker again and coasted to their fourth pennant in five years, defeating the Red Sox by 8½ games. Then they waited to see if the Giants could hang on to their early lead in the National League and meet them in the World Series once again.

≈ The Miracle Braves ≈

The 1991 Atlanta Braves were not the first worst-to-first miracle team—that honor belongs to the 1914 Boston Braves. In 1950 they were voted the greatest sports story of the half-century, outpolling even Babe Ruth's called-shot home run of 1932.

Woodrow Wilson was in the White House, pushing his new income tax through Congress. Black Jack Pershing was in Mexico, chasing Pancho Villa. Charlie Chaplin and Mary Pickford were in Los Angeles, making silent classics. Sinclair Lewis was writing *Babbitt.* Autos were

still rare on American streets, and airplanes were even rarer in the skies. From Europe came ominous news of the murder of the Austrian arch-duke, and armies mobilized across the continent.

And many strange things were happening to the Braves.

They were in last place, as usual, where they had finished for four straight years, 1909-12. A new manager, George Stallings, and some shrewd moves raised them to fifth in 1913. But they reverted to form in the early months of 1914. By July 4th the Braves were last again, 15½ games behind the powerful Giants.

Then the miracle began to unfold.

)(**The Chief**)(

George "Tweedy" Stallings, the 47-year-old manager of the Braves, was an anomaly in that era of roughneck, sometimes semi-literate ball players. He was a Georgia aristocrat, born on a 5,000-acre estate. His father, a Confederate general, had been a friend of Tecumseh Sherman, who spared the plantation on his famous march to the sea. Stallings went to medical school before deciding on a career in baseball, and his uniform on the bench was not the flannels of the players but a business suit with vest, bow tie, and straw hat.

For all his Chesterfieldian appearance, Stallings had a viper's tongue. "He was the cussingest man I ever knew," former catcher Bubbles Hargrave grinned admiringly. "Simpleton," "dunce," "bone-head" and "clown" were some of the printable names he used. "Invective," said catcher Hank Gowdy, "was an art with him."

"Bonehead," he once growled, "go up there and hit!" Six Braves jumped up and grabbed bats.

Stallings was a swarthy, moon-faced man with gleaming white teeth. In fact, his steal sign was to bare his teeth in the dugout. He sat on the same spot on the bench each day, knees and feet tightly together, getting more and more agitated as the game progressed. The more nerv-ous he became, the more he slid back and forth. Sometimes he fidgeted half the length of the bench and back, while his players huddled on the ends to give him room. Every year, they said, he wore out the seats of

several pairs of trousers.

In spite of his erudition, Stallings had one trait in common with most other baseball men of his day: He was deeply superstitious. Fred Lieb would remark on this 25 years later in his book, *Sight Unseen: A Journalist Visits the Occult*: "I often wondered whether a Negro nurse who cared for him in the days of his infancy had not inculcated on him her primitive superstitions of the African jungles."

One of Stallings' pet aversions was the sight of scraps of paper or peanut shells. Other teams quickly discovered this, of course. "I have seen him livid with rage," Lieb wrote, "when New York players tore up tiny bits of paper and scattered them in front of the Boston dugout. On hands and knees, he personally picked up every tiny scrap from among the Boston bats strewn on the ground, swearing loudly at the perpetrators of the dastardly deed. Stallings' unreasoning faith in these bits of paper actually had power to bring bad luck to his team, he thought such tremendous power into his superstitions."

Another Stallings idiosyncrasy was to freeze in whatever position he happened to be when his team made a hit. One day he was stooped over, retrieving a peanut shell, when a Brave drilled a hit, and Stallings froze. He remained stooped as the next man got a hit, and the next, and the next. By the time the rally was over, George had to be helped to straighten up and assisted as he hobbled painfully off the field. Another time, Stallings was looking toward the bullpen when a rally started. For 15 minutes he couldn't move, and players had to give him a play-by-play.

As a manager, Stallings' record was spotty. He had done well in the minors but indifferently in the majors. He won five straight pennants (1891-95) in California, Georgia, and Nashville. Promoted to the old Phillies of 1897, he finished a dead-last 10th. The following year he lifted them to eighth before returning to the minors. In 1901 he was in the American League, bringing Detroit in third. Then he dropped back to Buffalo in the International League; he led them to first-place finishes in 1904 and 1905.

Four years later Stallings took over the old New York Highlanders, forerunners of today's Yankees. They were no "Murderers' Row" then, however, having finished last in 1908. Stallings lifted them to fifth in

1909, then to second in 1910, 14½ games behind the Athletics.

Stallings dropped out of the big leagues once again until 1913, when he signed to manage the woeful Braves, who in 1912 had won only 52 and lost 101 to finish 52 games behind the Giants.

Stallings, or "Chief," as he was called, looked over his pitching staff and moaned. "I've got 16 pitchers, all of them rotten." Years later, back on his plantation, he was seized by a heart attack. To what did he ascribe it, the doctor wondered. "Bases on balls, you son of a bitch, bases on balls," Stallings growled. They were reportedly his last words.

The Braves' pitching was epitomized by lefty George Tyler, a fastball pitcher whose specialty was shooting BB's at teammates with a toothpick. He was better with BB's than baseballs, unfortunately; in 1912 he won only 11 games and lost 22, the most in the league. The Braves were a fair hitting team, however, with four players hitting better than .300. But they weren't winning games.

So Stallings started cleaning house. He picked up some promising rookies: Butch Schmidt, a burly first baseman, outfielders Joe Connally and Leslie Mann, and shortstop Rabbit Maranville, a light hitter but a sensational fielder and a future Hall of Famer. Best of all, Stallings discovered two fine rookie pitchers. One was 26-year-old Dick "Baldy" Rudolph, from Fordham University, with a good curve, good control, and a sharp-breaking spitter. The other was a 21-year-old, 6'3" Californian, Bill James, who threw the best spitball in the game. The Braves, Stallings announced, would not finish last in 1913. And they didn't. With James winning six games, Rudolph 14 and Tyler 16, the team finished fifth, a respectable step up.

Over the winter Stallings installed Hank Gowdy as catcher. In his biggest coup, he got Cubs veteran Johnny Evers, a .285-hitter and a scrappy second baseman, who had helped make "Tinker-to-Evers-to-Chance" a baseball legend. A pugnacious leader, Evers was hated by his foes but adored by his teammates. He was named captain, and he and Maranville turned more double plays than Johnny ever had with Joe Tinker.

I am ready for Fortune as she wills.

Dante
INFERNO

☲ The Summer of 1914 ☲

The Braves quickly fell to last place and stayed there into July. "Bad luck early in the season lost many a game," the *Boston Globe* would write later. "We'd done the best we thought we could," Maranville said, "but somehow we always came out on the losing end." The fans started calling them "Misfits" and "Butter Ball Tossers."

On July 4 the Braves lost a doubleheader in Boston. James was bombed for 17 hits while Tyler lost 4-3, and the team fell to 15½ games behind. It is axiomatic that the standings on July 4 are pretty much what they will be at season's end.

In desperation, Stallings obtained speedy outfielder Josh Devore, a veteran of the 1911 champion Giants, and third baseman Carlisle "Red" Smith from Brooklyn.

Embarking on a road trip to the west, the Braves stopped in Buffalo to play an exhibition against the Buffalo Bisons of the International League, who thrashed them 10-2. That night, on the Pullman to Chicago, Stallings stomped through the car, paused at his stateroom, and looked back at his hangdog players. "Big leaguers!" he sneered. "Baa. You couldn't beat a bunch of females!" Then he turned and slammed the door behind him.

The players looked at each other, stunned. Maranville broke the silence. "Can you play better ball than you have been playing?" he asked Evers. "Yes," said Johnny, "I think I can." "I think I can, too," Rabbit replied. Pretty soon all the players were nodding and, as Maranville recalled years later, "we all jumped in our berths and called it a day."

At about that time, Lieb writes, a friend of Stallings returned from Cuba bearing a gift, an innocuous looking 10-cent piece that had been blessed by "a fanatical Cuban from the island's interior who styled himself 'the Black Pope.' Money blessed by this mad religionist supposedly took on 10 times its face value." The friend gave the coin to Stallings, saying, "Here's something to bring luck to your team, George."

The next day Tyler beat the Cubs in 11 innings. Then James beat Hippo Vaughn, a 21-game winner that year, 3-1. Swiss-born Otto Hess, a veteran lefty, lost 11-6. But Rudolph won the fourth game, 5-2.

The Braves next split their four games at St. Louis, with Rudolph winning one in 12 innings. "Stick in there," Stallings said. "We'll show 'em." The Braves will be leading the league by September 1, he predicted.

In Cincinnati James won a four-hitter, 1-0. Rudolph also won, 6-3. By the morning of July 19 the Braves were just one game out of seventh. That day James, pitching on one day's rest, came on in relief with the Braves losing 2-0. Boston scored three runs in the ninth to climb out of the cellar. In Pittsburgh, they won four out of five, getting four shutouts from their staff—Rudolph's was a three-hitter, and James won 1-0 in 11 innings. That propelled the Braves into fourth place, 10 games behind, as the players headed home, having won 12 out of 16 in the west.

As headlines screamed of armies mobilizing in Europe, 10,000 Bostonians, the biggest crowd in years, came out to welcome the team back to brand new Braves' Field. However, Hess lost to Chicago, the Cubs' ninth straight victory. But Rudolph and James won the next two games and the Braves vaulted into third place while war erupted in Europe. Lieb says Stallings parked his car two blocks from the park that day. For the rest of the season he parked in the exact same spot, "and woe to any car owner who tried to squeeze in ahead of him."

St. Louis was next. Tyler beat them 2-1. Rudolph followed with a two-hitter, and James took another extra-inning game, 4-3, before a crowd of 20,000. Tyler won 1-0, and the Braves had climbed to .500, just 5½ games behind. Next Rudolph beat Pittsburgh 1-0, his second two-hitter in a row, and James followed with another shutout.

That night Maranville and Schmidt went to dinner and came home soused. Next morning, red-eyed, they struggled to the park. With the Pirates' Babe Adams on the mound, Rabbit stuck his bat out and somehow got two bloop singles. He also stole two bases.

In the 10th, he was gulping water at the water bucket when someone yelled to him, "You're up."

"Up where?" he asked.

Connally shoved a bat in his hands. "Go up there and hit," he ordered.

"Hit who?" Rabbit replied. "I'll fight anybody here."

They finally pointed him toward home plate, and he took his stance. "Don't get too close to the plate," the ump warned, "you're liable to get hurt."

Maranville squinted. When he saw Adams go into his windup, Rabbit went into his swing, and the ball sailed over the left field fence as Rabbit, with four homers all year, stood dumbly watching. At last Gowdy came out and gave him a push. "Run, Rabbit," Hank said. "You made a home run, and the game is over."

Reliever Paul Strand won the next day in the 10th as well. Then James beat last-place Cincinnati, 3-1. "BRAVES MOVE INTO SECOND AND DECLARE WAR ON GIANTS," the *Boston Globe* rejoiced as German armies marched through Belgium.

The next day Tyler battled the Reds for 13 innings before the game was called, 0-0.

On August 13 the Braves traveled to New York for the long-awaited showdown against the Giants. Skipper John McGraw led with Rube Marquard, a 20-game winner three years in a row, and Rudolph beat him 5-3. James beat Tesreau and Tyler completed the sweep, winning 2-0 in 10 innings.

Out west again the Braves swept four from Cincinnati. When Hess beat Pittsburgh, the Braves were only one game behind. The next day James hooked up in another extra-inning duel, losing 3-2 in the 13th. But Cincinnati beat the Giants twice, and the Braves were tied for first.

How to explain the amazing drive?

Stallings believed that the secret lay in his pocket, in the magic coin reposing there. "With each additional victory, the talisman gained in power," Lieb wrote. "I believe Stallings would have killed anyone trying to take it from him during that drive, and if the blessing increased the value of the coin ten-fold, Stallings would not have parted with it for many thousand times its face value. Had he lost it, Stallings' faith in its potency was so great that I believe it is conceivable the mad rush of this upstart team would have been checked."

Boston stumbled briefly in Chicago. Tyler lost twice, 9-5 and 1-0, and the Braves dropped half a game behind.

In St. Louis, Boston won three out of four. Rudolph lost in 10

innings, but James hurled another shutout, Strand won in relief, and Tyler pitched a one-hitter.

Then, with an off day on the schedule, the Braves went to scout the mighty A's. Defending world champions, the A's were heading for their fifth American League pennant, having won in 1905, 1910, 1911, and 1913. They were world champs the last three of those years. Philadelphia boasted the famous "$100,000 infield" of Stuffy McGinnis, Eddie Collins, Jack Barry, and Home Run Baker. McGinnis, Collins, and Baker were all .300 hitters. The A's also had a pitching staff with three future Hall of Famers—Eddie Plank (15-5), Chief Bender (17-15), and Herb Pennock (10-4).

While the Braves looked on, the A's easily whipped Cleveland, but Stallings remained buoyantly optimistic. He would mortgage his plantation and bet it all on the Braves to beat the A's four straight in the World Series, he declared.

The next day Rudolph and James beat the Phils while New York and Marquard were losing to Brooklyn, putting the Braves back into first. But then Tyler lost to Grover Alexander (27-15), and Boston fell half a game behind again.

That night Germany Schaefer, a veteran clown coaching the Washington Senators, took Maranville to dinner with a "lady friend." If possible, Schaefer was even nuttier than Maranville: He once "stole" first base from second, and on another occasion homered and ran the bases backwards. The two madcaps lingered over beers, swapping stories and laughs until midnight, when the lady suggested they go to an all-night club to "eat, drink, and be merry."

"It's O.K. with me," Maranville replied obligingly.

Schaefer excused himself. "Have a good time, both of you."

When the sun was creeping through the windows of the roadhouse, Rabbit crept back to his hotel. "Where the hell have you been?" Schmidt demanded. When Maranville told him, he snorted. "You big sucker, that's one of McGraw's pet tricks, and to think that you were dumb enough to fall for it."

Maranville arrived at the park still half asleep as James took the mound with two days rest.

That evening Rabbit put in a call to Schaefer. "Many thanks for the party," he said. "I had a wonderful time, but I paid for it."

"What happened, Rabbit?" Germany asked eagerly.

"I couldn't hit a balloon," Rabbit moaned, "and I made three errors. I couldn't stay awake."

"That's too bad," Schaefer consoled him. "What was the score?"

"Twelve to three in favor of us, and I got three hits which drove in four runs and was all over the diamond. Next time you try to pull any more of your tricks, you better get a Dutchman like yourself and not an Irishman like me!"

Two days later James dueled 12 innings to beat the Phils, 6-5. That was followed by a surprise victory from rookie Gene Cocreham. Then the Braves headed home to face the Giants in a doubleheader on Labor Day, September 7.

In the morning game 35,000 people filled the park, and thousands more were turned away as Rudolph faced Mathewson. Matty had them beat 4-3 with one out in the ninth when Devore, the ex-Giant, beat out an infield hit and Herbie Moran, recovering from a beaning, hit one into the standing-room crowd for a double. Then Evers hit a sinking line drive to left, scoring both runners as the Braves jumped in the air like bucking broncos. That afternoon another full house paid to see the second game, in which Tyler lost, 10-1. But the next day James easily beat Marquard 8-3, Rube's ninth loss in a row, and the Braves were back in first place to stay.

On September 9, Braves rookie George Davis, a Harvard law student who had won only three big league games in his life, pitched a no-hitter over the Phils. He got a scare in the fifth when he walked the bases full with no out. He got one big strikeout, but still had to face dangerous Gavvy Cravath, the league home run champ with 19, a large total for those days. Davis got him on a double play, and the crisis was over.

Boston kept pulling away until by September 29 they needed only one more win to clinch. Tom Hughes, called back from the minors, beat Chicago 3-2—the only game he won that year—and the Miracle had happened. From 15½ behind, the Braves had stormed to 10 games ahead. Of their last 75 games they had won 59 for a winning percentage of .787.

Not even the winningest club in history, the 1906 Cubs (116 wins, .763), could match that.

Wrote Lieb: "As the season wore on, Stallings' coin assumed greater and greater significance for George. He wouldn't have parted with it for his World Series share, and it was difficult for him to decide which was a greater factor in his sensational victory, the 'blessed' dime or the pitching arms of Rudolph, James and Tyler."

The Braves' Big Three had pitched heroically. Their records before and after July 4 look like this:

	JAMES	RUDOLPH	TYLER	TEAM
Before July 4	7-6	8-9	5–8	34-45
After July 4	19-1	19-11	1- 6	59-14
Total	26-7	27-10	16-14	94-59

Some of the batters' before-and-after marks:

	BEFORE	AFTER	DIFFERENCE
Whitted	.156	.253	+ .097
Mann	.208	.291	+ .083
Smith	.245	.314	+ .069
Cather	.254	.310	+ .056
Schmidt	.259	.302	+ .043
Gowdy	.236	.249	+ .013
Connally	.301	.309	+ .008
Evers	.280	.278	- .002
Maranville	.256	.237	- .019
Gilbert	.293	.180	- .113

Evers was voted the league's Most Valuable Player.

Stallings' club had already earned its immortal nickname, "The Miracle Braves," no matter what the outcome of the World Series against the A's and Louis Van Zelst. Although Van didn't know it yet, he was about to come up against a double whammy—Stallings' lucky coin and "Tessie."

When music arose with its voluptuous swell,
Soft eyes looked love to eyes which spake again,
And all were merry as a wedding bell.

Lord Byron

CHAPTER 22
Van vs. "Tessie"

THE SWAGGERING A's were 2-1 favorites as the 1914 World Series opened, but the Royal Rooters were chafing to get back into action. Ex-mayor Fitzgerald announced a Royal Rooters Special train to take 200 faithful to Philadelphia. The story ran on the top of page one, right next to the lead story of the German attack on Antwerp.

The day before the opening game, Boston owner John Gaffney called Stallings with a premonition of trouble. He was too late. Third baseman Red Smith (.314) had just broken his leg, and Charlie Deal, a .210-hitter, would have to substitute for him.

But the Braves were nothing if not cocky. Stallings himself told them they could win in four straight, something that had never been done before in World Series history.

When Harry Davis, captain of the A's, dropped by the Boston dressing room to congratulate them on their pennant, little Herbie Moran piped up: "I don't think you fellows will win a single game." Then Stallings ordered his players not to talk to the A's anymore. He even disdained to use the visitors' clubhouse in Philadelphia, dressing instead at another park and walking to the stadium.

George bought himself a new suit before the Series, and after each game he sent it out to be cleaned.

Maranville, who as usual was the focus of contention, wandered into a Philadelphia bar. Pushing through the swinging doors, he found a room full of 6'6" waterfront toughs, all talking about the Athletics. The 5'5" Maranville swaggered up to the bar and ordered a beer. When a muscular patron on the next stool growled, "Aren't you Rabbit Maranville?", the little shortstop shook his head and began looking for an exit. But the longshoremen bought him a round, and he bought the next. Six rounds later, Maranville was ready to whip the whole room. "Yes, I'm Rabbit Maranville," he said. "Who the hell are you?"

The bartender stepped out from behind the bar, took Chief Bender's stance, and demonstrated how the Chief was going to pitch to the

Braves the next day. The barkeep struck the first nine men out.

Then Maranville grabbed a broom and demonstrated how the Braves would hit Bender. Nine straight hits rattled off the Rabbit's bat, and he swaggered out of the bar.

The betting odds were 2-1 against Boston, but the Rooters arrived in high spirits. They were now as much a news item as the team itself, and the *Boston Globe* ran a four-column photo of the Rooters marching behind their banner and assigned a special reporter, Lawrence J. Sweeney, to cover them. The Rooters "are teeming with confidence," Sweeney wrote. "They are brim full of audacity, and... are placing great store in the fact that they have never yet trailed along with losers.... Everywhere the utmost feeling of good fellowship was displayed, and the Philadelphians jibed and jested with the Bostonians in a true spirit of brotherly affection." Nor did the Pennsylvanians get tired of hearing "Tessie" over and over again, as some New Yorkers had. However, the visitors warbled "Sweet Adeline" between the "Tessies" every so often.

The Rooters crowded into buses for the trip down Broad Street to Shibe Park (later Connie Mack Stadium), and blue Braves' flags waved madly as Rudolph and Bender warmed up. Had the Chief scouted the Braves? "No," Bender said airily, "there's no need scouting a bush league club like that." Before the first game the Chief complained of vertigo and gall bladder problems, but he set the Braves down 1-2-3 in the first.

The A's wasted no time hitting Rudolph. Danny Murphy singled, Rube Oldring sacrificed, and the dangerous Baker stepped in. "Everyone was getting ready to witness what they thought would be the slaughter," wrote J.G. Taylor Spink of *The Sporting News*. But Baker fouled out, and when Murphy recklessly tried to advance after the catch, he was doubled off, abruptly ending that threat as the blue Braves pennants fluttered furiously in time to "Tessie."

In the second Boston's Possum Whitted singled, Hank Gowdy doubled in one run, and Maranville singled in another as again the blue flags waved. Gowdy was fast becoming the Rooters' favorite.

The A's got one back when Moran let a single get through him in the outfield. As Herb trotted to the dugout at the end of the inning, the Rooters cheered him lustily.

"The utmost feeling of good fellowship was displayed," according to one paper. When the A's' Jack Barry made a dazzling one-handed catch, the Rooters' band broke out "in a tumult." And when the A's fans clapped to try to distract Rudolph, the Rooters refused to do the same to Bender.

Meanwhile, crouched on the Boston bench, as Damon Runyon wrote in *The Sporting News*, raged a madman—George Stallings. "His hat cocked over one ear, his face distorted, and his eyes glaring," he drove his men with "maniacal fury... with lingual lash and welting words. Invective streamed from his tongue in a searing stream, as he crouched there, conning the field before him," his fingers clenching and unclenching "as if grasping the throat of an enemy." He was, Runyon concluded, "mad—quite mad."

From the third inning on, Rudolph "completely mesmerized" the A's, according to *The Sporting News*. They could get only two hits.

Meanwhile, Gowdy smashed a single and a triple, and Gowdy and Schmidt, the slowest men on the club, each stole a base. The "bunch of tramp ball players" drove Bender off the mound in the sixth—the first time a Philadelphia pitcher had ever been knocked out of a World Series game. When the downcast Chief trudged off the mound, the Rooters gave a rousing cheer for him, too.

"They play pretty good for bush leaguers, don't they, Albert?" Connie Mack said quietly.

The game pushed the war news completely off the top of page one in Boston. It was "one of the severest trouncings ever given to a team in a World Series," Runyon reported, adding, "the odds came crashing downward to even money... When the poor Athletics had been thoroughly humiliated, the famous Stallings smile broke out over his bronzed countenance, as his players danced around him in victory."

As usual the Rooters paraded around the field, joined by Fitzgerald's pretty daughter, Rose, and her new husband, the dashing Joe Kennedy. Then they marched to their waiting buses, joined by Stallings, who pulled his auto into the line of the march. Evers and Maranville also caught up with the celebrants and demanded a banner to carry.

In the lobby of the Continental Hotel, Runyon found Stallings circu-

lating among the crowd, "a smiling, courteous, polished southern gentleman" again, while on the Roof Garden champagne flowed. The Rooters were called onto the stage to sing "Tessie," and Honey Fitz was dragged away from the newlyweds to sing a solo of "Sweet Adeline."

The odds had risen to even money when Bill James hooked up in Game 2 against Eddie Plank, who had pitched brilliantly in three World Series but had only a 2-4 record to show for it. James had a no-hitter going after five innings, but Plank matched him on the scoreboard 0-0.

In the sixth, Philadelphia's Wally Schang doubled with one out. When a pitch got away from Gowdy, Schang lit out for third and was called out, though the next day's photos showed he was safe. It was the turning point of the game as James whiffed Plank to end the inning.

In the ninth, the Bees got two big breaks. Cot Deal hit a fly which A's outfielder Amos Strunk misjudged, and Deal wound up at second. A moment later, Plank whirled and threw to second, catching Deal flat-footed. A dead duck, he broke for third and just beat the relay, and though the A's argued long and loud, it was to no avail. Then Leslie Mann lined a ball just out of Eddie Collins' reach for a 1-0 lead.

With one out in the last of the ninth, James walked the last two men in the batting order with Murphy up. Evers called time and waved Maranville to play behind second. Sure enough, Murphy slapped one through James' legs, but Rabbit hopped on it, touched second and threw out Murphy to end the game. Plank—and little Van—had lost again.

The hoarse Rooters snakedanced around the field with Evers at their head. Then they marched home past City Hall, though they refrained from a noisy parade out of respect for the crushed feelings of their hosts. "Even Jimmy Coughlan was prevailed upon to spare the cymbals."

The umpire's call on Schang was a bad break. But, The Sporting News said, "The Braves have made their own good luck.... The Athletics have acted like a beaten team.... The spirit is oozing out of the world champions."

As the teams prepared to move to Boston, the Braves' clubhouse man asked Stallings if he should leave their traveling uniforms in Philadelphia. "No," Stallings snapped, "we won't be coming back."

The Rooters marched to the train station, gave one last chorus of

"Tessie," and told the crowd, "Take your last look at us now. We won't be back." Late that night a throng of 10,000 fans, led by new Mayor Jim Curley, waited in the Boston station to cheer their heroes home amid "much jollification." The Athletics, according to Spink, "crept silently into the city and registered at a quiet hotel."

Prior to Game 3, the Rooters paraded from the newly opened Boylston Street subway station up Beacon Street to Fenway, which the Red Sox had offered to the Braves because it held more people than their old South End Grounds. (A new Braves Field was under construction.) Fitz posed with his Rooters, many of them in Indian headdress, then led them into the park to present Stallings with a diamond pin. This time their old seats had been reserved at the top of Duffy's Cliff.

Lefty Tyler went up against young Bullet Joe Bush (17-12) of the A's. "Tessie" was heard at the end of every half inning. Twice Philadelphia went out ahead, and twice the Braves came back to tie it. When the game went into extra innings, the band blared "Tessie" "until the players gasped for breath." In the 10th the A's filled the bases, and Baker hit a grounder to Evers, who inexplicably froze without throwing, as two runs crossed the plate. The game appeared as good as over.

In the dugout, the scrappy Evers began "crying like a baby," Maranville reported, but the others consoled him, saying he'd won many a game for them all year. A few minutes later Gowdy came to bat, and the air was filled with "Tessie." Hank had hit only three home runs all year, but he hit another one into center, where it hopped into the bleachers for the only homer by either club in the Series. Duffy's Cliff was in a frenzy. All that could be heard was a jumble of drums, brasses, and cymbals, though some reporters thought they could detect a slight suggestion of "Tessie" amid the cacophony.

After Moran walked, Evers strode to bat to a mingling of boos and cheers. He responded with a single past first, sending Moran to third, and Joe Connally hit a fly to tie the game again.

Finally, as darkness was falling in the 12th, Gowdy hit a double into the fans in left, his third hit and second double of the day. Moran bunted the next pitch, and Bush threw wildly as the winning run slid home. As Stallings leaped up to cheer, the seat of his pants ripped open from all his

fidgeting on the bench.

One paper screamed, "ROYAL ROOTERS MAD WITH JOY—'TESSIE' NEVER LETS UP IN EXTRA INNINGS." Tooting their tune, the Rooters marched to home plate, while Mayor Curley climbed onto the roof of the Boston dugout to lead the cheers. Then they paraded to the Fens, a large public park, where Honey Fitz brought two captives, Gowdy and Evers, who were forced to march along with him at the head of the parade. Schmidt and Rabbit were also soon made prisoners. While fans made a human chain hundreds of yards long to keep the crowds back, the players and their captors marched to the Copley Square Hotel, where the Athletics were staying, and gave a lusty cheer for the A's.

Both Mack and Collins insisted that it was not the Braves who had beaten them, but "Tessie." The incessant repetition had caused Bush to weaken in the crucial final inning. Henceforth, they muttered, "Tessie" ought to be barred from all World Series games.

The next day Dick Rudolph, a brand-new father, was locked in a 1-1 game against the A's Bob Shawkey (15-10). Good sportsmanship prevailed as usual. When one Boston fan booed Philadelphia's Rube Oldring, yelling, "You'll be carrying the hod [that is, laying bricks] next year, Rube!", the Rooters made him apologize.

In the fifth Evers drove in two runs with a single to give the Braves the first four-game sweep in Series history.

The A's, wrote Spink, "were not only outplayed, outpitched, and outfielded, but out-umpired, outlucked, and out-guessed." The Braves hurlers had handcuffed the A's hitting stars: Baker batted only .250, Collins .214, and McInnis .143. Meanwhile, Maranville (.246 in the regular season), batted .308 in the Series. Evers (.279), hit .438, and Gowdy (.243) batted .545, a Series record that would stand until broken by Babe Ruth in 1928.

After the last of the Athletics went out, the Rooters gave three cheers for the defeated foe. "Should I send your suit out to be cleaned?" the clubhouse atttendant asked the Chief. "No," Stallings replied, "it's done its job." Then he joined the parade back down Boylston Street, where every window was filled with cheering fans. At Symphony Hall they stopped and gave one final cheer for the new bride, Rose

Kennedy, looking radiant in an automobile.

Forgotten in the merriment was little Louis Van Zelst. He had met and vanquished Charlie Faust, but the twin forces of the Black Pope and "Tessie" apparently proved too much for one young boy to overcome.

♋ Epilogue ♋

Thirty-four years later Bender, then 64, looked back on the weird events of 1914 and recalled a luncheon that July with writer Grantland Rice and a stockbroker named Oswald Kirksey. "Chief," Kirksey said, "I'll lay you $75 to $25 that the Braves will win the pennant and the World Series."

Bender and Rice laughed. "You're crazy," they said, "the Braves are in last place."

Kirksey smiled. "I'll still take your money."

Revealing the story in 1948, Bender was still shaking his head. "I often wonder," he muttered, "what got into Kirksey that day, and how he could be so sure the Braves would win."

The most beautiful thing we can experience is the mysterious. It is the source of all true art and science.

Albert Einstein

CHAPTER 23
The Passing of the Mascots

GEORGE STALLINGS LOOKED FORWARD euphorically to another victory. But his coin's magic power, if that's what it was, would not work a second time. Bill James won only five games, hurt his arm, and never won another major league game. Lefty Tyler's victory total fell from 16 to nine. George Davis would win only three more big league games in his career; he died in 1961, taking his own life. The Braves fell to second, then to third in 1916, sixth in 1917, and finally seventh in 1918. In fact, they wouldn't win another pennant until 1948 or another world championship until 1957.

Connie Mack was also having his problems. He had counted on a long World Series to bring in much-needed revenue, but the four-game sweep left him strapped financially. That winter Home Run Baker demanded a raise and, when Connie couldn't agree, announced he would sit out the 1915 season. Chief Bender and Eddie Plank jumped at lucrative offers from the outlaw Federal League. To raise cash, Mack sold Eddie Collins to the White Sox. Still, Connie had pitchers Herb Pennock, Bullet Joe Bush, Bob Shawkey, and Rube Bressler, along with his entire World Series outfield and half of his $100,000 infield. Not a championship club, Connie conceded, but a good first division team nevertheless.

Louie Van Zelst did not go to spring training in '15. On March 19, he was suddenly taken gravely ill with heart trouble and Bright's disease. The next day he knew he was dying, and two days later his sad father wired Mack that Louis was gone. The whole team sent heartfelt condolences to the family of "the little chap who had magicked the team to championships."

When the season opened, nothing went right. The A's lost seven of their first eight games. By mid-May they were in seventh place; by June 1 they were eighth.

Then Mack seemed to come apart. He sold Jack Barry and Danny Murphy for pittances. He let Pennock and Shawkey go on waivers. At season's end the A's were last, 48½ games behind the Red Sox, the worst

showing thus far in American League history. The conventional theory is that the A's finished last because Connie broke up the team. Actually, they were last *before* the final breakup began.

The Athletics would spend seven straight years in last place. The 1916 club was the worst team of this century with a record of 36-117—40 games out of *seventh* place.

After 1914 Connie Mack would manage the A's for 36 more years and would finish last in 17 of them. He won only three more pennants, 1929-31. With Van, he had won four flags in five years. Without him, he won only five in 48.

Yet, curiously, for 14 years, 1915-1928, every American League champion except one would owe its pennant at least in part to stars who had played with Mack and Van in those glory years of 1910-14. All those former A's could win for someone else, but not for Mack.

☿ The Death of Charlie Faust ☿

In 1914 Charlie Faust had apparently scaled a mountain in California, for he arrived in New York demanding a mention in the record books.

That fall the Giants and White Sox barnstormed through the Northwest. In Seattle, Fred Snodgrass said, "Who should come down to the hotel to see me but Charlie Faust?"

"Snow," he said, "I'm not feeling very well. But I think that if you could prevail on Mr. McGraw to send me to Hot Springs a month before spring training, I could get into shape and help the Giants win another pennant." Nothing ever came of it, of course.

In June 1915, barely two months after Louis Van Zelst's sudden death, in an insane asylum in Fort Steilacoom, Washington, Charles Victory Faust also passed away suddenly at the age of 30.

That season Snodgrass' average plunged from .263 to .194, Chief Meyers' from .286 to .232. Christy Mathewson fell from 24 victories to eight, and Rube Marquard could win only nine games while losing 22; 19 of them came in a row, a record. Like the A's without Van, the Giants after Faust's death slid all the way to last.

In order to be a realist, one must believe in miracles.

David Ben-Gurion

ϒ **Epilogue** ϒ

In 1979 only two men of those Giants and Athletics teams remained alive, Rube Marquard and Stan Coveleski.

Once tall and ramrod straight, Rube was 89 years old and had to be wheeled, bent nearly into a fetal position, to the veranda overlooking Cooperstown's Glimmerglass Lake. I had to lean close to ask a question and hear the reply.

"Did Charlie Faust really help the Giants win the pennant in 1911?"

Marquard's lips moved. The answer came slowly, almost inaudibly: "When he was with us, we won," Rube said with a smile. "When he wasn't, we didn't."

Coveleski, like Marquard a Hall of Famer, was still trim and spry with a shock of gray hair at 90 when I wrote to him to ask about Louis Van Zelst. What was the true story on how Van was hired? And did he really bring the team good luck? The reply arrived inscribed with beautiful penmanship, as though dictated to a wife or daughter:

"Rube Oldring did ask Connie Mack to hire him," Coveleski wrote. "And we did regard him as lucky. It is all true, every word of it."

There is nothing so far removed from us to be beyond our reach or so hidden that we cannot discover it.

Descartes

C H A P T E R **2 4**
One Last Chorus

As THE BRAVES FADED TO SECOND in 1915, the Phillies' two stars were Grover Alexander, baseball's biggest winner at 31-10, and Gavvy Cravath, its best home run hitter, who popped 24 over the short (280-foot) wall at Baker Bowl. They also found a hunchbacked batboy of their own. Nothing is known of him, not even his name, except for a photo of him shaking hands with the Red Sox mascot in October. That's right: The Phillies won the pennant.

The Red Sox, meanwhile, rebounded from their fourth-place finish in 1913 and by '15 were back on top again. Smokey Joe Wood made a comeback with a 15-5 record and a league-leading 1.42 ERA, and a rookie lefthanded pitcher named Babe Ruth sported an 18-8 record. With a horrendously deep right field at Fenway Park (since shortened considerably), the Sox hit only 14 home runs all year—four of them by Ruth—and edged Detroit by 2½ games.

With the hated McRoy banished, the Royal Rooters prepared once again to accompany their heroes to the World Series. Several hundred converged on Boston's South Station, marching behind the Ninth Regiment band. The soldiers, of course, loudly played "Tessie," women waved handkerchiefs, and six singers with megaphones led the crowd in the chorus. Johnny Keenan was so excited, he got up out of a sickbed to be there.

Some 300 lucky Rooters with tickets were bedecked in red coats, trousers, and hats, with kelly green vests and white and blue badges with red socks hanging from them. They waved as the train pulled out to the strains of "On My Way to Dublin Bay."

Arriving under lowering clouds, the Rooters found their welcome less cordial than a year earlier, and they marched through a gauntlet of sarcastic jeers, defiantly waving their pennants. But at Baker Bowl, the reception was friendlier. The Quaker City fans, who had their own band, cheered the Beaneaters. As well-mannered guests, the Rooters struck up "Alexander's Ragtime Band" when Alex the Great took the mound. They also gave three cheers for Phillies manager Pat Moran, who was

not only a Massachusetts man but a Hibernian as well.

A few hours away, in the White House, the widowed President Woodrow Wilson was exchanging wedding vows with Mrs. Galt.

The Phils took a 1-0 lead into the eighth. When Tris Speaker scored to tie it, the Rooters erupted in "riotous joy." However, in the bottom of the inning the Phils went ahead on two walks and three infield hits to win, 3-1. Undaunted, with "Tessie" as their battle cry, the Royal Rooters marched defiantly around the field and out of the park.

The honeymooning First Couple spent their first day as man and wife at the ballpark for Game 2. As fans peeked curiously, Honey Fitz, a good Democrat, led the Rooters' salute to the chief, followed by "The Star Spangled Banner." The Rooters were, as usual, "always fair, always considerate, always sportsmanlike, noisy, hilarious, [and] orderly," in the words of the *Boston Globe*.

The Red Sox scored right away when Speaker crossed the plate as Ed Burns, the Philadelphia catcher, dropped the throw. The Phils tied it in the fifth, but thereafter Boston pitcher Rube Foster (19-8) was air-tight, holding the Phils to three hits. He himself drove in the winning run in the ninth.

Tootling "Tessie," the Rooters high-stepped out of the park and back to the railroad station. Wrote Lawrence J. Sweeney of the *Globe*: "'Tessie' has already begun to affect the nerves of the National League champions."

After an off-day the great Alexander came back before a record crowd of 42,300 at Braves Field, which had been loaned to the Red Sox in thanks for the use of Fenway a year earlier. It was perfect autumn weather, and Keenan insisted on leaving his bed to be there.

Alex again was superb. Philadelphia scored first on two singles and two bunts. Meanwhile, "there was never a letup in the booming of the brass, the thumping of the bass drum, and the clanging of the cymbals," the *Globe* reported. Philadelphians grumbled that "'Tessie' would unnerve a stone," and Alex was not immune to "the rattles."

In the fourth Speaker smashed a triple to right and scored on a fly to tie the game. To rest their frazzled vocal chords, the Rooters took to singing "Tessie" only at the beginning of each half-inning, and both

Alexander and Boston's Dutch Leonard pitched scoreless ball through the eighth.

In the ninth Leonard set the Phils down 1-2-3, getting the powerful Cravath on a grounder for the last out. In theBoston's half, Harry Hooper singled, a sacrifice moved him up, and Duffy Lewis singled him home for the game-winner.

Throughout the inning the loyal Royals had played and replayed the hypnotic refrain. "And it brought victory," wrote Sweeney, "as surely as Hooper's single and Duffy Lewis' timely smash, for Alex was visibly affected." The odds had now fallen to 10-3 on the Red Sox, and no takers. The spirit had gone out of the Phils.

For Game 4, fans climbed the walls and tunneled into the park to watch Ernie Shore (19-8) win another 2-1 victory, the third in a row. The teams went back to Philadelphia for Game 5, won by Boston 5-4—their fourth one-run victory in a row—as Alex warmed up on the sidelines for Game 6, which never came.

♌ The 1916 Series ♌

The Sox sold Speaker to Cleveland but still repeated, as young Ruth won 23 games and led the league in earned run average, 1.75.

In the Series they faced the surprising Brooklyn Superbas, also called the Trolley Dodgers or Robins, in honor of manager Wilbert Robinson. Back in 1911 "Uncle Wilbert" had been a Giants coach under McGraw and was credited with making a winning pitcher out of Rube Marquard. After Rube's awful 1915 season, Robbie picked him up, and he justified the manager's faith by posting a 13-6 record. Robinson also signed another old warhorse, Jack Coombs of Van Zelst's old Athletics. Coombs had won only one game in his last two years with Connie Mack; under Robinson in Brooklyn the veteran was 13-8 in 1916. The Robins also featured pitcher Jeff Pfeffer (25-11) and a merry madcap outfielder from Kansas City named Charles "Casey" Stengel (.279).

German U-boats were sinking ships not far off the New England coast as the 1916 World Series opened. Brooklyn borough president Louis Pounds led a contingent of Flatbush faithful, the "Brooklyn

Boosters," to the opening game in Boston. They marched with the players in a big send-off parade from Ebbets Field to the subway with flags flying from homes and stores.

At Braves Field "on the outskirts of the city," as the *Globe* put it, fans sat all night, in blankets and on stools, for the $1 standing-room tickets. A spot in line was going for $2. Police picked up one eight-year-old kid in a freight car with the price of a ticket in his pocket.

Meanwhile, the Rooters' red-coated band, led by drum major Jimmy Coughlan, just back from the Mexican border with the Ninth Regiment, gave the Boosters "a rousing welcoming serenade," according to one New York reporter, and escorted Boston Mayor Jim Curley to his box near the dugout. (Curley would later be imprisoned for fraud and win re-election from his cell.) Another guest of honor was Charles Evans Hughes, the Republican presidential candidate.

The *Brooklyn Eagle* found the Boston bleacherites less polite than their counterparts in Brooklyn and noted they didn't throw foul balls back as the Brooklynites did: "In fact, there were a few fights over them." But a Boston police captain denied the charge; Boston crowds are always well behaved, he said, "when there are ladies around."

The *New York Times* sniffed that the Boston band "played weird noises on the instruments," but it recognized one of the favorites as vaguely resembling "There'll Be a Hot Time in the Old Town Tonight."

Bill Dinneen, the hero of the 1903 Series, trotted out to third base in the blue uniform of an umpire.

Marquard started the game against Ernie Shore. When Stengel singled and scored on a triple, the Boston Rooters let out a cheer, which "both puzzled and pleased" the Robins.

The Red Sox rocked Rube for a 6-1 lead after eight innings. But in the ninth the Robins rallied for four runs and had the bases loaded. Their Boosters, "crazed with joy," rushed to the front of the stands, yelling and waving blue pennants. But submarine hurler Carl Mays rushed in from the bullpen to get the final out.

In Game 2 young Ruth dueled Brooklyn's Sherry Smith 1-1 for 13 innings. In the top of the 11th the Rooters broke out in a chorus of "Tessie," but when Brooklyn owner Charlie Ebbets told them to "cut it

out," they stopped abruptly and later apologized. Ebbets vowed he wouldn't let them in his park in Brooklyn if they didn't quiet down. (But, the Rooters noted, Boston allowed the Boosters to beat their dishpans when the Red Sox were at bat.) Ruth finally won the game in the 14th when pinch hitter Del Gainer knocked in the winning run.

After the game the largest contingent of Royal Rooters ever—600 men and some women, led by Nuf Ced—embarked by a special 10-car train for New York. It had been 13 Octobers since they had first entrained for Pittsburgh in 1903, and now they were, in the words of the *Globe*, "gray-headed, bald, bewhiskered fans of sedate age." The *New York Times* described them as "sane and conservative businessmen until a World Series begins."

They arrived at Grand Central Station at 1 a.m., and the strains of "Tessie" filled the big station. The Rooters marched up Broadway, loudly blaring "A Hot Time in the Old Town" and, of course, "their war song," "Tessie," while crowds stood 20-deep along the sidewalks to watch them. The parade ended at the hotel at 75th Street where the Red Sox players were vainly trying to get some sleep.

The Rooters arrived in red sweaters and red-striped socks for the first World Series game in Brooklyn history. They encountered the Boosters beneath their own green gonfalon with a baseball emblazoned on it in their own section behind first base. The Rooters were directed to deep left field, as far away as Ebbetts could put them, even though there were plenty of empty seats elsewhere in the stands.

Coombs faced Carl Mays, 6-5, who four years later would kill Ray Chapman with a pitch. When Brooklyn scored the first run in the third inning, the Boosters responded with tin horns, cowbells, and police whistles. The Royal Beantowners replied with calls of "we'll bet you 20-13, 20-15," but the Flatbush fans drowned them out with "musical jingles." The Robins went on to a 5-4 victory.

The Rooters waited for the Brooklyn fans to enjoy their victory, then left the stands to meet the Boosters, and the rivals "laughed and chaffed good-naturedly," Sweeney reported. Then they marched back down Broadway "not a bit disheartened."

The Rooters were up early for Game 4, eager to cover every cent of

Brooklyn money they could find. They assembled in front of the Elks Home on 43rd Street in Manhattan, where they boarded sightseeing autos for the trip over the Brooklyn Bridge. At first the Robins wouldn't open the ballpark gates to them, until a Boston detective in a commanding voice ordered them open. After the Rooters took their seats, the Brooklyn Boosters "cheered and roared, kicked and pranced, shouted and hooted," and marched to the Rooters' section and gave them "a wonderful ovation." The two sections cheered each other for five minutes "while the crowd watched spellbound." "Poor 'Tessie,'" wrote Sweeney, "was played out."

The game pitted Boston's Dutch Leonard (18-12) against Marquard. Brooklyn struck first with two quick runs as Brooklyn hats went into the air "in clouds." The odds suddenly changed, from 5-3 on the Sox to 4-1 on the home team, and the Rooters snapped up all the Brooklyn money they could find.

One ardent Rooter, Denny Griffin, fearing he was a Jonah, banished himself to the farthest seat in the upper deck. He was discovered several innings later when the band played "The Star Spangled Banner," and he rose, wildly waving his American flag.

The rest of the Rooters, however, seemed to have "an uncanny intuition" that Marquard would not last through the game. "Tessie" was played as never before, "and as usual she proved successful right then and there," as Boston's Larry Gardner hit his third home run of the year, a three-run drive on a 3-0 pitch, to put Boston ahead to stay. It "took the heart out of Rube," the *Globe* said. "What is worse, the fans lost heart, too." Boston went on to a 6-2 victory, and the Rooters did what was called a "Cherokee war dance," dodging cushions skimmed at them by the Brooklyn fans.

The Rooters boarded their special train happier and richer. They signaled that they didn't expect to return by the selection they played, "Auld Lang Syne." When their train pulled into South Station at 3 a.m., they paraded behind their red-coated band, cheering and singing, down Washington Street and through Newspaper Row, while a large crowd of late-night workers gave them a big hand.

In a chilly Columbus Day wind, the standing room crowd of 47,200

cheered "mostly to keep warm," said *The New York Times*. They cheered every play worthy of applause "and many that weren't." The Robins scored first off Ernie Shore, but the Sox retaliated with two runs in the third off Brooklyn ace Jeff Pfeffer and went on to win, 4-1.

Boston was the champion of the world, its fifth victory in five Series since "Tessie" first raised her voice in 1903. Before "Tessie" Boston had won one game and lost three in the Series. Since its Rooters began singing the song, its record was 21-5.

But "Tessie" would never again be heard in Fenway Park or Braves Field. In 1917 the Red Sox finished second. They reclaimed their crown in 1918 as young Ruth led the league with 11 home runs. The United States, however, had its eyes on the trenches of France, where American boys were dying. The season was cut short, and the World Series against the Cubs just didn't have the same magic of years gone by. Perhaps also the Rooters were getting old. For whatever reason, no mention is made of them in the 1918 Series, which the Sox won four games to two.

The next year Ruth hit a record-breaking 29 home runs, but the Sox fell all the way to sixth. That winter they sold the Babe to the Yankees and began 26 years of wandering in the wilderness. They wouldn't be in the World Series again until 1946, and in 78 years, through 1999, have never won another one.

Gone are the Royal Rooters, who, the *Globe* wrote, "hold a warm place in the hearts of [the fans] because they're recognized as a game bunch who have never been known to quit." In their place the Fenway stands became home to stentorian, beer-belly loungers, who yelled obscenities at Ted Williams and covered the diamond with negative energies.

The nosedive in the fortunes of the Red Sox has been blamed on "the Curse of the Bambino." Nonsense. When the Fenway organist strikes up a happy, lilting rendition of "Tessie" again, I believe, the Red Sox will return to the glory days of old.

Meantime, Tessie must be up there in that heaven where forgotten sweethearts go, tearfully pining for her lost loves, the leaping, sliding, dashing heroes of her youth, and their jaunty, prancing faithful who lustily sang her praises, the Royal Rooters.

CHAPTER 25
Connie's Last Mascots

IN 1920, STILL WALLOWING AT THE BOTTOM of the American League, Philadelphia's Connie Mack tried his luck with another hunchback, Lou McClone. It was a brief and tragic experiment. Quite the opposite of Louie Van Zelst, McClone fell in with bootleggers and was gunned to death in a gangland war.

The A's remained deep in the cellar, though they finally rose to seventh in 1922, fourth in '23, and fifth in '24.

In 1925, the A's suddenly soared. They surged into first place, held it through June, dropped back briefly behind the Senators in July, but regained the top by August.

Then they went into an unaccountable tailspin. By September 1 they had suffered seven straight losses and had fallen 2½ games behind. On September 2 Washington's Stan Coveleski, the ex-Athletic, beat them 8-5. The seventh-place Yankees shut them out for loss number nine. They dropped a heartbreaker to New York, 4-3, for their 10th defeat in a row. Rookie Jimmie Foxx, 17 and just up from the minors, failed to slide and was out at home in the ninth with what would have been the tying run.

The Senators came to Philadelphia for a Labor Day doubleheader September 7. The first game pitted Walter Johnson (20-7) against rookie Lefty Grove (10-12). With Philadelhia losing 2-1 in the ninth, the A's Bing Miller made a wide turn at third and was thrown out to end the game, sending his team to loss number 11.

In the second game, losing 7-6 in the eighth, the A's loaded the bases and Frank Welch slammed a long drive to the wall, where left fielder Goose Goslin seemed to make a great catch. The runners held their bases, but the umpire ruled that Goose had trapped the ball, and the confusion cost the A's two runs. Then first baseman Joe Judge erred and two runs scored—but the ump ruled that the batter had bumped the fielder, nullifying the runs. It was the A's 12th loss in a row. When would the run of bad luck end?

The next day Mack discovered two "grinning young" black kids,

whom he invited to sit on the A's bench. Next to rubbing a hunchback's hump, rubbing a Negro's hair was considered potent baseball magic. Babe Ruth often did it, as did Mack himself. The boys shook hands with the players, who gave them pats on the head. One of the boys, Eddie Cone, also did some comic dancing to the delight of the players. "There's nothing like a happy colored boy to bring good luck," coach Ira Thomas grinned. "It's the last resort a team has."

In the first, Washington's Sam Rice walked, stole, and took third when pitcher Slim Harriss' throw went into center field. A week earlier Slim had blown up after a similar play against Washington. This time, however, he calmly got the dangerous Goose Goslin on a soft fly as Rice died on third.

In the fourth Philadelphia's Jimmy Dykes walked. Mack signaled a hit-and-run, but the Senators responded with a pitch-out. Bill Lamar threw his bat out in desperation and hit a lucky double over third. Al Simmons then tapped a ground ball, and Dykes scored while the Senators chased Lamar in a rundown. The breaks were going Mack's way at last.

In the fifth Miller rubbed Cone's head for good luck, then socked the first pitch into the upper deck for a homer. With two out and Cochrane on first, Jimmie Dykes hit to the pitcher. The throw to first was late as Cochrane slid into third, then scored on another overthrow.

Harriss won a three-hitter, 6-1. The A's long victory drought was over.

On Wednesday the A's looked anxiously for their two new mascots, who unfortunately were in school and unable to get to the game on time. Washington's Roger Peckinpaugh, who hit only four homers all year, hit two against Grove to give the Senators a 6-3 lead.

Mack sent an emergency message to all gatekeepers to rush the boys to the bench as soon as they appeared. Apparently, however, someone didn't get the word, because the boys were stopped at the gate, but they scrambled under the turnstile and raced for the dugout.

There followed a "deluge" of Philadelphia hits that drove Washington pitcher Tom Zachary (12-15) to the showers. The fifth hit, a three-run triple by Simmons, gave the A's the lead that they never lost.

Final score: Philadelphia 9, Washington 7. Straw hats were sailing all over the field.

The A's were seven games behind. Could they catch the Senators?

The next day Mack left his two good luck charms behind and traveled to New York, where his team lost 7-3.

The boys, meanwhile, had disappeared. No mention was ever made of them again. The A's finished 8½ games behind.

Mack would have to wait until 1929 when his club—virtually the same one he had fielded in 1925—could at last bring him a pennant.

Tell the boys I've the luck with me now.

Bret Harte,
THE LUCK OF ROARING CAMP

 C H A P T E R   2 6

Eddie Bennett

LIKE LOUIS VAN ZELST, EDDIE BENNETT WAS A HUNCHBACKED batboy who seemed to bring success to every team he joined.

Eddie was born in Brooklyn's Flatbush in 1904. Like Van Zelst, he suffered a childhood accident—in Eddie's case, a fall from a baby carriage—that left his back permanently twisted and accounted for the hump that baseball players considered lucky. Eddie's parents died in the flu epidemic of 1919, leaving the boy an orphan at 15, with no living relatives.

On September 17, 1919, Eddie was hanging around the Polo Grounds, where the Yankees used to play their home games, on an afternoon when the White Sox were in town. Starring Shoeless Joe Jackson (.351), Eddie Collins (.319), and Eddie Cicotte (29-7), the Sox already had a virtual lock on the pennant; they were seven games ahead with 11 games to go. White Sox outfielder Oscar "Happy" Felsch spotted Eddie. "Hi ya, kid," he called. "Are you lucky?"

"Sure I am," Eddie answered, and Felsch took him into the park and sat him on the Chicago bench. That day they beat the Yankees 11-2 and 2-0, as Happy got five hits in nine at bats.

Chicago took Eddie along for the last nine games of the season, and in Boston he watched Babe Ruth hit his record-setting 27th home run. With Eddie along, Felsch slugged 13 hits in 27 at bats to raise his season's average to .275. Though the White Sox won only two of the nine games, they backed into the flag with ease. However, they wouldn't take Eddie to the World Series, which Felsch, Cicotte, Jackson, and five others threw to Cincinnati.

In 1920 Bennett talked his way into the office of Brooklyn manager "Uncle Wilbert" Robinson, who gladly gave him a job.

The Dodgers, or Robins as they were called in Robinson's honor, hadn't won a pennant in 23 years. In 1919 they had finished fifth, 27 games behind the Reds. Their stars were Hi Myers, Ed Konetchy and Zach Wheat, with Jeff Pfeffer, Leon Cadore, Burleigh Grimes, Al Mamaux, Sherry Smith, and the veteran Rube Marquard on the mound.

For 1920 Robinson made no major lineup changes. The only new face in the locker room was Eddie's. ("A real nice boy," Grimes would say, "polite, hard-working.") But after Myers took the kid in and gave him a home, the Robins started acting like a different team.

On May 1, Cadore battled the Braves for 26 innings to a tie, the longest game on record. The next day the Dodgers battled the Phils 13 more innings, losing 4-3. The day after that they went 19 more innings before losing 2-1. They were going to be tough.

The batboy for the visiting teams that year was 14-year-old Tommy Blomburg, later an Episcopal priest in, of all places, Cooperstown. Blomburg remembered Bennett well, although "he paid no attention to me at all. He was getting paid; I got paid in split bats or foul balls, which I could sell."

Blomburg himself used to wear "a little green cap." The Robins' reserve catcher, Harold "Rowdy" Elliott, noticed that whenever Tom wore the cap, the Robins seemed to lose. "I don't want to see that cap on you any more," he ordered.

But the trainer for the visiting Cardinals had a better offer. "You wear that tomorrow," he said, "and we'll give you two balls instead of one."

Sure enough, the Dodgers fell behind, and Tommy looked up to see Elliott advancing on him. "I think he wanted to give me a licking. I beat it to the exit and got lost for two or three days. I never told my father; he was a blacksmith, a very rugged man, and would have thrashed Elliott for good. But I'm sure I didn't come back with that green cap."

On August 15 the Robins climbed into first place ahead of the Giants. "The Giants had a much better team," Blomburg remembered. Ross Youngs hit .351, Highpockets Kelly led the league in RBIs, and three pitchers won 20 games—Art Nehf, Fred Toney, and Jesse Barnes. But they suffered a bad break when their third baseman, Frankie Frisch (.280), was stricken with appendicitis.

"One day the Cardinals scored two or three runs, so I started putting their bats away," Tommy recalled. "Boy, this game isn't over yet," St. Louis Manager Branch Rickey said, and sure enough, Brooklyn scored three runs to win.

The Robins went on a 10-game win streak to clinch the pennant to

finish seven games ahead of New York.

The sportswriters scratched their heads. It's true that Wheat added 31 points to his average to finish at .328, and catcher Otto Miller tacked on 63 points, from .226 to .289. But second baseman Pete Kilduff lost 14 points; outfielder Tommy Griffith, who had been dropped by the 1914 Braves, lost 19 points, and Ivy Olson, 24.

The pitchers blossomed, however. Grimes, a spitballer, had the best year of his life, 23-11, while Marquard rose to 10-7 and Smith improved to 11-9, as Brooklyn led the league in ERA.

Brooklyn didn't compare with the great teams of the past, *The New York Times* wrote, but made up for it in fighting spirit. How to account for the change in fortune?

♋ The Weird Series of 1920 ♋

The ungrateful Dodgers refused to cut Bennett in on a share of the World Series money against Cleveland. It turned out to be one of the strangest Series ever played.

The Indians boasted batting champ Tris Speaker (.388), plus the two best pitchers in the league, big Jim "Sarge" Bagby (31-12) and spitballer Stan Coveleski (24-14), the ex-Athletic who had pitched heroically down the stretch to edge out the White Sox just before a grand jury KO'd them for fixing the previous Series. But the Indians staff was tired, while Brooklyn's was considered the best in the league. "VICTORY IN SERIES HINGES ON BREAKS," opined *The New York Times*.

As in 1919, it would be a best-five-of-nine Series. The teams opened in Brooklyn on a blustery wintry day, and Coveleski beat Marquard, 3-1.

The two aces, Grimes and Bagby, hooked up for Game 2. Burleigh (or "Boily" in Brooklyn) had a 2-0 lead in the eighth, when he walked two men. Speaker then lined what he called one of the hardest balls he ever hit—straight to Pete Kilduff at second—and Grimes got dangerous Elmer Smith and Doc Johnston on spitters to win.

Brooklyn's Sherry Smith started Game 3 against Ray "Slim" Caldwell (20-10). Brooklyn scored two quick runs, thanks to an error and a nub hit by Myers, Eddie Bennett's pal, and the Robins won 2-1 to take a one-game lead.

Brooklyn had only to split the remaining six games—four in Cleveland and two at home—to win; the Indians needed to win four of the six. Brooklyn was installed as a 2-1 betting favorite.

The Robins decided not to take Eddie to Cleveland with them. Instead, they brought back their former batboy, 13-year-old Richard Claude. Bennett took the news hard, and Myers found him face down on his bed, a pillow over his head, sobbing.

In Cleveland everything went wrong.

In Game 4, the Indians knocked Cadore out in the first inning, and Coveleski baffled them again to even the Series.

Before the fifth game even started, Marquard was arrested for scalping tickets. Brooklyn owner Charles Ebbets swore Rube would never pitch for the team again. The game that followed saw: the first World Series grand slam, the first World Series homer by a pitcher, and the only World Series unassisted triple play, which was turned by the Indians' second sacker, Bill Wambsganss. "It took a lot of things that were sheer luck, or coincidence, or whatever you want to call it," said Wamby years later.

On a beautiful, summer-hot afternoon, Grimes ran into trouble in the first inning. But it wasn't his fault, said Wambsganss, adding that Cleveland's Charlie Jamieson got "what I would call a scratch hit" off first baseman Ed Konetchy's glove. Wamby was the next batter." He missed two bunts, then hit a two-strike roller between third and short for a freakish hit.

Speaker laid down a sacrifice, which Grimes fielded and then "fell on his can." All runners were safe. "But it was luck all the way around, you might say," Wamby said.

Cleanup man Elmer Smith was next up. Grimes threw him two spitters, and Smith missed them both widely. Next Burleigh decided on a fastball. Why did he throw to Smitty's strength? "For the simple reason," Grimes told me years later, "there was a fellow coaching for us, a friend of Robbie, who had been in the American League, and he told us to pitch low fast balls to Smith. In those days we didn't scout the other team at all." The coach was Jack Coombs, the Athletics veteran. "I don't see how it could have been an accident," Grimes said, "because Coombs

had been in the American League all his life."

On second base, Wamby shook his head. A fastball "was right down Smith's alley," he said.

To make matters worse, Smith knew it was coming. Back in Game 2 the Indians had discovered that Kilduff at second base grabbed a handful of dirt before each pitch, so he could throw the slippery spitter if it was hit his way. But if a fastball was called, Pete threw the dirt away. Now, with two strikes on Smith, Kilduff dropped the dirt, Grimes delivered, and Smith swung. The ball sailed over the short right field fence for the only grand slam in the Series' first 32 years. It wouldn't be done again until 1936, when Tony Lazzeri hit one for the Yankees.

Brooklyn responded with a barrage of hits but couldn't bring the runners home. In the second, Konetchy tripled but was thrown out trying to score on a fly. In the third, the Robins hit three singles and couldn't score.

In the fourth, Johnston singled, and after a passed ball ended the hope of a double play, catcher Steve O'Neill was walked intentionally to get to Bagby. "What they didn't know," Wamby confided later, was that Bagby (.252) was a pretty good hitter. Old Sarge swung and lifted "an easy fly ball that would have been caught ordinarily. But they had a temporary stand built out there in right field, and the ball dropped right in the corner of that stand. That accounted for three more runs. But it was just a matter of luck."

That was all for Grimes. Robbie lifted him for reliever Clarence Mitchell, setting up the final drama of that bizarre afternoon—the fateful fifth inning.

Kilduff opened with a single. Otto Miller also singled to center, but Speaker uncorked a splendid throw to hold Kilduff at second.

Next, "who should come to bat," Wamby asked, "but that same Clarence Mitchell?" Why didn't Robinson pinch-hit for him? Apparently because Mitchell was a lefty and a pretty fair hitter (.234), who often pinch-hit and played first base. He had hit .369 the year before and had pinch-hit a single in the first game of the 1920 Series. Still, Robinson had two other lefty swingers, Bill Lamar and Bernie Neiss, sitting on the bench.

Wamby "knew Mitchell was a pull hitter, pulled to the right all the

time," so Bill played him on the outfield grass and over toward first. The count ran to 3-and-2, the runners took off with the pitch, and Mitchell smote what the *Times* called "a smoking line drive." Wamby described what followed: "He hit a line drive somewhat to my right, over my head. I had to dash quickly to my right. I was just in stride and leaped into the air and caught the ball. That made the first out. I was on my way to second and saw Kilduff running to third." So Bill touched the base to double Pete. Out number two. He was about to throw to first to double Miller when he heard rookie shortstop Joe Sewell shout, "Tag him, Bill! Tag him!" "I turned to my left, and Otto Miller was standing there within arm's reach of me." Wamby put the ball on him for out number three.

As Grimes remembered it: "Miller was running on the 3-and-2 and ran right into Wambsganss. That's the kind of play it was. With a little luck... " He shrugged. "But it doesn't work that way, see? The house just fell in."

(One writer emerged from the men's room to hear the crowd roar. "What happened?" he asked. "Wambsganss just pulled a triple play," he was told.)

Oddly, Mitchell came to bat one more time that day and slapped another hard line drive for a double play. Two swings, five outs.

"We were hitting a lot of line drives off Bagby," Grimes moaned. Actually, the Robins outhit the Indians, 13 to 12. Their leadoff men singled in five of the nine innings but were rubbed out by two double plays and one triple play.

Final score: Cleveland 8, Brooklyn 1. "So they weren't very lucky that day," Wamby conceded.

For Game 6, Cleveland fans set up a bedlam at the park, and cheerleaders paraded the stands with megaphones. But the Robins' confidence was almost gone. "Brooklyn lacked fight," the *Times* wrote. "The club acted as if it expected defeat."

Brooklyn sent Smith against Cleveland's sensational rookie, Walter "The Great" Mails (7-0). Four years earlier Mails had been riding the Brooklyn bench and even helped paint the outfield fence out of boredom. The Robins released him—and what was worse, wouldn't pay him for the paint job, either. After four years in the minors, he wanted

revenge. "Boys," he said, wiping his face with a towel before the game, "all you have to do is get me one run." (Mails was nothing if not cocky; they didn't call him "the Great" for nothing.)

In the second Brooklyn loaded the bases, but Smith flied out. In the sixth the Indians got Mails his run. Speaker singled with two out, and George Burns, a cast-off from the last-place A's, hit a long double to score him.

In the eighth Robinson let Smith, a righthanded batter, hit for himself against the lefty, Mails. He grounded out. Ivy Olson followed with a double, which was wasted. In the ninth, Myers reached on an error and advanced to second, but Kilduff flied out to end the game with the Robins losing again, 1-0.

Sherry Smith had been complaining about the umpiring throughout the game. He deserved to win, Speaker said. "He had far more stuff than in Game 3, and we didn't hit him nearly so hard."

Robinson said he didn't want to alibi, but muttered that he had to admit that "the breaks have been few and far between since we reached Cleveland."

Starting Game 7 was Grimes, coming back with one day's rest against Coveleski, who had given up only one run in 18 innings against Brooklyn. "From the moment Coveleski walked out on the pitching mound, Brooklyn was a defeated team," the *Times* wrote; the players were already talking about going home for the winter. Coveleski shut them out, 3-0. Only Christy Mathewson, with three shutouts in 1905, had ever done a better job in the World Series.

With Eddie Bennett on the bench, the Robins had won two and lost one. Without him, they lost four straight—5-1, 8-1, 1-0, and 3-0. Cleveland committed 10 errors, but Brooklyn couldn't capitalize on them. With a little luck in games 5 and 6, they could have been leading four games to three and heading back to Brooklyn.

Without Bennett, the Robins played like the fifth-place team they had been the year before. As the philosopher Wambsganss put it many years later, "Everything is made for us by chance—our ancestry, our birth. It's just a matter of chance that you're here at all."

Eddie was also following the news of the Black Sox scandal

involving his old friend, Felsch, and the others. "Felsch was not a bad fellow to me," he insisted. "Most of the Sox were good to me. They treated me better than the Brooklyns did." Bennett left that winter, and the Dodgers fell back to fifth place, exactly where they had been before he joined them.

In 1924 Da Bums won 15 straight games to storm from third place to catch the hated Giants. But on the next-to-last game they lost to the seventh-place Braves 3-2 and finished 1½ games behind.

In 1930 they led the league through mid-September. But the Cardinals made a rush from fourth place to first as Brooklyn faded to fourth.

Brooklyn wouldn't win a pennant again until 1941. Thus, for 44 years, 1897-1940, the Dodgers captured only one flag, and that was the year Eddie Bennett brought his good luck hump to Ebbets Field.

Meanwhile, what happened to Eddie? He was doing just fine. He had accepted a better offer.

II **The Babe's Bat Boy** II

Bennett had made friends with Yankees pitcher Waite Hoyt, a Brooklyn native, who suggested that the kid move over to tend bats for the Yanks at $25 a week.

You guessed it—the Yankees won the first pennant in their history.

Most historians believe that Babe Ruth's 59 home runs were the reason. However, Babe had been there in 1920 and hit 54 homers, but the Yankees finished third, the same as they had in 1919 before Babe arrived. Not until Bennett joined the team did Ruth's power bring a pennant.

Eddie became the Babe's personal favorite. They played catch before the game; no one but Eddie could hand Babe his bat. They knelt in the on-deck circle together; Ruth rubbed the boy's hump before going to bat, and if Babe hit a homer, Eddie was the first one at the plate to shake his hand at home plate. When Ruth wooed his second wife, it was Eddie who carried the *billets-doux* between them.

"Babe and Eddie were always talking," said Yankees pitcher Lefty

Gomez. "Babe would take him to dinner. Eddie was one of the nicest men I ever met. Everybody on the Yankees was crazy about the guy. If you felt bad, you could go over and talk to Eddie. He talked to me a lot when I was a rookie.

"I never went any place people didn't ask me how Eddie was," Gomez continued. "You went downtown to a restaurant, everybody knew him. He was very friendly with a lot of the movie actors— Jack Oakie, George Raft. Eddie dressed in well-tailored clothes and bright ties."

Eddie "was close to everybody, he did favors for everybody," Waite Hoyt agreed.

Several players wouldn't let anyone but Eddie touch their bats. Pitcher Wilcy Moore always threw his first warmup toss to Eddie. Pitcher Herb Pennock always rubbed the hump before he pitched. Another pitcher, Urban Shocker, insisted on rooming with Eddie on the road.

Bennett had a sharp basketball eye, Hoyt said. He could stand in the middle of the floor and shoot baskets while the fans showered him with money.

With Eddie on duty, the Yanks won three straight pennants, 1921-23. Then they won three more in a row, 1926-28. The last four flags were world championships as well. Eddie's pay was gradually increased to $100 a month, plus World Series bonuses.

Eventually Eddie hired other kids to do the actual batboy duties, while, in the words of one paper, "he devoted himself to his important function, giving luck. This he does mostly by crouching in front of the dugout and concentrating."

Was he lucky? "We always thought he was," Gomez shrugged.

In 1932 the Yanks won their seventh pennant in 12 years with Eddie. It was also Eddie's last year. He was hit by a taxi and hospitalized with a broken leg, and he took to drinking to ease the pain. When it hurt too much go to the park, the Yankees continued to support him, and he hobbled to the World Series on crutches to watch the Yankees win again.

Without Bennett, the team lost the next two pennants, in 1933 and '34, as some of the Yankees nodded their heads knowingly. One paper said Bennett's absence "was held by many to be the reason for the

Yankees' failure to win the pennants those years."

In 1935 Ruth and Bennett left the Yankees together. Babe went to the Dodgers. Eddie was found dead in his bed, surrounded by his baseball photos and autographed balls. He was 31. His death was widely reported, and the Yankees arranged his funeral, though none of the players was in town to attend.

Sportswriter Joseph Hezberg wrote that the Yankees won pennants on the hitting of Ruth, Lou Gehrig, Bob Meusel, and Wally Pipp, the pitching of Pennock, Gomez, and Moore, and the fielding of Everett Scott, Tony Lazzeri, and Joe Dugan. "But ask any of those Yankees what was chiefly responsible, and the answer would be Eddie Bennett, whose luck was so good, it even won a pennant for Brooklyn."

Part V

Curses

Out flowed the web and floated wide;
The mirror cracked from side to side.
"The curse has come upon me," cried
The Lady of Shalott.

Alfred Lord Tennyson

The great enemy of truth is very often not the lie—the deliberate, contrived and dishonest—but the myth, persistent, persuasive and unrealistic.

John F. Kennedy

CHAPTER 27
The "Curse" of the Bambino

THE MOST EFFECTIVE AND LONGEST-LASTING CURSE in sports history was attributed to the Olympic wrestler Oboetas, who put the whammy on his hometown of Achia when it failed to welcome him home as a hero after his victory. Achia went 300 years without another Olympic victory.

One of sports' most potent modern curses was hockey's Curse of the Muldoons, laid on the Chicago Black Hawks in 1927 by coach Pete Muldoon, who was fired for not winning the Stanley Cup. "Fire me, and ye'll never finish first!" he cried as he stormed out. Although the Black Hawks did win the Stanley Cup in 1934, their goalie, Charlie Gardiner, died two months later of a brain tumor. They won the Cup again in 1961, but it was another tragic victory—not long after, forward Murray Balfour died of cancer. In 1967, Muldoon himself died. That day the Black Hawks went into first place and stayed there to win their first Prince of Wales trophy.

Baseball's best known—and phoniest—curse is the "Curse of the Bambino," which has supposedly dogged the Red Sox since they sold Babe Ruth to the Yankees back in 1920.

Red Sox pitcher Bill "Spaceman" Lee takes credit for suggesting the idea to Boston writer Dan Shaughnessy, who asked Lee why he thought the Red Sox couldn't win a World Series. "Why don't you dig up Babe Ruth and ask him?" Lee replied. Shaughnessy liked the idea and made it the title of a book. Catchy title. Bad history.

In Babe's last year in Boston, 1919, the Red Sox finished sixth; the Yankees finished third. In his first year in New York, the Yankees finished third again; the Red Sox rose to fifth. Hardly a "curse."

Of course losing Ruth didn't do the Red Sox any good and explains why they were so bad throughout the 1920s, and why the Yankees were so good. But it's not the reason Boston hasn't won a World Series since 1918. The reasons are four-fold:

1. Boston fans don't sing "Tessie" anymore.

2. World War II. In 1943 the Red Sox were a young club, all coming into their primes at the same time. Ted Williams was 24, at the peak of

his career. Johnny Pesky was 23, Bobby Doerr 25, Dom DiMaggio 26, and pitcher Tex Hughson 27. Dave "Boo" Ferriss was 22 when he joined them in 1945.

By contrast, the Yankees, who seemed invincible, were an aging team, still good but just passing out of their prime years. Joe Gordon was 28, Joe DiMaggio 29, Tommy Henrich 30, Lefty Gomez 31, Red Rolfe 34, Bill Dickey 36, and Red Ruffing 39. Though the Yanks repeated as American League champs in '43, the young and charging Cardinals had knocked them off in five games in the '42 World Series.

Without a war, I believe, the Red Sox could have won two or even three pennants. (Imagine Ted Williams in the World Series in cozy Ebbets Field or Sportsman's Park!) Just how good they were became obvious in 1946, when they walked to the pennant, 17 games ahead of the Yankees.

3. Fenway Park. The infamous "Wall" has forced the Red Sox to load up on righthanded power-hitters and righthanded pitchers. This leaves the Boston batters victims of Yankee Stadium's yawning "Death Valley" in left and their pitchers victims of the notorious "short porch" in right.

4. With two exceptions, 1946 and 1998, every postseason series the Red Sox have lost, they lost to a better team—usually a much better team:

OPPONENT / WINS	RED SOX WINS	DIFFERENCE
1946 Cardinals 98	104	+ 6
1967 Cardinals 101	92	- 9
1975 A's 98	95	- 3*
1975 Reds 108	95	-13
1988 Angels 95	92	+ 3 *
1986 Mets 108	95	-13
1988 A's 104	89	-15
1990 A's 103	88	-15
1995 Indians 100	86	-14
1998 Indians 89	92	+ 3
1999 Indians 97	94	- 3 *
1999 Yankees 98	94	- 4

* Red Sox won

What is conveniently forgotten is that the underdog Red Sox battled the superior Cards, Reds, and Mets to seven games before finally succumbing.

Also, they played each Series with key injuries. In 1946 Williams was nursing a swollen elbow; in '67 young slugger Tony Conigliaro was out after a career-ending beaning; in '75 rookie sensation Jim Rice missed all seven games; and in '96 Bill Buckner played on a gimpy leg. If each had been healthy, how might history have been changed?

Perhaps, one could argue, these, plus World War II, are manifestations of a curse.

The legend of the "curse" began in 1946 and grew with three last-day regular-season losses in 1948, 1949, and 1978. Let's examine those and other heartbreaking seasons.

⚖ 1946 ⚖

Boston, the hottest team in baseball for five months, cooled off in September. Meanwhile St. Louis got hot, knocking off Brooklyn in two straight playoff games.

In Game 7 Dom DiMaggio, the best outfielder in baseball, was carried off the field with a charley horse, and an inning later Enos Slaughter made his famous dash home. "I wouldn't have tried it if Dom had been in center field," Enos said. "I think I'd have had a shot at him at third base," Dom added. (Incidentally, films show that Pesky didn't hold the ball.)

⚖ 1948 ⚖

Almost all Boston's starting pitchers developed sore arms in '47, and the Sox fell to third.

In '48 they got off to a horrible start but relentlessly climbed back into a three-way race with the Indians and Yankees. Williams' inside-the-park homer knocked the Yankees into third place. (A Yankee "el foldo"?) Cleveland won in a sudden-death playoff when Denny Galehouse (8-8) lost to Gene Bearden (20-7).

⚹ **1949** ⚹

Boston collapsed again in the first half, then made another dramatic comeback. In late September they swept New York three straight games as the Yankees complained about the umpiring. But three straight wasn't enough; the Red Sox had to make it four-out-of-five, and New York won the final two to win the pennant. Did the Red Sox get credit for a gallant comeback? Of course not. Overlooking the Yankees' September stumble, New York writers hailed them for their clutch play.

From 1946-49 the Red Sox were the best team in baseball:

TEAM	WINS
Red Sox	379
Yankees	375
Dodgers	371
Cardinals	369

Yet the Sox were called losers and the Yankees winners. The power of the New York press.

♉ **1967** ♉

Boston stormed from ninth in 1966 to win a terrific four-way fight on the last day, when the Sox beat Minnesota in a doubleheader. The Yankees finished ninth. (Where is the ghost of the Bambino when the Yankees lose?)

Boston's ace, Jim Lonborg (22-9), pitched in the final doubleheader. He had to pitch Game 7 of the Series on two day's rest against a better-rested Bob Gibson (13-7). Gibson won. But to hear the writers tell it, Boston choked again.

That winter Lonborg broke his leg skiing, and dreams of a new Boston dynasty were over.

♉ **1978** ♉

In a topsy-turvy season, the Yankees suffered several key injuries early in the year and fell 14½ games behind. In the second half, it was the Red Sox' turn to be hit with injuries while New York surged into the lead. The Yankees seemingly KO'd the Sox in a crucial September series, but Boston fought back to finish in a tie. In one of the greatest games ever played, Boston lost by one run with the tying and winning runs on base. *(See Chapter 11.)*

♑ **1999** ♑

The playoffs were a good example of how the press feeds the myth.

The Red Sox lost their big star, free agent Mo Vaughn (.337, 40 homers in '98); his replacement was long-time minor leaguer Brian Daubach (.294, 21 homers in '99). Boston won a Wild Card berth in the playoffs anyway, with less regular season victories (94) than any other playoff team.

Yet, each time the Red Sox lost a game, the TV airwaves were filled with pious clucking about "the Curse of the Bambino." (When both Texas and Houston were eliminated with one win in seven games, nobody dredged up a "Curse of Santa Anna.").

In the Division Series against Cleveland, Boston ace Pedro Martinez (23-4), baseball's best pitcher in a decade, faced the most powerful hitting team in five decades. He was leading, 2-0, when he suddenly walked off after four innings with a painful back spasm and the Indians won, 3-2. They also won the next night, 11-1.

Cleveland would have to win only one of the final three games. Instead, Pedro's brother, Ramon, won 9-3. Kent Mercker won a blowout, 23-7. And Pedro Martinez limped back in in relief to pitch six hitless innings for a 12-8 victory.

With their pitching in shreds and Martinez's back still stiff, the Red Sox appeared to be no match for the Yankees in the American League Championship Series.

In the 10th inning of the first game, New York second baseman

Chuck Knoblauch bobbled the ball on the pivot, but the ump gave the Yanks a double play anyway, and they won in the bottom of the tenth. "We stole one from them tonight," New York's Derek Jeter said. (Hmmmm. Maybe there is a curse after all.)

In Game 2, two Red Sox hit balls within two inches of being home runs and couldn't score. ("You have to feel lucky," said Yankees pitcher David Cone). The Yanks won on a bloop single by Paul O'Neill. "It was a big break for us," he admitted.

In Game 3, Martinez, "hurting on every pitch," whipped turncoat Roger Clemens, the former Red Sox star, by a score of 13-1. It was the worst drubbing in Yankees postseason history.

With the Yankees ahead by one run in the eighth of Game 4, Knoblauch missed a tag by about three feet, but the ump gave him another double play anyway, and the Yanks went on to win, 9-3. After a third blown call—this time at first base—Boston skipper Jimy Williams was ejected and fans bombarded the field with whatever they could throw, something the Royal Rooters never would have done.

In Game 5 Babe Ruth's daughter threw out the first ball and assured the Sox that her father wouldn't put a curse on anybody. The umpires, she shrugged, were another matter. The Yankees won the game and pennant, 6-1.

"Curse of the Bambino?" Or an underdog's gutty battle to upset "the Team of the Century?"

Though the Curse of the Bambino is a sportswriter's myth, baseball has many bonafide curses. They include the hoodoo on six teams: the Brooklyn Dodgers, the Chicago Cubs, the Houston Astros, the Cleveland Indians, the Atlanta Braves, and the California Angels.

I have set before you life and death, blessing and cursing; therefore choose life, that both thou and thy seed shall live.

Numbers 30:19

CHAPTER 28
Brooklyn, Barucha, Branca

AFTER EDDIE BENNETT LEFT them following the 1920 World Series debacle, the Dodgers would not win another pennant for 21 years. To the many Jewish fans in the borough, the team was often a *barucha*—a blessing—but it was also, all too often, a *barucha leh-vataleh*—a blessing in vain. Only the Cubs and Red Sox have visited on their faithful fans so much heartbreak.

The three teams did carry a curse: their parks. The Cubs, in particular, insisted on playing day games at home long after other teams had installed lights. That left the Chicago players drained of their strength in the dog-day afternoons of August, while other teams relaxed in the cooler evening contests and entered the September stretch fresh for battle.

But in the case of the Dodgers, there may have been additional explanations. Could the source of their bad luck possibly have rested, ironically, on the backs of two of their best pitchers, Kirby Higbe and Ralph Branca, both of whom insisted on flaunting a big blue number 13?

The Dodgers finished seventh in 1938. That winter a dynamic executive, Larry MacPhail, bought the team and hired fiery Leo "the Lip" Durocher as manager. Da Bums jumped to third in '39, then second in '40.

In '41 the Dodgers picked up three players from the Cardinals—catcher Mickey Owen, pitcher Curt Davis, who would win 13 games, and young Pete Reiser, who would win the batting title at .343. From the Cubs they got second baseman Billy Herman. And from the last-place Phillies they obtained hard-hitting Dolph Camilli, who would top the league in homers and RBIs and win the MVP, plus big fastballer Kirby Higbe, who would have the best year of his life, 22-9. All season long they battled the Cardinals before finally pulling ahead at the end to win.

The World Series against the Yankees was a classic.

In Game 1, the Yanks went ahead 2-1 against Davis. The Dodgers got one back on Owen's triple in the fifth. They could have gotten another, with two on and one out, but Camilli struck out and Medwick

grounded out. In the seventh the Brooklyns again cost themselves the tying run when Pee Wee Reese was out trying to advance on a short foul fly. In the ninth they left the tying run on second when pinch hitter Herman Franks hit into a double play.

The next day Brooklyn tied the Series with a 3-2 win behind their ace, Whitlow Wyatt (22-10). Moving home to Brooklyn for Game 3, Durocher bypassed his other 22-game winner, Higbe, in favor of 40-year-old Fat Freddie Fitzsimmons. For seven innings Fitz knuckleballed the Yankees into silence, but it was still tied 0-0 when a savage liner hit him in the knee and knocked him out of the game.

The Yankees jumped on relief ace Hugh Casey for two runs. Although the Dodgers got one run back in the eighth, they left the tying run on second as Pete Coscarart, subbing for the injured Herman, popped out. In the ninth, the heart of Brooklyn's order—Reiser, Medwick, and Cookie Lavagetto—went out feebly, leaving Camilli in the on-deck circle. Except for the injury to Fitzsimmons, the Dodgers might have had a two-to-one lead. Instead, they were behind two to one. Then came the heartbreaking Game 4.

Higbe, wearing number 13, walked out to the mound and was soon knocked out. However, the Bums regained the lead 4-3 and Casey held it until the fateful ninth.

With two outs New York's Tommy Henrich missed Casey's sweeping curve for strike three, but catcher Owen, who was expecting a small curve, let it squirt through his glove as Henrich streaked to first. The sudden break jolted the Yankees awake. Joe DiMaggio doubled, Charlie Keller singled, Bill Dickey walked, and Joe Gordon (.500 for the Series) doubled, as the Yanks scored four runs for victory.

If the Dodgers had gotten the breaks in games 3 and 5, they could have been ahead three games to two in a good position to win the Series. Instead, the Yankees whipped Wyatt 3-1 in the final game, and Brooklyn's hopes were gone.

Then came World War II. The Armed Forces took Higbe as well as the Dodgers' two young stars, Pete Reiser and Pee Wee Reese, and the team fell far behind the Cards, who won in '43 and '44 as Stan Musial luckily escaped the draft. In '45 the Bums finished third behind the Cubs.

In those three wartime seasons, could the Bums have won another pennant or two? After St. Louis beat the Yankees handily in '43, the Dodgers could probably have done the same, Brooklyn historian Ron Gabriel points out.

As soon as the war ended, Brooklyn and St. Louis resumed their pennant battle.

One of Brooklyn's few bright spots for the future was 19-year-old Ralph Branca, an NYU student who pitched part-time in '45 and compiled a 5-6 mark. That winter the penny-pinching general manager, Branch Rickey, sent young Branca a contract for $3,000, the same salary he had received in '45. The kid sent it back unsigned, the press ridiculed Rickey as "El Cheapo," and Ralph was sent to the doghouse—the bullpen—where he was given thankless mop-up relief chores.

Again the Dodgers broke in front, but the Cards stuck with them until late August, when St. Louis edged ahead. Should the Dodgers have brought up their sensational Negro rookie, Jackie Robinson, who was leading the International League in batting? He could have plugged holes at first base (Ed Stevens, .242) or third (Cookie Lavagetto, .237). Perhaps it would have been too drastic a move and might have upset the chemistry of a team with several southern stars.

At any rate, the Dodgers finally caught the Cards. Ill-fate hit the Dodgers in September, however, when Pete Reiser broke his ankle. On September 11 the Dodgers struggled for 19 innings to a 0-0 tie against the Reds. The next day, exhausted, they lost to the Cards 10-2 and tumbled out of first.

At last Branca got his chance to start. Durocher told him he would pitch to one batter to fake the Cards into starting a left-handed lineup, then lefty Vic Lombardi would come in. Angry, Ralph got the side out on five pitches and ended up tossing a three-hit shutout to move the Dodgers back into first. Three days later he hurled another shutout over seventh-place Pittsburgh.

The Dodgers and Cards battled on. Brooklyn could have won it on the final day, but the Boston Braves beat them behind their new pitcher obtained from the Cardinals, Mort Cooper. It was Mort's 13th win.

Thus the Dodgers and Cards finished in a dead heat, the first in

history, forcing a three-game playoff. The Dodgers won the toss and could select the site of the first game. For reasons unknown, they chose St. Louis, so the weary team hopped on an all-night Pullman for the long ride to Missouri, while the Cards enjoyed a day of rest.

St Louis started its sore-armed ace, Howie Pollet (20-10). Higbe was exhausted from the pennant drive, so Durocher turned to Branca (3-0). Ralph started out confidently, striking out two future Hall of Famers, Red Schoendienst and Musial, the batting champ at .365. But singles by Terry Moore and Enos Slaughter brought up the hometown kid, Joe Garagiola. Joe hit a grounder behind third, and one run scored.

The Dodgers tied it, but in the Cards' third, with one out, Musial walked and Slaughter singled. Whitey Kurowski was up, and a double play would end the inning. Branca got the grounder, but the Dodgers just missed the DP as Musial scored. It cost Ralph the game.

The Bums spent another night on the train back to Brooklyn and lost again, giving the Cards the pennant. It was an especially galling defeat for Branca, who had spent most of the season on the bullpen bench. "They blew the pennant because they were ticked off at me," he would later say.

Nineteen-forty-seven was a season of turmoil for the Dodgers. Robinson joined the team, Durocher was suspended for consorting with gamblers, and old Burt Shotton sat in for him.

Higbe was sent to Pittsburgh, and Branca asked for Kirby's old number 13 in honor of his 13 brothers and sisters. He had a great season, 21-12, showing what he could have done the year before. This time, the Dodgers easily beat the Cards for the pennant, and Branca opened the World Series in Yankee Stadium before the largest crowd in Series history.

In Game 1 the Dodgers got Branca a quick 1-0 lead, and Ralph reeled off four perfect innings. He struck out five, including Tommy Henrich, Yogi Berra, and John Lindell. He got DiMaggio and George McQuinn on easy grounders. "Branca was mowing down the Bombers with machine-like precision," wrote *The New York Times*. But in the fifth DiMaggio grounded to Reese and beat it out. Then Branca walked McQuinn, hit a man, and gave up a double to Lindell, putting the Yanks

ahead 2-1. Phil Rizzuto walked, loading the bases, and Branca came out. The Yanks won 5-3.

Was number 13 unlucky? "I didn't see any infielders getting killed out there today," Branca said defiantly.

The two teams traded one-sided slugfests in the next two games. Then, in Game 4, New York's Bill Bevens (7-13) had a sloppy eight-walk, one-run no-hitter going for eight innings. With two out in the ninth, he walked two men, and Lavagetto pinch-hit a fly ball off Brooklyn's short right field wall to win the game with the Dodgers' only hit. But the Yanks came back in Game 5, winning 2-1 as Reese and Lavagetto both struck out with men in scoring position.

Down three games to two, the Dodgers won the must-win sixth game 9-8 as Al Gionfriddo made a great catch against Joe DiMaggio. Branca picked up the victory in relief. But the Yankees won the seventh game 5-2, and Brooklyn had lost again.

In 1948 the Dodgers had finished third, Branca going 14-9. But in '49 the Bums and Cardinals staged another dogfight. By July 1 Branca's record was 10-1 when he developed a sore arm and went 3-4 the rest of the year.

The Cardinals blew their lead in the final week, losing four straight to sixth-place Pittsburgh and last-place Boston (though no one called it the "Curse of Rogers Hornsby"). The Dodgers won the pennant in the 10th inning of the last day on a single by rookie Duke Snider.

Once again, the World Series pitted the Dodgers and the Yanks. The teams split the first two games, and Branca started the third game in Brooklyn with two perfect innings, whiffing both Yogi Berra and DiMaggio. He gave up a run in the third, but resumed his perfection for the next four innings, and the teams went into the ninth tied 1-1. Branca led off the home eighth, and at this point a modern manager, counting pitches, would probably have lifted him for a pinch hitter. He struck out, killing what might have become a big inning, because the next two men got on, with Carl Furillo and Robinson due up. Both went out to end that hope.

Now the tired Branca took the mound for the ninth. He got Henrich and DiMag, but then loaded the bases. He had thrown 124 pitches so far,

but still Shotton made no move. A lefthanded pinch hitter, John Mize, ripped a single off the short scoreboard for two runs, and at last Shotton brought in a reliever, too late. Branca had pitched well, but he was tagged with another big loss. The Yankees won the next two games and another championship.

In 1950 Branca had a bad year, 7-9, and the Dodgers ended up chasing a new rival, the Philadelphia "Whiz Kids" of Robin Roberts, Curt Simmons, and Del Ennis. It had been 35 years since the Phillies had won a pennant—which, coincidentally, was also the last time a filly had won the Kentucky Derby. In May another filly, Middleground, won the Derby, and the Phillies beat the Bums on the final day on Dick Sisler's 10th-inning home run.

Then came the epic season of '51. On August 13 the Giants were 13½ games behind the Dodgers, who were breezing behind Preacher Roe and Don Newcombe, each 15-2. Rookie Clem Labine, called up from Montreal, won his first four games, two of them by shutouts. But when manager Chuck Dressen saw Clem go into a stretch with the bases full, the skipper rushed to the mound and demanded he use a windup. Clem said he could control his curve better from a stretch, but Dressen spat out an obscenity. Clem wound up, and the Phils' Willie Jones hit a grand slam. Labine spent the rest of the season on the bench, even though he felt he never had better stuff in his life.

Branca was 9-3 when he and Dressen went over to the door that separated the dressing rooms in Brooklyn. Together they sang loud enough for Durocher to hear, "Roll out the barrel, the Giants are dead."

Far from dying, New York made one of the greatest comebacks of all time, rising from the casket and reeling off 16 straight wins. Throughout the long rally, Leo shared George Stallings' 1914 fetish of picking up all scraps of paper on the field. He also refused to change his uniform. "I'm wearing the same socks, shirt, and underwear too!" he boasted.

The Giants' 34 year-old Sal "the Barber" Maglie had almost single-handedly kept New York in the race in the first half with a 15-5 mark. He was even more magnificent in the stretch, when he was 8-1, including three wins over Brooklyn, 2-1, 8-1, and 2-1.

Larry Jansen (23-11), pitching with a chronic backache, was 8-3 in

the stretch. Jim Hearn, 10-7 before the drive, had a strained ligament, but with a new sidearm delivery was 7-2 in the stretch, including two over the Dodgers.

Brooklyn meanwhile collapsed. Only the allegedly spitballing Preacher Roe stood tall, with a 7-1 record. Newcombe fell to 5-7. Carl Erskine (8-4) developed a sore arm and was only 4-4 in the stretch.

Branca himself took the mound with two days rest, strained for a no-hitter, and hurt his arm. He never threw as hard again, he said. To make it worse, almost every game he pitched in September the Dodgers got him only one run. He lost one crucial game to the Giants, 3-1. In his last 13 decisions, he was 4-9 for a total of 13-12.

The Giants, meanwhile, were developing an almost mystical belief that some higher power was in control. Beginning September 25, Boston beat Branca, Erskine, and Roe. On the 28th, Erskine took a 3-0 lead into the eighth against Philadelphia but lost, 4-3. The race was now all tied up with two games remaining.

On the season's final day, Jansen beat the Braves to put the Giants half a game ahead. It was New York's 37th win in 44 games. Meanwhile the Dodgers struggled into the 12th inning in twilight so dark many of the 31,000 fans couldn't see the ball. The Phils loaded the bases with Eddie Waitkus up and the count 3-2. A single or walk would end the season. Waitkus slashed a liner up the middle, where Robinson made a miraculous backhand catch.

The teams squinted on for two more innings until Robinson blasted a Robin Roberts pitch into the upper deck for a 9-8 victory. The playoff began the next day in Brooklyn.

≈ The 1951 Giants–Dodgers Playoff ≈

As in '46, the home advantage would be determined by the toss of a coin, and in those few seconds the outcome of the coming drama may have been determined. Brooklyn's brass were out of town, so the Dodgers' ticket manager, Jack Collins, called the toss and won. Of course everyone thought he would elect to play the first game in New York and the next two at home.

However, Collins remembered the '46 playoff, when the Dodgers had made the same decision against the Cards with disastrous results. But there would be no exhausting train trip this time. Momentarily confused, Collins said Brooklyn would open at home.

It would be Branca against Hearn. Both were well rested, but as he warmed up, Hearn felt a sharp pain in his side. He ducked into the training room to get "a big blob" of hot stuff poured on it.

Brooklyn took a one-run lead in the second when Andy Pafko hit a homer. Branca pitched out of a jam in the third, getting Al Dark on a foul with two men on. He lost his lead in the fourth when Bobby Thomson hit a fastball over the center field wall for his 31st homer with Monte Irvin on base. If the game had been played in the Polo Grounds, where center field was 485 feet away, it would have been an out.

As so often in the past, the Dodgers couldn't give Ralph the runs he needed. In their half of the fourth, with two on and no out, Roy Campanella, Andy Pafko, and Gil Hodges were coming up. But Campy hit a ground ball for a DP as he limped into first with a charley horse, and the big inning turned into a goose egg.

Meanwhile, Branca was pitching strongly. In the sixth he put two men on with two out, then struck out rookie Willie Mays. In the eighth he gave up a homer to Irvin to make the score 3-1, Giants. An error and a sacrifice put another runner on second with Mays up again, and Branca whiffed him again.

Brooklyn manager Chuck Dressen finally took Branca out. In eight innings he had given up five hits, but the Dodgers' sluggers just couldn't bring the runners home.

Dressen sprang a surprise in Game 2, calling on Labine to work on a cold, rainy afternoon in New York. Clem's curve was crackling. In the second he loaded the bases with two out, Thomson up, and the count 3-2. Labine threw an overhand curve, which Thomson swung at and missed. Brooklyn won, 10-0, setting the stage for one of baseball's greatest games.

Each team chose its ace, Newcombe against Maglie. Newk would be pitching without his regular catcher, Campanella, still nursing the charley horse. Backup catcher Luke Walker was behind the plate. "I was

dead," Newcombe recalled, remembering how he felt before the game. "My arm felt like an old ham hock." Dressen told him to give all he had for five innings, but Don didn't think he could go that far.

The score was 1-1 after seven. In the eighth, the Dodgers scored three runs.

Newcombe was still "throwing aspirin tablets," thought Bill Rigney, the leadoff man. Don whiffed him on three fastballs. He got Hank Thompson on a grounder, and then fanned Eddie Stanky.

"I don't think I can make it for the ninth," Newcombe told Dressen. "I just don't have it any more." The Dodgers just joked and responded, "Hang in there, Big Newk." As Don warmed up for the ninth, he called Robinson over. "My arm ain't got nothing left," he said. Jackie cut him short with an anatomically interesting suggestion of what he could do with his arm. In the coaching box, Durocher was holding his throat in the choke sign.

The first batter, Dark, a religious man, thinks today that the Lord was guiding him. He looked for a pitch on the outside corner and pushed it to the right side, where it glanced off Hodges' glove for a hit.

The next man, Don Mueller, noticed Hodges holding Dark close, a strange ploy with a three-run lead. Mueller slapped the ball into the hole, and Hodges, an excellent fielder, missed it by inches. If he'd caught it, it probably would have been a double play. Instead there were men on first and third.

Monte Irvin came up, thinking home run. If he had hit it over the wall, it would have been a new ball game, Dressen would have brought in a new pitcher, and the whole script might have turned out differently. Instead, Monte swung on the first pitch and popped it up.

The PA in the press box came on with an announcement: "Press credentials for the World Series in Brooklyn may be picked up at six o'clock." In the bullpen Erskine and Branca jumped to their feet and began throwing.

Lefthander Whitey Lockman lined a hit to the opposite corner as Dark scored and Mueller slid into third, breaking his ankle. The game was held up while medics carried Mueller off and Dressen mercifully took Newcombe out.

"Are they ready?" Chuck phoned the bullpen. At that moment, Erskine happened to break a curve into the dirt. "Erskine's bouncing his curve," coach Clyde Sukeforth said.

"Give me Branca," Dressen barked.

Walker, the catcher, says he would have brought in Labine, who had a good curve, to pitch to Thomson, who didn't hit curves too well. But Labine was not even warming up, nor was Bud Podbelian, the Dodgers' best reliever.

Next Walker asked if they should put Thomson on, setting up a double play with the nervous rookie, Mays, up next. Dressen refused; it was against the book to put the winning run on base.

"Throw fastballs," Dressen ordered Branca. "Fast and tight." Ralph's plan was to get ahead of Thomson on the first pitch, move him back on the next one, then break a curve to get him out.

Thomson had hit a slider for a homer in Game 1, so he probably wouldn't see that again. "I think he'll throw you a fastball, high and tight," Durocher told him. "Be ready." It was a fastball, down the middle. Strike one. Thomson looked at Durocher and rolled his eyes in disgust.

At this point, Irvin suggests, an experienced catcher like Campanella would have gone to the mound to slow his pitcher down. However, Walker just squatted and put down one finger for another fastball. At that moment, Thomson says, he had a sudden flash of inspiration: Ralph was going to throw the same pitch again! This one, however, was higher and inside; it might even have been a ball.

Bobby swung and hit a low line drive that just did reach the seats above the low wall 315 feet away. If the game had been in Brooklyn, where the foul poul was 348 feet, it would probably have been an out. Instead, it was one of the shortest, and most heartbreaking, home runs of all time.

While delirious fans hoisted Thomson to their shoulders, Branca somehow made it back to the clubhouse, he doesn't remember how. The next day's paper showed a jubilant Thomson while Branca, his head buried in his hands, repeated again and again, "Why *me*?"

Next season, Brooklyn fans demanded that Branca throw away his number 13. He agreed to exchange it for number 12, and the Dodgers

won the 1952 pennant with ease. But they lost the World Series to their old foes, the Yankees, in seven games. For the Brooklyn faithful, it was "wait till next year" again.

There was one change, however: Number 13 would be gone. That winter Ralph Branca was waived out of the National League to the Detroit Tigers.

≈ "Next Year" ≈

The Dodgers and Yankees met again in October 1955. This time, playboy pitcher Johnny Podres (9-10) won two games, and Sandy Amoros made a great catch against Yogi Berra in Game 7. That's the kind of thing that used to happen to the Dodgers, who finally had vanquished both their nemesis and their Fate. Eddie Bennett and Ralph Branca had been exorcised. Brooklyn had a *barucha*, a blessing, at last.

But the blessing was short-lived. In 1958, owner Walter O'Malley moved the Dodgers from Brooklyn to Los Angeles, leaving behind wounds of the heart and the psyche that still have not healed. Of all the curses visited upon the Dodgers, this was the cruelest.

The lust of the goat is the bounty of God.

William Blake

CHAPTER 29
The Billy Goat Curse

FOR 49 YEARS, 1946-94, THE CUBS HAVE WANDERED in the wilderness without winning a pennant, the longest such drought in baseball history.

They've had great players—Ernie Banks, Ferguson Jenkins, Billy Williams, Ron Santo, Hank Sauer, Bill Madlock, Dave Kingman, Bill Buckner, Rick Sutcliffe, Andre Dawson, Ryne Sandberg, Greg Maddux, and Sammy Sosa.

They came close several times—1969, '72, '84 and '89. But somehow they just couldn't win. Some fans knew the reason: It was the infamous Billy Goat Curse, one of the longest-running curses in sports annals.

It began in 1945.

╳ The 1945 World Series ╳

In September 1945, with a week left in the pennant race, the Cubs opened a 1½-game lead over the Cardinals, thanks to the heroic pitching of Hank Borowy, acquired from the Yankees. After going 10-5 for New York, Hank was 10-2 with Chicago. "Hank had pitched some tough ball games in September to keep us in the race," recalled Cubs second baseman Roy Hughes. "We just couldn't get any runs for him. All through September all we could get poor Hank were two-three runs. He was the victor 2-1, 3-2, 3-1."

In a final showdown against St. Louis, Borowy toiled 11 innings under a hot sun before winning 6-5, virtually clinching the flag.

Chicago's World Series opponents would be the Detroit Tigers. The Cubs, with 98 victories on the year, should have been heavy favorites over the Tigers, with 88, although ex-GI Hank Greenberg returned in time to bolster Detroit in the pennant drive. Because of wartime travel restrictions, the two champions would play three games in Detroit followed by four in Chicago, with no travel day in between.

On October 3 Borowy opened the Series, winning 9-0. The Tigers won Game 2 to even it up. Chicago's Claude Passeau then pitched a one-

---

hitter, only the second ever recorded in the World Series, to give the Cubbies a two-to-one lead. They needed only to split the last four games at home to be world champs.

The next day, October 6, 42,923 persons jammed Wrigley Field. Well, actually, it was 42,922 persons and one billy goat. The goat, named Sonovia, was the mascot at the Billy Goat Tavern in Chicago's Loop, across from the Tribune building. The eccentric owner, Billy Goat Sianis, boasted not only a goat that butted customers but a cat that slurped beer and a phone that gave electric shocks.

Sianis bought two box seat tickets to the Series and arrived with Sonovia dressed in a blanket saying, "Let's Get the Tigers' Goat." The adjoining customers were not amused, however, and, holding their noses, summoned the usher. He got on his new-fangled walkie-talkie and eventually reached Cubs owner Philip K. Wrigley, himself. "Either the goat goes, or he goes," Wrigley barked, and soon both goats— Sonovia and Sianis—were given the bums' rush out the gate.

Chicago lost the game 4-1, and the Series was all tied up.

Sianis pasted Sonovia's ticket over his bar and put the *kakos inos*— Greek for "evil eye"—on the Cubs. They will never win another pennant, he predicted.

But the Cubs weren't worried. They still had their two aces, Borowy and Passeau.

The Tigers knocked out the tired Borowy in Game 5, however, to take a one-game lead. The Cubs now had to sweep both remaining games.

Passeau started Game 6 and was hurling a two-hitter after five innings. Then the Tigers' Jimmy Outlaw, who was 2-for-20 in the series, stepped to the plate. "I threw him a knuckleball on which he broke his bat," recalled Passeau. When Outlaw hit the ball back to the box, Passeau knocked it down with his bare hand and threw him out. But the ball had torn a nail off Passeau's middle finger. No longer able to grip the ball properly, he was yanked.

After eight innings the game was tied 7-7, and manager Charley Grimm desperately called on Borowy, who had pitched the day before. Hank held the Tigers scoreless for the next four innings before Chicago's

Stan Hack hit a ball that struck a sprinkler faucet in the outfield and bounced over Hank Greenberg's head to tie the Series at three games apiece.

After a merciful day off, Grimm had no choice but to call on Borowy again to pitch his third game in four days. Hughes and Borowy drove to the park together along Lake Shore Drive. "Hank, how you feelin' today?" Roy asked. "I'm tired," Borowy admitted. He didn't get a man out, as Detroit blasted him for five runs and won the game and Series.

The next day a dejected Wrigley opened a telegram. "Who stinks now?" it read, and it was signed "Billy Sianis."

The next year Borowy developed blisters on his fingers and finished 12-10, while the Cubs fell to third. They dropped to sixth in '47 and last in '48.

♈ 1959 White Sox ♈

Sianis made another trip to the ballpark with Sonovia, or at least a goat that looked like him. However, the park was not Wrigley Field, home of the fifth-place Cubs, but Comiskey, home of the White Sox. Sure enough, the 1959 Chisox went from 10 games behind in '58 to win the pennant, ending Casey Stengel's string of five straight flags.

The Sox went into the Series with 94 victories, six more than their foes, the Los Angeles Dodgers, but they made the mistake of not asking Sianis to the Series, which they lost, four games to two.

The White Sox have never won another pennant.

The Cubs, meanwhile, slid to seventh (next to last) in 1961. A couple of promising rookies, second baseman Ken Hubbs and outfielder Lou Brock, joined them in '62, and in '63 they finished seventh in a 10-team league. But Hubbs was killed in an auto crash after the season, and in '64 Brock was traded to the Cardinals for Ernie Broglio. Broglio won nine games for the Cubs; Brock went on to the Hall of Fame. St. Louis won the pennant, and the Cubs slid to 10th in '66.

The next year Leo Durocher took over as Cubs manager and, with Ernie Banks, Fergie Jenkins, Ron Santo, and Billy Williams, lifted the Cubs to third in '67 and '68. The Cards won the pennant both years.

♉ 1969: Cubs vs. Mets ♉

On August 15, 1969, the Cubs had opened up an 8½-game lead over the surprising New York Mets. Chicago was ecstatic. But not Billy Goat Sianis. "Don't bet on it," he said calmly, wiping the bar.

In early September the Cubs lost three straight to third-place Pittsburgh. The last one was an 11-inning heartbreaker. In the ninth the Pirates' Willie Stargell hit a two-strike home run that tied the game. In the 10th the Cubs' Billy Williams doubled but was erased on a sacrifice attempt that turned into a double play. The Pirates went ahead in the 11th on an error and a single that Chicago's second baseman Glenn Beckert just missed. In the bottom of the inning, the first two Cubs singled, but Beckert lined into a DP to end the game. The Cubs were only 2½ games ahead.

On September 8 Chicago arrived in New York. With the game knotted at 2-2 in the sixth, the Mets' Tommy Agee hit a ground ball to left, but the wet grass held it up and he took second and scored on a single on a close play at the plate.

In the eighth Beckert and Williams singled, but Santo hit into a DP and Banks struck out. It was Jerry Koosman's 13th victory of the year, and the Cubs were only 1½ games ahead.

The next night Mets manager Gil Hodges posed with a snowshoe rabbit—the team hadn't lost since he got it. Behind his desk hung a scroll from Pope Paul exhorting the Mets.

For the Cubs the portents were not good. Ken Holtzman (17-13) would not pitch on Rosh Hoshana, so Durocher had to call on Jenkins (21-15 on the year) with two days rest.

Before the game a New York fan let a black cat out of a bag. It fled into the Cubs' dugout, and the Mets promptly scored two runs. In the seventh New York scored on "two weird hits that bounced strangely" past Willie Smith, subbing for the injured Banks at first base. Finally, Art Shamsky's homer—his 13th—sent Jenkins down to his 13th defeat. The Mets were now only half a game behind.

On September 10 the demoralized Cubs went to Philadelphia to face the fifth-place Phils. Holtzman threw a change-up to rookie Dave

---

Watkins, because the scouting reports said Watkins couldn't hit it. He did, for a two-run home run as the Phils' Rick Wise won his 13th game. The Cubs fell out of first place to stay.

The next night the Cubs were leading 2-1 in the ninth with a man on second and Philadelphia's dangerous Dick Allen (32 homers) up. Durocher decided to pitch to Allen, who hit it over the fence, and Chicago lost its eighth in a row.

The Cubs lost again the following night when a routine ground ball hopped over Beckert's glove.

They lost their 10th straight to St. Louis when ex-Cubbie Brock hit his first home run in two months. In the Loop, Sianis quietly collected on his bets and poured the cat another saucer of beer.

♋ **1973** ♋

It was July 4. Billy Goat Sianis had died; his nephew, Sam, was tend-ing the bar, and the Cubs were in first place, 5½ games ahead of the Cardinals. They were 5-1 betting favorites to go on and take the pennant at last.

The Mets were last, 11 games behind.

"A lot of people call me," Sam said. "Why don't you get together with Wrigley?" they begged him.

"I want to buy a season ticket for the goat," Sam replied, "but they turn me down." However, he finally relented and agreed to give the Cubs one more chance.

"I buy two box seats," he said and dressed his goat, Sinovia XII, in a new blanket sporting this message: ALL IS FORGIVEN. LET ME LEAD THE CUBS TO THE PENNANT. BILLY GOAT.

Sam hired "a big, black limousine, cost me a hunnert bucks. I try to bring the goat and take it to Cubs park and be nice and take the hex off." With TV, the press, and radio waiting, "the limousine stop in front of the park. The driver open the door and roll out a red carpet, and the goat come out of the limousine and walk on the red carpet straight up to the gate."

Sam flourished two tickets. "But usher say no goat allowed in park.

I say, 'I got two tickets and the goat stay right there and go in to see the ball game. If you don't apologize to the goat and let him in the park, you're not gonna win the pennant.'"

Ferguson Jenkins walked by, read the sign, and, said Sam, "was very entoosiastic." Fergie petted the goat gingerly and offered to take him into the clubhouse, but the cops closed the door firmly. So Sianis and Sinovia XII climbed back into their limousine. "I'm a Cubs fan," Sam said, "but you know, they don't even give me a refund for the tickets, so we just keep the hex on."

That day Chicago shortstop Jose Cardenal, batting .319, was hit by a pitch and taken out of the lineup. The next day the Cubs lost to the Phils. Then Jenkins beat San Diego, 8-5, but Chicago lost the following day. On Sunday, July 8, they lost again, on a suicide squeeze executed with two strikes.

By August the Cubs were under .500 and in fourth place. The Mets, meanwhile, performed another miracle, storming into first place while the Cubs faded to fifth.

"It seem to me," said Sianis, "the hex work pretty good."

♈ 1974: The A's ♈

The Cubs were dead last.

But if Wrigley was not listening, another Chicago citizen was. He was Charley O. Finley, owner of the Oakland Athletics. The A's, with ex-Cubbie Ken Holtzman winning 19, 21, and 19 games, had won three straight pennants, 1972-74, the team's first flags since 1931, when they were in Philadelphia.

Oakland went into the '74 Series against the Dodgers seeking a rare three straight world titles. But the team was torn by dissension. Star pitcher Catfish Hunter said Finley owed him back pay and threatened to quit. Slugger Reggie Jackson and pitcher Vida Blue openly sneered at the owner. Pitchers Rollie Fingers and Blue Moon Odom got into a fistfight in the locker room before the opening game.

Still, Holtzman won 3-2.

But the Dodgers beat Blue in the second game, and Finley put in a

call to Chicago and the Billy Goat Tavern. Could Sianis and Sinovia fly to Oakland for the rest of the Series?

"I fly the goat TWA in a crate," Sam said. "Didn't cost much, a hunnert bucks." The two were ushered to a box seat next to movie star Karl Malden. Before the game Sam paraded Sinovia around the field, then deposited her in the pen behind the outfield wall, where she joined Finley's mule, Charley O, contentedly munching grass. Sam predicted the A's would sweep the last three games.

In the third inning, Oakland loaded the bases, and Jackson hit a bouncer in front of the plate which the Dodgers' catcher kicked away, letting two runs in as the A's won 3-2.

Sam's box-seat mate for Game 4 was Rock Hudson. With Holtzman pitching, the Dodgers' Bill Buckner, the ex-Cub, doubled with one out, but Ken got Jim Wynn and Steve Garvey on strikeouts. In the third inning, Los Angeles put a man on third with one out, but Holtzman struck out Davey Lopes, and Buckner popped up a squeeze bunt.

In the bottom of the inning, Holtzman, who hadn't batted in three years because of the DH rule, hit a home run to give himself a 1-0 lead.

Wynn led off the Dodger sixth with a double, but Holtzman got Garvey, Joe Ferguson, and Ron Cey on three ground balls. The A's won 4-2. They needed only one more victory.

They got it the next day by a score of 3-2. A Dodgers error gave them one run. In the eighth Buckner singled, and when Oakland's Bill North lost the ball, Buckner sprinted toward third, to be gunned down by a great throw by Jackson. The A's were world champs again.

Sam talked about it all winter long.

The Cubs, meanwhile, kept stumbling along. They finished fourth in 1976 despite the presence of two-time batting champ Bill Madlock. They were fifth again in '79 despite Dave Kingman's 48 homers, and slipped to sixth in '80 despite Buckner's league-leading .324. The club fell to last in '80 and '81.

♉ **1984** ♉

In 1984 the Cubs got a new general manager, Dallas Green, a new manager, Jim Frey, and three new pitchers—Dennis Eckersley, Rick Sutcliffe, and Tim Stoddard. Green invited Sianis and his goat to attend opening day ceremonies as a sign that the curse was lifted.

The Cubs opened on the road, splitting eight games—it looked like the same old Cubs. Then they came home to Wrigley Field to face the Mets' hot rookie, Dwight Gooden.

The fans sat through infield practice in a drizzle, then announcer Jack Brickhouse took the microphone to describe the lugubrious history of the Billy Goat Curse. At that, the right field gate swung open to reveal Sam and his latest goat—this one named simply Billy. As Sam and Billy marched to the pitchers' mound and accepted the cheers of the crowd, the rain suddenly stopped.

The Cubs beat Gooden 11-2. (Dwight would go on to a 17-9 record for the year.)

With Sutcliffe giving the Cubs a sensational 16-1 season, good for the Cy Young Award, Chicago went on to win the division and prepared to meet the San Diego Padres in the playoff.

The first two games would be in Chicago. "I'm gonna give you both games if the goat come to both games," Sianis told Green. It was a deal.

In Game 1 Bob Dernier, with three home runs for the year, drove the second pitch over the wall for a homer, and Sutcliffe won 13-0, the most lopsided game in playoff history. Joked San Diego's Steve Garvey, "At least we blocked the extra point."

Sianis and Billy were watching from their box seat as the Cubs won Game 2, 4-2. "The goat, he wants to stay at the game," Sianis smiled. "I have a hard time getting him to leave. Every game the goat come to, they win."

So the triumphant Cubs prepared to fly to San Diego, needing only one victory in the last three games, while the phone at the Billy Goat Bar began ringing off the hook. "Everybody call from San Diego, said, 'Don't come around with the goat, because we gonna kill the goat.'"

The California fans shouldn't have worried. The Cubs scoffed when

San Diego's Gary Templeton predicted a three-game Padres sweep. So confident were they that they left Sam and Billy behind.

In the first game on the Coast, the Cubs faced their favorite Padres pitcher, Ed Whitson, whom they had already battered three times that year. They took a 1-0 lead after two, but their own pitcher, Eckersley (10-8), was driven out in a barrage of seven runs, and the *Chicago Sun Times* nervously recalled the 1945 debacle.

After an off day, the two teams took the field for what proved to be one of the most dramatic playoff games yet. Cubs outfielder Dernier just missed a shoestring catch, and San Diego went on to score two runs. Chicago went back in front on two homers. The Padres tied it with a ground ball off the pitcher's glove, a sacrifice, a ground out, and Garvey's single. They added two more in the seventh.

The Cubs evened it and had two on and two out with pinch hitter Rich Hebner at bat against San Diego reliever Goose Gossage. Hebner fouled out.

That brought the teams to the ninth tied 5-5. Facing ex-Cubbie Craig Lefferts, the Cubs loaded the bases with righthanded Ron Cey, their top RBI man with 97, at bat. Cey grounded out.

In the last of the ninth, Chicago's ace reliever, Lee Smith, took the mound to face Tony Gwynn, the batting champ at .351, and Garvey. Tony singled. Garvey had already knocked in three runs for the day, but he hadn't had hit a home run in two months. So of course he hit one to the opposite field, and the playoff was all tied up.

In the final game, the Cubs sent their ace, Sutcliffe, back and took a 3-0 lead. In the seventh, with a man on second, San Diego's Tim Flannery hit a gounder to first baseman Durham, normally an outfielder. The ball didn't bounce but went through his legs for an error—his only error with the glove all year—and the game was tied.

After a bloop single on a checked swing, Gwynn came up. Tony lined a savage grounder to second baseman Ryne Sandberg, the league's MVP. It looked like a certain double play. Sandberg put his glove down for a low hop, but the ball took a high hop and bounced off the mitt for a double to score the go-ahead run.

The Cubs had lost again on two bad hops. "These things haven't

happened to us all season," moaned Frey. "I had decent stuff," protested Sutcliffe. "I wasn't getting hit that hard, but they happened to find holes."

Would the balls have bounced differently if Sam and Billy had been there?

Thereafter it was the old familiar story. Billy went back to butting customers at Sam's bar, and the Cubs slipped steadily to last in '87.

Sam's quiet life was interrupted once, when the Chicago Sting soccer team invited him and Billy to attend their championship game against Montreal. Of course, Chicago won.

♉ **1989** ♉

In 1988 the Cubs' new manager, Don Zimmer—the Red Sox skipper in the 1978 Boston Massacre—brought the team in fourth with a 77-85 record. For '89 the team traded Rafael Palmiero for reliever Mitch Williams. Once again the Cubs asked Sam Sianis for help, and he and Billy watched the Cubs win the opener against the Phils 5-4 as Williams loaded the bases in the ninth, then struck out the side. Sam and Billy now had a perfect 9-0 record.

That year outfielder Andre Dawson fell more than 50 points in his batting average, to .252. But Sandberg batted .290 with 30 homers, Williams gave the team 36 saves, and Chicago won the division title. One would think the Cubs had learned their lesson as they prepared to meet San Francisco in the playoffs, which opened in Wrigley Field. But though Sam Sianis waited by the tavern phone, no call ever came.

In the opener, the goatless Cubs were losing 4-3 after three innings when their ace, Greg Maddux (19-12), loaded the bases and the Giants' Will Clark slammed a home run to break the game open.

The Cubs won Game 2, 9-5.

Moving to San Francisco, the Cubs took a 2-0 lead in the first inning. But the Giants came back with three runs against Sutcliffe (16-11), though they hit only one ball out of the infield. Brett Butler singled, Robby Thompson got a scratch single, and Clark hit an easy grounder back to the box. The ball rolled just under Sutcliffe's glove. "If I get a true bounce, we get a double play," he said. Instead, the bases were loaded

with no outs. Kevin Mitchell (47 homers) was walked intentionally to pitch to Matt Williams (.202). Matt squibbed a DP ball to Sutcliffe, who slipped and had to settle for one out as a run scored. Zimmer raised some eyebrows by ordering an intentional walk to Terry Kennedy to load the bases for Candy Maldonado. The decision backfired when Candy also walked, forcing in the second run. Jose Uribe hit an infield chopper to score the third run.

The Cubs went ahead 4-3 in the seventh. In the bottom of the inning, with one man on, Zimmer brought in reliever Les Lancaster to pitch to Thompson, apparently unconcerned that Robby had homered off Lancaster in Game 2. On the hit-and-run, Thompson knocked the ball over the fence for a hit-and-run homer.

The Cubs threatened to tie the game again in the eighth. Mark Grace singled, and when Dawson drove a long fly to the wall, Grace tagged up and made a daring dash for second. He was out by a whisker on a great throw. After an error, Shawon Dunston singled—a hit that could have scored Grace and tied the game if not for Mitchell's throw—and the Cubs lost, 5-4.

The next day the Cubs sent Maddux back to the mound, but bad luck continued to follow them.

Chicago scored a run in the first. In the bottom of the inning, with a San Francisco runner on third and Clark on first, Mitchell hit a double-play ball to second. However, Clark slid into second, waving his arms, to force a wild relay throw to first. The umpire should have called Clark out, ending the inning, but he didn't, and one run scored.

In the fifth with the score tied, lefthander Steve Wilson (6-4) was on the mound for Chicago with a man on second and the righthanded Mitchell up. Should Zimmer walk him? Should he lift Wilson for a right-hander? Zim did neither, and Mitchell whaled the ball over the fence for a 6-4 lead.

In the ninth Chicago loaded the bases with two out, but Dawson whiffed on three pitches.

One more Chicago loss, and it would be over. Zimmer went with his biggest winner, Mike Bielecki (18-7), against San Francisco's Rick Reuschel (17-8), an ex-Cub. As usual, Chicago scored first, and for six

innings Bielecki hurled two-hit ball, protecting a 1-0 lead. But in the seventh Clark lined a long drive just out of Dawson's reach for three bases, and Mitchell's fly tied the score 1-1.

"When I went out in the eighth, I felt tired," Bielecki later admitted. With two outs, he gave up two straight walks on 3-2 counts. On the Chicago bench, Zimmer stood up and walked to the mound. Bielecki fully expected the skipper to take him out, but Mike mumbled the obligatory, "I feel great," and Zimmer walked back to the bench. Bielecki gave up another walk, this one on four pitches, with the red-hot Clark (.632 for the series so far) coming up.

With the count 2-0, Zimmer finally waved for Lancaster. "I thought the count was 3-0, not 2-0," Lancaster said later. If he had known the true count, "I would have thrown a slider." Instead he threw a fastball, and Clark lined a single for a 3-1 lead.

The Cubs would not surrender. With two out in the ninth, they lined three straight singles for one run, with their best hitter, Sandberg, at the plate. Ryne drilled a grounder to end the Cubs' final hope.

They had outhit the Giants by 10-4. But once again they couldn't hit when it counted.

♉ 1998 ♉

Sammy Sosa was making a run at 60 home runs, and the Cubs were part of a three-way race for the Wild Card berth in the playoffs, when Sianis appeared on Jay Leno's TV show and announced he was going to lift the curse. Strangely, there was no response from the Cubs.

Sammy ended with 66 home runs, second to Mark McGwire's 70, and the Cubs defeated San Francisco in a one-game playoff. Next were three games against the Braves in the first round of the National League Championship Series.

John Smoltz (17-3) easily beat them in Atlanta, 7-1.

In Game 2, Chicago's Kevin Tapani (19-9) dueled Cy Young winner Tom Glavine (20-6) and had a four-hit, 1-0 lead after eight innings. Hoping to save a tired bullpen, skipper Jim Riggleman decided to leave Kevin in for the ninth, and Javy Lopez slugged a game-tying homer. In

the 10th reliever Terry Mulholland missed touching first, thus putting a man on second, and Chipper Jones hit a line drive just inches inside the foul line to win it, 2-1.

Still the Cubs refused to call Sianis. They sent their rookie sensation, Kerry Wood (13-6), against Greg Maddux (18-9). Wood lost 6-2, and the Cubs were history. For the series, Sosa batted .182 with no home runs.

In 1999 the Cubs had the highest payroll in the National League Central division. Wood developed arm trouble and didn't pitch a single game. Despite 63 homers by Sosa, Chicago dropped deeper and deeper into last place. Still no *billet-doux* arrived for the Billy Goat. The Cubs ended up losing 95 games—only three teams in the major leagues lost more.

The once-mighty franchise, which had won seven pennants from 1906-1945, still has not captured a flag since then.

There was that fatal and perfidious bark,
Built on th'eclipse and rigged with curses dark.

John Milton,
LYCIDAS

CHAPTER 30
Two Tainted Teams

꒰ The Angels' Curse ꒱

WHEN THE CALIFORNIA ANGELS' bus ran off the Jersey Turnpike in May 1992, almost killing manager Buck Rodgers, it was just the latest in a long line of accidents to the team. That same year coach Deron Johnson died of lung cancer, and pitcher Matt Keogh was hit by a foul ball while sitting in the dugout and required emergency surgery to save his life.

It was almost as if the Angels were under some kind of curse.

1961: Pitcher Johnny James broke his arm throwing a curve and never pitched again. The Angels came in eighth.

1962: Ken Hunt swung a bat in the on-deck circle and broke a collarbone; he never played a full season again.

1963: All-Star pitcher Ken McBride was 13-2, with 10 wins in a row, when he suffered whiplash when his car was hit from behind. He was 4-28 for the rest of his career. Reliever Art Fowler was hit in the head during batting practice and lost vision in his left eye. The Angels finished ninth in a 10-team league.

1964: Rookie Rick Reichardt had a kidney removed. Tom Hegan broke his jaw when hit by a pitch and never regained full vision.

1965: Rookie pitcher Dick Wantz died of a brain tumor in mid-season. The Angels finished seventh.

1968: Pitcher Minnie Rojas, 12-9 in 1967, had his spine severed in an auto accident that killed his wife and three children. Don Mincher (25 homers in '67) was beaned, virtually ending his Angels career. Hurler Paul Schaal had his jaw broken by a pitch. The Angels finished eighth.

1972: Infielder Chico Ruiz was killed in a car collision. The Angels finished next-to-last.

1973: Infielder Bobby Valentine, batting .302, was switched to the outfield, crashed into a fence, broke his leg, and was out for the rest of the year. California finished fourth in the six-team division.

1974: Lee Stanton hit three home runs in one game, then broke his hand. Rookie catcher Charlie Sands, a .300-hitter in the minors, hurt his

knee and never regained his form. Another rookie, pitcher Bruce Heinbechner, was killed in another of the by now spooky auto accidents. The Angels finished last.

1975: First baseman Bruce Bochte broke his hand. Star pitcher Nolan Ryan was coasting with a 14-4 record when he injured his arm and lost his next eight games. The Angels finished last again.

1976: The Angels obtained Bobby Bonds (32 homers) from the Yankees. He broke his hand, missed half the season, and hit only 10 homers. The Angels finished fourth.

In 1977, a Los Angeles journalist enlisted the help of a witch to help break the hex on the Angels. We'll pick up that story in Chapter 37.

ⅠⅠ The Star-Crossed Astros ⅠⅠ

Like the Angels, the Houston Astros seemed to have a curse hanging over them almost from the time they were born in 1962.

1963: Jay Dahl, a 19-year-old bonus baby, was killed in a car accident after pitching only one game.

1964: Pitcher Jim Umbricht, 33, succumbed to cancer.

1967: Walter Bond, 29, a former Astro, died of leukemia.

1970: Outfielder Jimmy Wynn was stabbed in the stomach by his wife. His average fell to .203 in '71.

1971: Former Astros' vice president George Kirksey was killed in an auto accident.

1973: Outfielder Cesar Cedeno was convicted of shooting a woman in his hotel room in the Dominican Republic. He was let off with a fine. A .320 hitter, his average fell next season to .269.

1975: Don Wilson, 29, a two-time no-hit pitcher, committed suicide from carbon monoxide poisoning. His five-year-old son died with him.

1977: Popular ex-pitcher Turk Farrell, 43, was killed in England while driving on the wrong side of the road.

1980: J.R. Richard, 30, one of the fastest pitchers in baseball, was felled by a stroke in the Astrodome, ending his career and almost ending his life. Houston won the pennant but lost the NLCS to Philadelphia.

In the strike year of 1981, the Astros shared the division lead with

the Dodgers but lost the playoff three games to one.

In '86 they won 96 games and met the powerful Mets (108 victories) in one of the most thrilling and dramatic playoff series of all time. The final game went 16 innings, and the Astros had the tying and winning runs on base when Mickey Hatcher struck out to end it.

♊ Jim Deshaies Breaks Murphy's Law ♊

The *Houston Post* called it "Murphy's Law." The Astros just couldn't seem to win in San Diego's Jack Murphy Stadium. By June 27, 1988, Houston had suffered 10 straight losses there. The Astros had been outscored 54-17; they had lost their last three games 3-1, 4-0, and 3-0.

That night a tall lefthander, Jim Deshaies, was scheduled to pitch. Jim was better than his 7-6 record appeared; his ERA was a strong 2.89. But Houston bumped into the jinx early when its leadoff man, Gerald Young, doubled and then was picked off second. Randy Bass followed with a double in vain. Meantime, Deshaies' high fastball was singing; he whiffed four men in the first three innings.

In the fourth the Padres put a man on, and Deshaies got Dickie Thon to tap a double-play ball to the front of the plate, but rookie catcher Craig Biggio double-pumped before throwing and the play was able to nail only one of the runners. Deshaies got Tony Gwynn on a fly, which would have been the third out of the inning, but, given the two extra outs, San Diego went on to score four runs in all.

When the Astros finally got a run in the eighth, it was the first they'd scored at Jack Murphy in 31 innings. Deshaies went down to his seventh loss. "The most frustrating thing about it is I had great stuff," he said.

The next morning, Deshaies later recounted, "I was in a book store down at the mall looking around." He picked up a little volume on magic spells, saw "some little incantation for breaking evil spirits in a building," and brought the volume to the park.

There, he recalled, "Dave Smith and a couple of the guys were play-ing around in the clubhouse" before batting practice and decided to give it a try—"just something to have some fun with." "You were supposed to collect twigs from a certain tree, light 'em, and spit on them. We didn't

get the right tree," but they lit a fire anyway and read the spell. Some of the other players got upset about the "devil worship." Glenn Davis, the team's batting star, who already had 22 homers that season, told them, "You shouldn't be messing around with that stuff."

That night Houston's Nolan Ryan (12-11 on the year) faced Ed Whitson (14-7), going for his seventh straight win for the Padres. Bass got the Astros off to a quick start in the first with a two-run homer.

In the second Davis smacked a line-drive single, but on the way to first, "it felt like someone shot me in the leg.... Nothing like this has happened to me before." He had to be assisted off the field with a pulled hamstring. The Astros won 4-1 as San Diego left 11 men on base. "We turned it around for a day, anyway," Deshaies said.

Davis, who had been on a hot streak (.422 in the last 13 games), would be out for two weeks, and the Astros' hopes for a pennant seemed gone. "He's the one person we can least afford to lose, Bass moaned.

But Houston won again the next night, 3-2. Shortstop Craig Reynolds, playing first base for Davis, saved the game with a good pickup to nip a runner at home as the Astros pulled to 5½ games behind the Dodgers.

Moving to Los Angeles the following night, Houston's Mike Scott (14-8) won 3-1. Third baseman Buddy Bell replaced Davis at first and knocked in two runs. Next the Astros mauled the Dodgers' Fernando Valenzuela to draw 3½ games behind. Los Angeles catcher Mike Scioscia couldn't understand it: "With Davis out, we should be beating them."

"I don't know what turned it on or how it happened," Houston's Doran shrugged. "But we don't walk on the field wondering what's going to happen any more. We walk on the field expecting something's going to happen."

Unfortunately, the magic didn't last. Davis returned, but in the last two months hit only eight homers with 27 RBIs. Deshaies won only four more and lost seven as Houston faded to fifth. He never tried another spell again.

The Great Spirit sees everything, hears everything, and forgets nothing.

Chief Joseph, Nez Perce

CHAPTER 31
Chief Wahoo and the Indians

IN 1993 THREE CLEVELAND PITCHERS—Steve Olin, their top reliever with 29 saves; Bobby Ojeda, and Tim Crews—were drinking and speed-boating in Florida when they slammed into a pier. Olin and Crews were killed instantly; Ojeda survived but was severely injured.

This was the worst is a long series of bad breaks to hit the team, which had been, and continues to be, the target of Native-American protests against its mascot, a toothy, grinning caricature known as Chief Wahoo.

In 1911 the Cleveland club changed its name from the Naps to the Indians. In the next 89 years they won only two world championships, 1920 and 1948.

Chief Wahoo was unveiled in 1947 and apparently brought good luck, as the team upset the favored Red Sox in a sudden-death playoff for the pennant the following year and went on to defeat the Boston Braves in the World Series, four games to two. But that was the last Series the Indians ever won. In fact, they got into only two more, 1954 and 1997.

From 1951-56, they had the best pitching staff in baseball but, alas, came up against the Yankees, who were even better. Cleveland finished second in five of those six years and had to win a then record 111 games to finish first in '54. Then they lost to the Giants and Willie Mays in the World Series.

Some fans blame the team's woes on "the Curse of Rocky Colavito," but that's ridiculous. The hard-hitting Rocky didn't join them until 1956, and in his four years there, they finished second, sixth, fourth, and second before trading him to Detroit. The trade may have hurt, but it was hardly a Ruthian curse.

By the 1990s Native Americans were actively protesting Chief Wahoo and even the name, Indians, as insulting. Whether for this or other reasons, the Tribe did seem to have the Indian sign on them.

A year after the boating accident, the Indians moved into a new stadium and were probably cheated out of the pennant by the players' strike. They had the best home record in the league, and the strike cut

them off with many more home games left than their rivals. At 66 and 47, they were in a good position to pass the White Sox for the division title, and could have tied or passed the Yankees, too.

In 1995 the Indians did win the pennant, but lost to Atlanta in the "all-Indian" World Series.

In '96 they won their division but lost to Baltimore in the ALCS.

In '97 the Tribe had their best chance and blew it. They won the AL Central with only 86 victories but upset the powerful Yankees (96 wins) in the divisional playoffs.

In Game 4 the Yanks were leading, two games to one, and were only four outs from winning the playoff behind their star closer, Mariano Rivera. But Sandy Alomar homered to tie it. In the ninth, Cleveland's Omar Vizquel hit a hard grounder that glanced off pitcher Ramiro Mendoza, knocking in the winning run and tying the series.

Cleveland won the division the following day, when reliever Jose Mesa stopped a New York rally in the eighth, then ended the game in the ninth when Bernie Williams flied out with the tying run on second, another Yankee choke in the clutch.

Then Cleveland knocked off Baltimore in six games, when Tony Fernandez slapped a homer in the 11th inning for a 1-0 victory.

Against another upstart Wild Card team, the Florida Marlins, in the World Series, the Indians split the first two games in Florida.

A freezing wind greeted the teams in Cleveland, where Native-American pickets were out in strength. With the score 7-7 in the seventh, Florida's Gary Sheffield made a leaping catch to rob Jim Thome of a home run. Then the Marlins exploded for seven runs and victory.

The Tribe came back to win Game 4. But in Game 5 they went into the ninth losing 8-4, knocked out rookie Livan Hernandez, but couldn't get the tying run home. It was their second loss in three games at home.

Back in Florida, the Indians won the must-win sixth game, 4-1.

In Game 7, the Indians were two outs away from the world championship when Florida's Craig Counsell lifted a sacrifice fly off Mesa to tie the game. Charles Nagy loaded the bases in the 11th, and Edgar Renteria hit a line drive an inch above Nagy's glove as the Indians suffered perhaps their most stunning defeat yet.

In 1998, the Yankees overpowered the Indians in the ALCS. Cleveland again lost two out of three at home, where Native American protesters once more turned out in force.

In 1999, the Indians took a two-to-nothing lead against the Wild Card Red Sox by scores of 3-2 and 11-1. With Boston's ace, Pedro Martinez (23-4), and MVP Nomar Garciaparra (.357) out with injuries, all Cleveland needed was to win one of the last three games. They would face Pedro's older brother, Ramon (2-1), Kent Mercker (2-0), and Bret Saberhagen (10-6), who had been blasted in Game 2.

Instead, Ramon beat them 9-3, Mercker triumphed 23-7, and a pain-wracked Pedro pitched six hitless innings of relief to beat them, 12-8.

Had the Curse of Chief Wahoo struck again?

I will go to Detroit, I will stamp my foot and shake down every house in Tukubatchi [Alabama].

Tecumseh,
predicting the great quake of 1814

CHAPTER 32
Chief Noc-a-Homa

THE ATLANTA BRAVES WERE THE BEST TEAM IN BASEBALL from 1991 to '99. Yet they won only one world championship and four pennants in that period.

While Native Americans picketed and protested both the team's nickname and its tomahawk chop, Atlanta lost two playoffs to inferior teams, in 1993 (the Phillies) and 1997 (the Marlins), and World Series to two other inferior teams (Minnesota, 1991, and Toronto, 1992).

Could Atlanta be under an Indian hex? It's not the first time the Braves have seemingly angered native spirits. The most famous incident was in 1982, and it almost cost them the title.

That year an Ottawa-Ojibway Indian named Levi Walker—"Chief Noc-a-Homa"—watched from his mascot's tepee just beyond the wire left field fence. He sprang out of the tent at each Atlanta home run to do a foot-stomping, ululating war dance.

The Braves were running away with the league in '82—until they took the Chief's tepee away to sell more seats, and the team went into a tailspin.

"I can't claim any power to make this happen," Walker has insisted.

Still, it makes you wonder.

The original Noc, in 1967, was a black man in a chief's headdress. The Braves finished seventh.

The next year, 1968, the old Noc was replaced by Big Victor, a 60-foot styrofoam mechanical chief. With each Braves home run, he waved a tomahawk, turned his head back and forth, and blinked his red eye bulbs. Unfortunately the light bulbs kept blowing out, and batters kept zeroing in on him in batting practice, sending divots of styrofoam flying. The Braves finished fifth. Their home run star, Hank Aaron, hit only 29. Pitcher Phil Niekro, a future Hall of Famer, posted a 14-12 mark.

That winter Walker asked for the job, and the Braves signed him for $50 a game.

And so, on Opening Day 1969, dressed in feathers and buckskin, a new Noc-a-Homa trotted from the dugout to left field. Manager Lum

Harris had an inspiration. "Chief," he said, "why not stop at the mound and do a little dance and then go to the tepee?" So, Walker recalled, "I did a little prayer dance and raised my hands to the Great Spirit: 'Whatever is your will.'" Then Levi raced to the outfield as the crowd cheered.

As he raced, the opposing bullpen sometimes threw coolers of ice water on him. When Levi began carrying a fire extinguisher to keep them at bay, they sneaked into his tepee and nailed his mocassins to the floor. Once they even burned his tepee down, delaying the game for half an hour.

Walker could also swallow burning torches on the mound and blow flames from his mouth. He fired a Civil War cannon, though he had to stop after he hit a fan with the wadding. Levi installed carpeting in the tepee, then TV, air conditioning, a refrigerator, a totem pole, lounge chairs, and finally even an Indian princess.

With Walker thus ensconced, Aaron soared to 44 homers, Niekro won 23 games, Rico Carty batted .342, and the Braves finished first in the new Western Division, though they fell to the "Amazin' Mets" in the playoffs.

But then the Braves went into a dive. They plunged to fifth in 1970 and were still there at the end of the 1975 season. Then Ted Turner bought the team. The Braves promptly went into a 13-game losing streak and fell to last place, the first time they had suffered that indignity since moving to Atlanta.

The next year, outfielder Jeff Burroughs said, "I'll tell you one thing for sure: This team won't lose 13 in a row." He was right. It lost 17 in a row. Turner himself managed number 17 and lost 2-1.

Turner tried everything. He got down on all fours and barked like a dog at home plate. He raced in a motorized bathtub against a team of broadcasters. He staged greased pig chases. He had a chimpanzee sweep the bases between innings. He sponsored a wet T-shirt contest (won by a minister's daughter). He had a Blind Date Night. He married 34 couples in a mass ceremony. (After the couples left to enjoy their first nights, they were followed on the diamond by professional wrestlers— "wedlock and headlock," as someone said.) He staged camel and

ostrich races with riders throwing cow chips at each other. A DJ dived into the world's largest ice cream cone and almost drowned.

Nothing helped. The Braves lost 101 games, their most since 1935, when they were in Boston.

Meanwhile, in addition to 82 home games a year, Levi was also making 260 public appearances with no increase in pay. He went to PTAs, Little Leagues, Boy Scouts and Girl Scouts. Once, he recalled, he made five appearances in one day, whipping his car at 80 and 90 miles an hour to get to them all.

Amid the clowning, Walker had a serious message. He wanted to tell the real story of Native Americans—"their job opportunities, problems on the reservations, lack of education, lack of funds," he said. "The average educational level is fifth grade, average income is $1,500 a year, the mortality rate of babies is so high they don't even acknowledge it. On the reservations, we're incarcerated without bars. I wanted to bring the problems to the public. At the same time we could also celebrate winning a baseball game."

In '78 Bobby Cox took over as manager but couldn't lift the team, even with two new long-ball hitters, Dale Murphy and Bob Horner. The Braves suffered two more last-place finishes, making four in a row.

In 1980 and '81 Cox got them as high as fourth and fifth, an achievement for which he was fired. Turner brought in Joe Torre as skipper for the fateful 1982 season.

♍ Turner Takes Away the Tepee ♍

Besides hiring Torre, the 1982 Braves also brought up rookie pitcher Steve Bedrosian, who may have had the fastest ball in the league. But in January Steve was in a head-on collision; doctors put 65 stitches in his head and removed two pieces of glass from his eyes. Then 12 days before opening day, Phil Niekro, 43, was hit by a batted ball and knocked out of the lineup for a month.

Nevertheless, the Braves won their first 13 games, a major league record. Rich Mahler was pitching shutouts, Bedrosian and Gene Garber were pitching brilliant relief, Dale Murphy was making spectacular

catches and hitting homers, and the batters were coming from behind time and again.

Aaron called them better than the '69 champs and as good as the world champion '57 Milwaukee Braves, for whom he had starred along with Ed Mathews and Warren Spahn. The '82 club would win by 10 games, Hank predicted.

Sports Illustrated put the handsome Murphy on its cover—a dubious honor feared by some as a sure jinx. Then *Time* put Turner on its cover. But if that was a double whammy, the happy Braves didn't show it. Beginning July 27 they swept four games from the second-place Padres. Murphy went 8-for-12 with two home runs; it left him batting .301 with 26 home runs. Horner had 20 homers. Bedrosian hadn't given up an earned run in 24 innings. "Braves become bullies," the *Atlanta Constitution* crowed.

"This should be the start of a dynasty," Turner predicted. Instead, it was almost the end.

It would be three weeks before Walker would go into his dance again. For, tucked at the bottom of the game report was a tiny note: The chief would be losing his tepee to make room for 250 more seats for the big Dodgers doubleheader two days hence. "Noc-a-Homa will be circulating in the stands," the front office announced. "Those are good seats and we need them now."

Then their luck turned.

On July 30 the third-place Dodgers, 10½ games behind, arrived for a doubleheader before a sell-out crowd. "Hey, Chief," Dodgers outfielder Dusty Baker winked knowingly, "they took your tepee down."

"You don't believe in that, do you?" Walker replied.

Baker shrugged. "We'll see."

In the first game the Braves took a 9-6 lead into the ninth, and Bedrosian strode in to save it. Instead, Los Angeles battered him for four runs to win. The Dodgers also won the second game, 8-2.

On the 31st the Dodgers' Fernando Valenzuela whipped Atlanta 3-0, and L.A. moved up to 7½ games behind.

On August 1, Niekro was winning 4-0 when he left the game in the fourth inning, but the Dodgers came back with nine runs for a four-game

sweep. The next day the Braves beat San Francisco, 7-3.

Against San Francisco on August 3, Atlanta took a 3-2 lead after eight innings. But in the ninth the Giants' Tom O'Malley, the youngest player in the league, hit a fly that just cleared the fence for two runs to put the Giants in front. It was Tom's second and last homer of the year. Even the angelic Murphy lost his temper, and no wonder. In his last 24 at bats he had only one hit, a scratch hit at that.

Murphy broke out of his slump on August 4, and Horner smacked a homer to send the Braves into the ninth with a 2-2 tie. But Bedrosian lost it on a stolen base against catcher Biff Pocoroba, who had thrown out only one man in 14 attempts all year.

It was Atlanta's sixth loss in eight games since the tepee had been removed. Their lead was now cut to 5½ games.

In Dodger Stadium on August 5, the Braves' Pascual Perez (2-9 lifetime) was beating Valenzuela 2-1 with two out in the last of the ninth, when substitute second baseman Jerry Royster, subbing for the injured Hubbard, fumbled an easy grounder, letting in the tying run. "I've never made an error with two out in the ninth before," he moaned. "I may never do it again." In the 10th, the Dodgers won on a bloop single, a passed ball, a sacrifice, and a fly.

"Braves blow another one," the *Constitution* sighed on August 6. Tied 3-3 in the 10th, Atlanta's Claudel Washington lifted a home run for a 4-3 lead. But in the home half, the Dodgers put one man on with one out when Atlanta first baseman Chris Chambliss dropped an easy throw. The Dodgers' Ron Cey hit a popup that fell for a double. Bill Russell then singled in the tying run, and shortstop Rafael Ramirez booted a grounder as the winning run scored. It was the fourth straight day Atlanta had lost in the final at bat. The Dodgers moved into second place, 3½ games behind.

On August 7, for the sixth time in seven games, the Braves took the lead, and for the sixth time they lost it, this time on an error by Horner. But they came back in the ninth as Murphy drove in the tying run, his first RBI in 39 at bats.

With the score still tied in the bottom of the 11th, Bedrosian came in. With a man on, two outs, and two strikes on pinch hitter Mike Marshall,

Bedrock gave up the game-winning single, and the Braves went down to another defeat. The Dodgers were only 2½ games behind.

Everything was going wrong. For the past 10 games Atlanta had batted a meek .195. Their three, four, and five men were batting .156 with runners on base. In the last four games, the Braves had made five errors in the ninth inning or later. Horner was mystified: "We're the same club that won 13 straight" in April, he said.

Atlanta's Rick Camp pitched a strong game on August 8, but lost 2-0. Murphy went hitless again—he was 2-for-19 with men in scoring position during the slide. A possible rally died in the seventh, when Terry Harper was thrown out at home by five feet. Atlanta's 10½ game lead of 10 days before had now shriveled to 1½.

Meanwhile, as Walker drove to appearances around northern Georgia, he was greeted by tepees in the yards of rural trailer homes and on the roofs of downtown Atlanta hotels. "There was a public outcry," he recalled. "People were saying, 'We want the tepee back up.' "

On August 9 in San Francisco, the Braves lost as Jim Barr pitched his first shutout in six years, a three-hitter. The lead had shrunk to only half a game.

"Mad as hell," Torres berated his players for their "lifeless" play. Claudell Washington admitted the team had been infected by a defeatist attitude. "We come out with our heads down," he said. "The 'death march' continues," the *Constitution* intoned.

The Braves' once-commanding lead disappeared completely on August 10. Murphy's first home run in almost two weeks put them ahead briefly 2-0, but once more they couldn't hold it. Murphy couldn't catch a wind-blown triple, which led to one Giant run. In the fifth Mahler uncorked two wild pitches to tie the game. In the seventh, the Giants' Milt May smacked a homer against the Braves' "Mad Hungarian," Al Hrabosky, to knock Atlanta out of first place.

Atlanta had accomplished something no team had ever done before—they had blown a 10½-game lead in only 12 days. Wrote Furman Bisher in the *Atlanta Journal*: "The Braves' next road trip will be to Lourdes."

"The Chief's ancestors may be behind it all," read the headline of

John McGraith's column in the *Constitution* the next morning. He wrote, "I don't believe in voodoo, the supernatural, ESP, ouija boards, good vibes, bad trips, Zen... or anything else they don't keep statistics for in *The Sporting News*... [But] I want to ask you a question: Has it occurred to you that the Atlanta Braves might be under a jinx? That... they are effectively stymied by forces beyond their control?

"Now I'll be the first to admit that I don't know anything about any other ancient culture than the one [commissioner] Bowie Kuhn rules," McGraith continued. "But I do know this: When the Atlanta Braves' front office removed Chief Noc-a-Homa's tepee from the left field stands two weeks ago—to gain access to 250 seats—they caused a row in the skies enough to instigate the team's current skein of 'inexplicable' bad luck."

"I don't know if it's true or not," the Chief shrugged. "But I will say that there are an awful lot of people who recognize me and say, 'You know what's wrong with the Braves? It's the tepee! We've got to get them to put back the tepee!'"

On August 11 Horner, with three hits in 22 at bats, was benched, but the Braves lost another heartbreaker on what Gerry Fraley of the called a "witches' sabbath." Two errors and a passed ball gave the Giants four unearned runs. The usually sure-handed Hubbard dropped an easy popup for one run. Braves fielders had now made 22 errors in 14 games.

However, Niekro was leading 5-3 when he retired with two men on. Bedrosian let both runners score, and Gene Garber gave up another run in the seventh. Meanwhile, Atlanta batters twice left runners on third with fewer than two out. But still they fought for 12½ innings until the Dodgers' Reggie Smith smashed a shot over the fence to send the Braves' to their ninth straight loss. It shoved them 1½ games behind the Dodgers.

"It's bizarre, really," Tim Tucker of the *Journal* wrote.

On August 12 Atlanta moved to San Diego, where the Padres were coming off a three-game losing streak. The Braves lost 8-2.

Then came Friday, the 13th of August. Atlanta took a 1-0 lead in the first, the fourth game in a row in which they had taken the lead.

The Padres' rookie pitcher, Dave Dravecky, who had batted only three times in his professional career, singled past first to drive in two

runs (the fifth game in a row that opposing pitchers had batted in a run). San Diego got another run in the third on a single by Joe Lefebvre, an infield out, and two wild pitches, the sixth by the Braves in six games.

Atlanta tied the game, but Hrabosky couldn't hold it, and the Braves lost 7-4. The team had gone "from the penthouse to the outhouse," Frank Hyland wrote.

Back in Atlanta, the front office, responding to "a deluge of telephone calls," said Noc-a-Homa would get his tepee back when the team came home on the 17th.

In San Diego on the 14th, the Braves seemed to gain some strength from the news and scored three runs in the first. But in the bottom of the inning, Washington stumbled chasing a hit, and the Padres tied it 3-3. Atlanta's rookie reliever, Donnie Moore, just up from Richmond, gave up an unearned run to put the Padres ahead.

In the eighth the Braves loaded the bases on two walks and an error, and Rufino Linares pinch-hit a single to put them ahead. Murphy protected the lead with a great catch in center field, Garber slammed the door in the ninth, and the Braves had won a game!

They lost the next day, though, and, wrote Tucker, once again "there was something bizarre about it."

Horner broke out of his slump with a three-run homer to give Niekro a 4-1 lead. But once again the lead vanished. Ramirez lost a popup in the sun. After a walk, Niekro needed a double-play ball and got it—right back to himself. He fired to second, where Ramirez and Hubbard both stood aside and let the ball sail into center field. San Diego scored four runs and went into the 10th tied 5-5. Bedrosian gave up a single just under the diving Chambliss' glove. Murphy lost a fly in the sun, and a single over the drawn-in outfield beat the Braves again. "EL FOLDO," the *Constitution* called it—one of the worst turn-arounds in baseball history.

After a merciful day of rest, the Braves prepared for a doubleheader at home against the Expos, third in the NL East, as Noc-a-Homa returned to his tepee. But it didn't help. Atlanta gave up eight runs on five errors and was slaughtered in the first game, 13-7.

The Braves were winning the second game 2-1 in the ninth when Montreal's Andre Dawson lifted a fly down the right field line.

Washington just missed it as the ball landed on the line for a triple. Al Oliver, leading the league in batting average and RBIs, singled over a drawn-in infield to tie the game.

An inning later, with a man on first, Chambliss dropped a DP relay—"It was a perfect throw, I just missed it," he said—and when Warren Cromartie singled past a diving Hubbard, the Braves had lost another.

Of their last 18 losses, six had been by one run; seven had come in the ninth inning or later.

On August 18, Atlanta's two big guns went 0-for-8, the Braves lost 12-2, and dropped four games out of first. The next day starter Pascual Perez got lost on the beltway, and Niekro was rushed into the game on three days rest. Miraculously, Phil had not lost a game during the long losing streak—four times he had left with a lead before the Braves blew it. This time he was losing 4-3 when he left after seven innings. But this time the Braves tied it. In the ninth Washington's two-out single off Montreal's relief ace, Jeff Reardon, gave Atlanta the victory, and Noc-a-Homa sprang from his tepee in joy.

The win brought the Braves back to only three games behind the Dodgers. Gratefully, they looked forward to the last-place Mets.

Perez, who had by now found the stadium, was good-naturedly hogtied by a teammate and led to the mound to be sure he wouldn't get lost again. The veteran responded with a masterpiece, 9⅓ innings of scoreless ball. Then, in the 10th, New York rookie Brian Giles (.210) hit the first home run of his life to put the Mets ahead.

In the home 10th, the Braves put two men on, but Ramirez was thrown out trying to score on a single. Then Harper hit a grounder to third baseman Hubie Brooks, who threw it away to let the tying run in. An intentional walk brought up the slumping Murphy, who walked on four straight pitches to force home the game winner.

Atlanta got the breaks again on August 21 and won its third straight. Tied 5-5 in the sixth, an error by New York pitcher Randy Jones put Linares on second. Then the catcher threw wild to put him on third, whence Royster singled him home. Atlanta was three games behind the Dodgers, with six weeks left.

A month later they were still three behind, but they pulled even, and

on the last day of the year they beat the Padres on Chambliss' 20th homer to win the division.

Did Noc-a-Homa and the tepee make a difference? Atlanta's record with and without the tepee looked like this:

	W	**L**	**PCT**
With tepee up	60	37	.619
With tepee down	2	17	.105
With tepee back up	27	19	.587
Total	89	73	.549

Murphy was voted MVP, though his numbers without Noc-a-Homa's tepee had been disastrous. The Braves' slugger hit .288 with 35 homers when the tepee was up, and .232 with a single home run when the tepee was down.

Atlanta finished second the next two years. Meantime, Levi Walker thought that, after 16 years as a part-time employe, it was time he began getting some benefits, such as medical insurance. The Braves listened sympathetically, and then fired him. He had missed three public appearances, they said. Levi protested that he missed them because the fans wouldn't let him leave one appearance in time to make the next one.

The Braves were unimpressed. "We were never very fair to Noc-a-Homa," admitted general manager Bob Hope.

Levi used his $5,000 severance pay to study for the Postal Service exam. "I wanted a better job and benefits," he says. "I got a better job and benefits."

Meantime, without their mascot the Braves slid to fifth in '85 and last in '86. They were still there in 1990 when Bobby Cox returned as manager in mid-season. They finished last again.

≈ The Braves in the '90s ≈

The three teams with the best winning percentages in baseball from 1991-99 were the Braves (.618), the Yankees (.560), and the Indians (.537). The Yanks won three World Series in those years; the Braves, one,

and the Indians, none. Why haven't the Braves and Indians been more successful?

Bobby Cox guided Atlanta "from worst to first" in 1991 and in the World Series met another dream team, the Minnesota Twins, who had also gone from last to first.

"The fans wanted me there," Levi Walker recalled. "They voted 2,016 to 64 by telephone for Chief Noc-a-Homa to come back." The Braves turned a deaf ear, however, and Atlanta lost in seven games.

In the 1992 Series against Toronto, Native Americans picketed Atlanta Stadium to protest the fans' "tomahawk chop" and Indian-style chanting. The Braves won the opener, but dropped the next three. After a win in Game 5, they returned to Atlanta, where Native Americans were back on the picket line, for Game 6. They lost the game, and the Series, in the 11th inning.

In the 1993 NLCS, Atlanta outhit, outpitched, and outscored the Phils but couldn't beat them. After two easy Braves wins, the protesters were back in Atlanta, where the Braves lost two close ones. The Phils wrapped it up back in Philly, 6-3.

Atlanta met the Cleveland Indians in the 1995 World Series. Cleveland was another target of Native-American protesters, who objected to the team's name and a cartoon caricature symbol, Chief Wahoo. The Cleveland protesters proved to be stronger, as Atlanta won four games to two.

In the summer of 1996, at Atlanta's Olympic Stadium, I ran into Noc-a-Homa in full regalia, his now gray hair in braids, hawking souvenirs to the crowds. No, he scoffed, he didn't believe the Braves were under a hex. But in the World Series that October, after crushing the Yankees in the first two games in New York, Atlanta lost three straight at home and the final game in Yankee Stadium.

Next fall the Braves (101 wins) faced the upstart Florida Marlins, the Wild Card with 92 wins, in the 1997 NLCS. In the opener in Atlanta, five unearned runs beat Maddux, 5-3. In Game 5, Florida's Cuban refugee, Livan Hernandez, whiffed 15 Braves, staking the Marlins to a one-game lead. Atlanta lost the pennant at home, 7-4, on a gutsy performance by Kevin Brown, pitching with the stomach flu.

In '98 Atlanta, the best team in the league with 106 victories, was upset in the NLCS in five games by San Diego.

In 1999 disaster struck. Andres Galarraga (44 homers in '98) was out with cancer. Closer Kerry Ligtenberg blew out his elbow in the spring; catcher Javier Lopez (.316) went out in mid-season with a knee injury, and John Smoltz injured his shoulder and finished 11-8. Still, the Braves won 103 games, tops in the majors. But after beating Houston in the Division Series and the Mets in a hard-fought NLCS, the Braves again succumbed to the New York Yankees in the World Series.

♍ A "Self-Inflicted" Curse? ♍

Since 1947, when Cleveland adopted the Chief Wahoo logo, the Indians have played 52 years. They have won three pennants and one World Series, in 1948.

Since 1913, when the former Boston Doves became the Braves, the team has played 86 seasons in three cities. They have won eight pennants and three World Series—one in 40 years in Boston, one in 13 years in Milwaukee, and one in 33 years at Atlanta.

How does one explain it?

Richard Velky, chief of Connecticut's Schaghticoke Tribal Nation, had his own explanation: The Braves and Indians, he said, are victims of a "self-inflicted" curse.

Addressing Braves owner Ted Turner after the '99 Series, Velky warned: "There are some who believe this sham of a chant has created much anger among the spirits. The chant and the [tomahawk] chop are "obnoxious, mechanical, and dysfunctional." They have "no connection whatever to any Native American heritage." The latest Atlanta defeat is "a dramatic reminder that your war chant is more of a lament than a victory cry." What's the solution? If I were Cleveland GM John Hart, I'd change my name to the Cleveland Maroons. And if I were Turner, I'd write Georgia Peaches on my uniforms and immediately put in a call to Noc-a-Homa.

Part VI

Witches

Soon fades the spell, soon comes the night;
Say will it not be then the same,
Whether we played the black or white,
Whether we lost or won the game?

Thomas Babington,
Lord Macauley

*The mind of man is capable of anything—because
everything is in it, all the past as well as the future.*

Joseph Conrad,
HEART OF DARKNESS

CHAPTER 33
A Clash of Witches

ON SEPTEMBER 13, 1975, the Red Sox were 4½ games ahead of the Orioles. They had blown a similar lead the year before. Would they blow it again?

To help ensure that they would, a Baltimore disk jockey named Johnny Walker of WFBR grabbed a plane and flew to Nairobi, Kenya, to the home of witch doctor John Agunga, to put a curse on the Red Sox. It set up a historic clash of psychic thunderbolts between the African shaman and Laurie Cabot of Salem, the most famous witch in America.

When I met Agunga two years later, I was in for a surprise. Far from wearing a headdress, loincloth, and a bone through his nose, Agunga met me in a black business suit with white shirt and tie. He said that, working with "the power of God through spirit," he could make opponents become weak or "dizzy" so they stumble, run slower, or fail to perform. One report, difficult to credit, said he could even make a soccer ball disappear in mid-field. When Kenya's national team went to the All-African championships, Agunga said, he sent them his power and they won every match but the final, which they lost 1-0. Sometimes, of course, the opponents hire their own witch doctors. In that case, he shrugged, "sometimes I beat them, sometimes they beat me."

Walker arrived bearing a Boston team photo, a ball autographed by all the Red Sox, a cap once worn by Carl Yastrzemski, and six cases of his sponsor's beer. Agunga went to work immediately. Chanting, he put the cap on top of a cleft stick in the ground, then rubbed it and the ball with earth and roots, plus something he poured from a can labeled "Shell Brake Fluid." He sprinkled them with dust, wrapped the ball in a monkey's paw, and tied it with a monkey hair. Walker waved the ball triumphantly and told the press: "The Red Sox will go temporarily blind; they won't see the ball. They'll have trouble running, they'll get dizzy and [won't] run as fast, and the ball will seem to swerve a little bit."

For the spell to work, Agunga said, the Orioles must do three things:

1. Do something different before the game, such as spinning in the batter's box.

2. Have no meat or sugar for seven hours before the game.

3. Have no sex for 12 hours.

O's general manager Frank Cashen rubbed his chin. "I don't know about the other things," he said, "but I don't see how a ballplayer can get along without meat."

"I also kinda took the whole thing seriously," Cashen confessed, adding that he prayed to Baltimore's recently canonized Mother Seaton, "just to touch all bases."

Following the first game played after Walker returned, the Associated Press reported: "It might be the witch doctor helped, as the Orioles defeated Detroit 8-0, while Boston split a doubleheader with Milwaukee. As a result, Baltimore moved within four games of the division leader."

In Boston someone called on Cabot to come to the rescue. The Red Sox deny it, but a male voice identified himself as someone from the Sox. "I think the whole thing is sheer commercialism," Cabot said, "but it could do some damage, psychologically if not metaphysically. I think it's hokey, but, between you, me, and the Red Sox, I think this guy can do it." She didn't want to get involved, but said, "I would definitely help out if this guy casts a spell on the Red Sox. I wouldn't do anything to harm the Orioles, because we don't believe in using witchcraft for manipulation, but I would put up a shield just to neutralize what he's doing.

"You shouldn't project for someone to lose, you should project for someone to win," Cabot continued. "You don't do harm. I don't believe in 'zapping,' but if he does use a hex, it will work. I can make it unwork just as easily."

It set the stage for the showdown against Baltimore in Fenway. Each team would send its ace—Luis Tiant (18-14) for Boston vs. Jim Palmer (22-11) for Baltimore. The two had met four times before, and Tiant had won three.

The Red Sox were 4½ games ahead again, with time running out. Said O's manager Earl Weaver grimly: "We're not dead yet. We've gotten out of the casket more times than Bela Lugosi." He herded his team onto a plane to Boston and the crucial two-game series.

The Red Sox waited confidently. A fan sent 25 Italian good luck

medallions to Boston's Rico Petrocelli, who distributed them to every team member. A full crowd of 34,000 was in the stands, and the Orioles took the field needling the Sox about the witch doctor. A little Bostonian with a magic wand and a flowing cape retaliated with a war dance on the roof of the Orioles dugout, along with an old man dressed in red Bermudas.

In the third Petrocelli made a stumbling stop of a hard line drive to save a double. Carlton Fisk and Petrocelli hit home runs, and the "surprisingly loose Red Sox," as one reporter described them, beat the Orioles 2-0. "I've never seen Tiant better," Weaver declared. The Orioles were 5½ games behind.

Score one for Cabot.

The next day, Boston fans paraded an effigy of the Orioles around the infield, chanting, "Go back to Nairobi." Baltimore's Mike Torrez and Boston's Rick Wise were both going for their 19th wins.

In the first inning the O's played "like rigor mortis had set in," wrote Tom Boswell of the *Washington Post*, as they "butchered" two ground balls to let in two quick Boston runs.

But that was it. Torrez pitched strong ball, Tommy Davis smacked a homer and two singles, the O's kicked two balls out of infielder's gloves and stole home for the only time that year to win 5-2.

Agunga and Cabot were even and the O's 4½ behind again.

A week later the Sox arrived in Baltimore for the final showdown. The Orioles' public address system played the recording of Agunga's chant as the Boston players walked onto the field, but it did no good. The Red Sox scored the winning run without even getting a hit, and the Orioles were counted out.

Boston went on to win the division and the pennant.

I am that which is, that which was, and that which will be, and no mortal may lift the veil from my face.

Attributed to Isis,
Egyptian mother goddess

CHAPTER 34
The Salem Witch

THE 1976 SEASON HAD BARELY BEGUN before the Red Sox quickly fell out of the race. By May 12 they had lost 10 straight games, the longest losing streak in modern Red Sox history, and were in last place. "We weren't playing up to our potential," manager Darrell Johnson shrugged. "We had the same personnel that we went to the World Series with, and they weren't playing the game the way they should. I don't know the reason."

Carl Yastrzemski thought he knew. "It's not poor hitting," he said, "but mental laziness, an overall failure to concentrate."

A Boston TV station, WBZ, called on Laurie Cabot to help again, and she agreed to fly to Cleveland, where the Red Sox would meet the Indians.

Over the years, Hollywood has given us such indelible images of "witches" that it's been hard to persuade people to take an objective look at them. But I wanted to learn more about this mystery woman, so I drove to Salem to a weatherbeaten clapboarded old house just off the waterfront and not far from Nathaniel Hawthorne's House of the Seven Gables. With three of my kids, we climbed the well-worn stairs to the third-floor landing and a door marked "Salem Research Center," decorated with a witch's pentacle, a five-pointed star enclosed in a circle.

Laurie met us in full black robe and shoulder-length black hair. Around her neck hung a pentacle and an ankh, the Egyptian symbol whose loops represent reincarnation or a circuit of psychic energy. Inside her cramped apartment, filled with bric-a-brac, a gentle black mastiff sat on his haunches. Two cats (black, naturally) curled up asleep; two parakeets chirped in their cage. Herbs hung from the ceiling—angelica, camomile, goldenseal. They would be dried, powdered, and kept in jars.

In a corner beside the door stood a collection of brooms, which, Laurie explained, were always being sent to her by people. In another stand rested a variety of canes. Some were "energized," making them magic wands; others were just plain canes. "If I want to send energy for

JOHN B. HOLWAY

healing, I can use that piece of wood," she said, nodding to her special wand leaning against the sideboard. It looked more like a four-foot knotted shillelagh than a fairy godmother's wand.

On one wall hung a shield with witches' runes written on it, warning those who entered to do no harm and proclaiming that a protective shield surrounded the house. The ancient bare boards of the living room were painted with a pentacle. That space was where Laurie did her projecting.

She smiled and directed us to seats around a large wooden table. The table was charged with pink light, she told us, symbolizing love and life "to make everyone feel more comfortable in the house."

"Just what is a witch?" I asked.

In a lilting, somewhat sultry voice, Cabot said it took a while for her to realize she was a witch, because the dictionary says a witch is "an ugly old hag who cavorts with demons and makes a pact with the devil in blood, which has nothing to do with witches. I'm not green. I don't cackle. I don't have a wart on my nose or wear a pointed hat. And I don't have scraggly teeth. Witches go to the dentist just like everyone else. I'm a human. I care a lot about people." She told us her black robe absorbs all the colors of the spectrum. "That means I'm picking up all the vibrations of the world around." Priests, nuns, and rabbis wear black for the same reason. During the Inquisition, or "the burning times," witches also wore black in order to do their rituals more safely in the woods at night.

The word "witch" comes from the Celtic word *wicca* and means "wise person," Cabot explained, adding that to its practitioners it's a religion, like Presbyterianism or Episcopalianism. That's why many witches capitalize "Witch." In Massachusetts Cabot is legally authorized to perform marriages.

Witchcraft is the old pre-Christian religion of Europe. King Arthur's Merlin was a witch (both males and females are called witches, incidentally). Witchcraft survives today, according to Cabot, in such Christian traditions and symbols as Christmas trees, yule logs, mistletoe, the Easter bunny, and Easter eggs.

Was she a good witch or an evil witch?

Cabot smiled in response. "Do I look like a good person? I don't

think if you were to interview a fireman you would ask him if he was a good fireman or an evil fireman. Witches are not Satanists... There are 6,000 witches in the United States, and none of them is Satanic or evil; they're all individuals. We don't worship anything, never mind Satan. We believe in God as being perfect, whatever God is—we don't know what God is, no one does."

On a TV talk show once, Cabot was baited by an evangelist until she snapped: "It's a good thing I'm *not* a bad witch, or you'd be in a lot of trouble now."

According to Cabot, some 600 witches were living in Salem at the time of our interview. Some were lawyers, psychologists, writers; some were also practicing Catholics, Protestants, Jews, and Zen Buddhists. Most of them dressed like everyone else. "They're just like you and me. They don't drink blood or eat babies. They don't do anything weird. They use nature and the stars and herbs and their own psychic abilities to guide their lives.

"We use potions and herbs to make ourselves better and have everything we really want in our lives without doing harm to anyone," she continued. "We're wonderful, beautiful people who care about ecology, the planet and other people. I'm like an Earth Mother. I'm everybody's mom."

Cabot blamed the King James Bible for much of the prejudice against witches. Exodus 22:18 says, "Thou shalt not suffer a witch to live." The original meaning, she said, is "Thou shalt not allow a murderer to live." In Europe, she added, "they had nine million people burned and hanged because of that."

Why not call herself something else and avoid unnecessary trouble? "Yes," Laurie agreed, "we could call ourselves anything else and make it easier for people to understand. But if they'd rather live with their ignorance and deal with me on a superficial basis, that's their problem."

She said she didn't go in for nudity. "That's a lot of baloney. If I can penetrate walls [that is, travel out of body], why should I take my clothes off? Sex and all those things have nothing to do with Hermetic law. If you want to run around nude, that's fine, I'm not opposed, but we have never found a reason to do it. It would scare everybody off."

Cabot said she was descended from the venerable New England family that traditionally spoke only to Lowells. She came from "a good religious background," she added. "I was born a Catholic and a Baptist simultaneously." Witchcraft was not only a religion to her, but a science, "and I also come from a very scientific family."

Forty-three at the time of our conversation, Laurie claimed that by the age of three she knew what people were thinking, could see the future, and "make things happen." She had been studying and teaching witchcraft since she was 17.

Cabot told me she traced her philosophical roots back to the Nazarenes and Essenes, mystics who came out of Egypt. The Essenes, who authored the Dead Sea Scrolls and instructed John the Baptist, taught Hermetic law. According to Cabot, Hermes, the classical Greek messenger of the gods (Mercury to the Romans), was a being from another solar system and made three trips to Earth to help colonize it. Hermes taught the Natural Law of "perfect creative energy." It's all explained in the Kybalion, a book about Hermes that was "the number-one required book" in Cabot's courses.

Cabot had written her own book, *The Power of the Witch,* and had hosted a radio show. She'd been interviewed by CBS, NBC, ABC, *The New York Times,* the *Los Angeles Times*, the *London Times*, and *Sports Illustrated*. She was also teaching two classes at the time, Witchcraft I and Witchcraft II, at Salem State College. "I have a waiting list for my classes a mile long."

Even hard-bitten cops have marveled at Cabot's powers. In 1975 detective Ken Downing arrived from Joliet, Illinois to enlist her help in solving a grisly murder. The decomposed body of a girl had been found, apparently murdered ritualistically by a Manson-like cult of Satanists. With five of her students, Cabot went into alpha (the relaxed state when brain waves slow down, like the first stages of sleep). "The description of the murder I gave them fit perfectly with their pattern of the case," she said. She also gave Downing descriptions of people, "and even the exact day and time of the killing."

I called Downing, who said Cabot's information was confirmed by the police's own sources. "That," he said, "was what was strikingly interesting."

Cabot had even been known to change the weather 40 degrees. She was asked to do it, for example, in the summer of '76, when a searing heat wave knocked out air conditioners in the Boston area. Nursing homes were particularly hard hit, and appeals reached Laurie to bring relief. So at dusk one Saturday night Cabot and three friends gathered at the historic Derby Wharf, along with photographer Ralph Turcott, whose wife Sheila was one of the witches. "It was over 100," Turcott told me, "and both the short-term and the three-day forecast called for more of the same. One of the witches had a long stick, possibly a cane, possibly a wand. I got an impression—I'm not sure—that one had one of those old short broom sticks of the kind used to sweep out the fireplace, and dipped it into the water. I don't remember any incantations. They treated the whole thing as though they were having fun."

Yes, it was a broom, Cabot said, explaining that wood is a great energy catalyst. A dowsing rod is a magic wand, a catalyst between the dowser and the water. "Science has proven it works," she said. "It's really your own thought patterns that make it work. If you hold it long enough in the alpha mental state, you can transfer your aura into the piece of wood. We treated the broom like a dowsing rod and made circles in the water. We drew in the energy and changed the weather just by directing our thoughts."

Turcott scratched his head. "The next day," he said, "it was about a 40-50-degree drop. All I know is that it was impressive."

Cabot told me she had done experiments with learning-disabled children, showing them how to go into alpha and then teaching them spelling in that relaxed state of mind. "Their teachers said they could never have made any progress like that without this method." She wanted to experiment further, and then offer the technique to the public schools.

She believed she could diagnose illness and heal it, all mentally. One four-year-old patient facing open-heart surgery underwent healing by Cabot for a year to clear his lungs so he could have an operation. At year's end the lungs were clear, "and the hole in his heart was much smaller than suspected. Those things happen to us every day," she said. "They're not unusual."

Yet when Cabot was invited to address Harvard University, the professors arrived with bags of popcorn as if they were going to a circus. They didn't even pay attention to what she had to say.

I noticed that Laurie's fingers were heavy with rings. One had a red carnelian stone for protection. During our visit, she indicated her right index finger, "my projection finger." It focused energy: "You can stop dog fights with it." Her daughters learned quickly that when she'd scold them and absent-mindedly wagged her finger, they'd better duck.

On her sideboard Cabot kept a black crystal, a scorpion preserved in a bottle of alcohol, and a bat preserved in a Lucite globe. There was also a jar of bee pollen, which she claimed to eat every day, as some athletes do, for protein. In ancient armies, she told us, soldiers carried pouches of pollen for "go" energy.

Rows of bottles contained her potions. Each had a different power, a different astrological trait. For success and attainment of goals, for instance, Cabot would prepare a Leo potion, made during the sign of Leo, on the day of Leo, and in the hour of Leo. Leo is the sun, so Laurie would seek a golden yellow color. She used goldenseal (which doesn't smell very good), plus some cloves and frankincense. Goldenseal is a cure-all, she said; if you rub it on an open cut, the wound will soon heal.

Her popular love potion, she said, should ideally be made under the influence of Venus. It consisted of dried rose petals, symbolizing Venus and love; mandrake root, which she said has been known for centuries for love and amiability; basil, a common kitchen spice also known for its love properties; narcissus oil, jasmine, frankincense, and dragon's blood. She'd also add an old bone, though she admitted it had no special significance. She'd mix them all in a pot and boil them to make the potion, which was essentially an organic perfume—not as refined as modern filtered perfumes, and with a pungent, medicinal smell. Cabot called it an "attraction potion," noting "love potion" would be too manipulative, "and we don't do that."

What about a love affair for Laurie herself? "That's not hard to do," she laughed. "I've had quite a few."

To believe in what you can see and touch is no belief at all, but to believe in the unseen is a triumph and a blessing.

Abraham Lincoln

≈ Breaking the Skein ≈

Before leaving for the game in Cleveland, Cabot sat down with Amy Konowitz of WBZ-TV. "I don't know anything about baseball, the teams, or the players," Laurie confessed. But she went into the alpha level, the clairvoyant level, "to scan the team in my mind's eye and try to see what was wrong. I saw a group of men, and one stood out very much on my 'screen.' I got the feeling that he was a very good player, had kept the team together last year, but this year had a very bad atitude and was very political, dispersing the energies of the team." To Konowitz she added, "If you can show me a picture, I can point him out."

Amy produced a team photo, and Cabot pointed to Carlton Fisk, the World Series hero of the year before and now leader of a holdout by several Series stars. "Oh, no," Konowitz protested, "he's the Red Sox's fair-haired boy."

"I'm sure it's him," Cabot replied. "This is what I see."

In Cleveland, Laurie flounced down a stadium aisle toward the field, a tall, attractive woman in her traditional black robe. She paused at the three-foot drop to the field, waiting for a hand. "What do you expect me to do, fly down?" she quipped. "I came here on United Airlines, not a broom." Hopping down, Cabot donned a Boston cap and posed for the photographers fluttering around while the Red Sox players looked on diffidently. Manager Darrell Johnson shook her hand and said a curt hello. Luis Tiant, however, "asked some very sensible questions, like why I wore black and why I called myself a witch."

Carl Yastrzemski was also nice, in contrast to most of the other players. "If you can do it," he smiled, "I'll leave you box seat tickets for every game." Another receptive player was outfielder Bernie Carbo, who brought his bat to Cabot. "Touch it," he said, "and make it magic." She complied.

"But guess who threw a tantrum on the field?" Laurie asked. "Carlton Fisk!" He complained loudly that Cabot had no business on the field, that she was making a laughingstock of the whole team. "He threw his bat on the ground, threw a tantrum," she says. WBZ announcer Len Berman exchanged looks with her. "Oh my God," he said, "you were right."

"Carlton is an angry young man," Cabot said, recounting the incident. "He's obnoxious. He's a brat. Stubborn. He's a Capricorn? Oh my God, no wonder he's a tyrant. Anyway, that was the first indication that what I said was true."

The Cleveland players were much nicer, Laurie reported. "I told them I was going to project aura energy, or group team energy, around the Red Sox. I made it very clear to them that I wasn't going to hurt them."

When the game began, Cabot and Konowitz retired to box seats behind the Red Sox bench. "I projected psychological balance," Cabot said, "sort of an orchid light for self esteem. Their energy on the physical level would be aumented by their aura energy of the white light, which is God, or universal mind energy. That's what makes us walk and talk."

Cecil Cooper, the first Sox batter, had been in a horrible slump. He tapped the ball between the legs of shortstop John Lowenstein for an error, one of three he would make that night. Cooper scored a moment later on a groundout by Fisk.

"It was fascinating," Konowitz said. "I'm a real cynic, a non-believer, but she was concentrating very, very hard on each player and each pitch." Whenever someone came up to ask for her autograph or to pose the usual question, "Where's your broom?" Cabot's concentration was broken and "something horrible happened on the field. The Red Sox would make an error or someone would strike out."

There must have been a lot of interruptions in the third inning. The Indians struck for four runs. The first scored on a double plus an error by Fisk. Another scored on a wild pitch.

"Carlton Fisk was in the middle of every scoring play that evening," Konowitz said. "He obviously was the person who seemed to disrupt the plays. We could see the Boston pitcher [Reggie Cleveland] getting very nervous every time a player would get on and Fisk was behind the plate. You could see an 'evil eye' sort of thing that would throw the pitcher off completely. He'd throw two balls and somebody would hit a double off the wall. Laurie at one point said she was going to make recommendations to the Red Sox management."

Cleveland's fourth run came in on a wild pitch. Fisk retrieved the ball

and threw to Cleveland, but slow-footed Rico Carty kicked the ball out of his glove. "That's the way things were going," Fisk shrugged after the game. "A guy who can't run trying to score on a ball 10 feet from home and getting away with it."

With Boston losing 4-3 in the fifth, Fisk was hit by a pitch, then Carbo smashed a long hit off the right field fence and bumped into Lowenstein as he raced around second. The umpire awarded Carbo third base and waved Fisk home with the tying run. Lowenstein had had a hand in three of Boston's four runs with what the *Boston Phoenix* called "three of the most bizarre errors on record."

"I didn't do anything to the Indians," Cabot insists. "If they made errors, it could be the law of polarization. It would weaken their energy a little bit. But I didn't set out to do that."

The Red Sox suffered a blow in the 10th. Their best hitter, Fred Lynn (.414 at game time), protested a called third strike and was thrown out of the game. Rick Miller (.212), suffering from a sore back, replaced him.

In the 11th the Indians put a man on second with one out, and Tom House relieved. House had never won a game since joining the Sox, but he struck out the next two men, and the clubs went into the 12th as a cold post-midnight wind off the lake sent temperatures plunging.

In the top of the 12th Boston's Doug Griffin—"a forgotten man," the *Boston Globe* would write—hit a bloop single over the infield and was sacrificed to second. Cooper hit a weak ground ball between short and third for a single, and Yastrzemski drove in Griffin with a long fly.

"We did it! We did it!" House cried, after setting down Cleveland in the bottom of the 12th, jumping up and down on the mound as the Red Sox poured out of the dugout and swarmed over him. "It was like V-E Day in Times Square," the *Globe* said. "The whole thing was bizarre," added the paper's Larry Whiteside.

Konowitz scratched her head. "Admittedly, it was a publicity stunt," she said. "But it worked."

In the locker room the jubilant players squirted beer at each other and filled the air with raucous noise and laughter. "We were a different team tonight," Yaz shouted. "We went after them. We did some things that we hadn't been doing during the losing streak. We were the aggressors. A

couple of runs were the direct results of us running. We made things happen. And the best thing is that everybody contributed. This thing has been haunting us all."

Johnson had almost forgotten what to say after a victory. "I know we didn't exactly crash that ball around," he told reporters. "We got a bloop and a 'chalk hit' [on the foul line] and a 'tweener' [between the infielders] to win it, even a balk. But it's about time those things broke our way."

In the Indians' locker room, manager Frank Robinson shook his head in wonder. "I was like everybody else," he said. "I looked at their talent on paper, and I really couldn't understand why they had lost 10 in a row."

The final out of the game, incidentally, was made by Cleveland catcher Ron Pruitt, number 13. Laurie was sympathetic. "Is this really a bad luck number?" she asked rhetorically. "No. It's a geometrically sound number. There are 13 acres under the pyramid of Cheops, for instance. I'd like him to understand that it's a very powerful number, that his great fear of losing was what made him lose; it wasn't the number on his back."

It was 2 a.m. when Cabot arrived at the hotel where the Boston players were celebrating. Several were pretty drunk, and a few were hostile. "You'd better not try to take credit for this," pitcher Bill Lee snapped, half joking but with a biting, hostile undertone.

Actually, Cabot didn't want credit. "There's no way I can maneuver the ball," she said. "The Red Sox did that themselves. I was just catalyzing their ability. If the Red Sox weren't good players on the physical level, the power wouldn't have worked."

In the morning paper, Whiteside ended his account: "Oh, yes, the witch lady. She sat behind the Red Sox dugout in her Count Dracula outfit and screamed and yelled. She seemed happy. And who is to say it wasn't her presence that did it?"

The Red Sox won the next night without her. ("Sometimes the energy stays around for a while," she said.) And they won without their leading hitter, Fred Lynn, who hurt his shoulder.

"In many ways this was a Laurie Cabot game," Peter Gammons

wrote in the *Globe*. "Lynn's replacement, Rick Miller, merely got three hits, two singles and a triple on balls that bounced over the center fielder's glove, and Tiant pitched a good game until he tired." The Red Sox began talking about a winning streak.

The magic was still working when the Sox returned to Boston and a crowd of 25,000 for a game against last-place Milwaukee. Lee was supposed to pitch but reported with a 101-degree temperature and was replaced by Dick Pole, a journeyman who had never won more than six games in a year in his career. Miller was still in center field. In his first at bat, he walked, advanced on a passed ball, and scored on Yaz's fly. He later scored the winning run as well. Carbo got two more hits.

The next day Boston made it four in a row. Carbo had two hits, giving him six for 14—a .429 average—since Cabot had touched his bat.

A week later the Red Sox erupted in a free-for-all fight with the Yankees, in which Lee hurt his arm and was out for most of the season. Laurie thought the injury had a psychological basis. "He's a nice person, but he just seems to be so messed up. He wasn't doing well, and it's easier to have his arm hurt and use it as an excuse for failure." A cure was open if Lee wanted to take it, Cabot said. "If we can give him a psychological balance so he'll realize he can succeed and that he's a good pitcher and a good person—and heal his arm too—dynamite!"

(Ex-San Francisco '49ers quarterback John Brodie, a student of Scientology, has a similar theory. In his book *Open Field*, he writes that he injured his arm in an auto accident for the same subconscious reasons. In general, he adds, good football teams don't get injuries; bad teams do. It's bad playing that causes injuries, not the other way around. When he realized that, Brodie said, his injury cleared right up.)

Meanwhile, the Red Sox kept stumbling along and finished in third place, 15½ games behind the Yankees. Johnson was fired. Much of the blame fell on Fisk, who hit 50 points below his 1975 figure, plus Lynn and Rick Burleson, who were holding out for more money.

Summed up Yastrzemski: "When I first came here and it seemed like the Red Sox were finishing last every year, I thought talent was the whole key to a strong team. But since then I've changed my opinion. Sure, it takes talent. But it also takes pride, attitude, character,

whatever you want to call it. Whatever it is, we haven't had it this year. That's what we need to regain."

♎ The Aftermath ♎

If the Red Sox were red-faced about accepting Laurie Cabot's help, others weren't. A Boston Little League team, the Back Bay Bears, perennial losers, sent an appeal plus locks of their hair. A sandlot team from Ipswich, Massachusetts asked for help, and then went from last-place to the playoffs. Even a Red Sox farm club, the Bristol Red Sox, came calling. Cabot told the official curtly, "Look, I'll work with you, but what I want is to teach each player to do it himself, have a formal class and sit down and learn to project. They could learn it in four days." She never heard from him again. "He just wanted an instant zap," she said.

Then Laurie forgot about baseball. She resumed her classes, her radio shows, her work with children, and her healing. And she took up work with football's New England Patriots, where her results (as noted at the end of chapter 3) were even more stunning than with the Red Sox.

But there's still more to the story. Beginning with the Red Sox series, the Indians went into a slump of their own. On May 21, 1976, an error had let in the tying and winning runs, their ninth loss in 12 games. Next day they lost again on a bloop single. The Indians loaded the bases in the ninth, but a strikeout ended the game. "I don't know what's wrong," Frank Robinson shrugged. "It's always one play that opens the door and hurts us."

A Cleveland disk jockey, Jack Reynolds of station WWE, decided to act. A close friend, an elderly Sicilian woman, said the Indians had the evil eye, the *malocchio*, left by Laurie Cabot.

Laurie denied it. "The Indians were super guys," she insisted. "I liked them better than the Red Sox as people."

At 2 a.m. the night of May 22, Reynolds recalled, "a black limousine pulls up to Cleveland Stadium. All the gates are locked." The old lady, well known among her friends for the power to heal with prayer and holy water, got out of the car and began blessing each gate

with holy water and olive oil.

That afternoon the Indians beat Milwaukee 2-1 in the first game of a doubleheader as John Lowenstein scored the winning run. He batted in four runs in the second game, which Cleveland won 8-5. Indians catcher Alan Ashby saved three wild pitches with great stops, and two good catches in the field robbed Milwaukee's great Hank Aaron of extra base hits.

"It's good to see those plays made," Robinson beamed. "We always played good defensive baseball, but it seemed we'd always let one play hurt us. Today we didn't."

Still glowing, the Indians flew to Baltimore and won two more in a row. They won the first 4-1. Dennis Eckersley gave up only one hit, then put two men on base in the ninth, but reliever Stan Thomas struck out three straight, including Reggie Jackson. They won the second game over Jim Palmer (22-13), the best pitcher in the league.

Beginning with the Sunday doubleheader, the Indians won 16 out of 18 games. "It was their hottest streak of the season," said Dan Coughlin, sportswriter for the *Cleveland Plain Dealer,* who had been told the story of the Sicilian woman by Reynolds. Coughlin, however, decided not to print it. "I didn't think anyone would believe it," he shrugged.

All those wild witches, those most noble ladies....

William Butler Yeats

CHAPTER 35
Ruth Revzen

ON THE SUNNY SUMMER AFTERNOON of July 9, 1976, a vivacious brunette in a diaphanous white gown and a garland of flowers atop her curls traipsed onto the grass at Wrigley Field to dab some magic potion onto four embarrassed Cubs players.

Her name was Ruth Revzen, psychic and palm reader. She looked more like Snow White than the wicked witch, and she called herself simply "a nice Jewish girl who makes potions." "She can't be a witch," said Howard Cosell, "she's too beautiful."

Disk jockey Bob Sirott of WLS had asked Ruth to help the fourth-place Cubs by putting a hex on San Diego pitcher Randy Jones, the hottest pitcher in baseball. Jones boasted a 15-3 record with his sixth-place team and seemed on his way to a rare 30-victory season.

While Jones watched, Ruth dabbed a secret Old Testament concoction of magnolia, cinnamon, and cypress onto the players' foreheads and arms. "It was the most God-awful smelling stuff," winced outfielder Rick Monday, who received the potion along with Bill Madlock (who'd repeat as batting champion with a .339 average), pitcher Bill Bonham, and catcher Steve Swisher.

As she daubed, Ruth chanted voodoo incantations learned in New Orleans. She doesn't remember exactly what she chanted. "I just put it together like some people write songs. The words I usually say are voodoo, like Damballah, an African god."

Cubs manager Jim Marshall didn't like the idea. "We don't need it," he sneered. Indeed, the Cubs, with a four-game winning streak going, had just shut out San Diego three games in a row. San Diego's Cuban shortstop, Tito Fuentes, scoffed. He knew more about witchcraft than Revzen, he said, and would exorcise her.

Ruth was not the only jinx Jones faced. He had just been featured on the cover of *Sports Illustrated*, and many athletes so "honored" had injuries soon after or other dire catastrophes befall them.

Unfazed, Randy strode to the mound and beat the Cubs 4-1 as Bonham got bombed out of the box.

"It wasn't Randy who beat us," muttered Madlock, "it was the &*%$#@ witch." Bill was held to one hit in four at bats; Swisher went 0-for-4, although Monday got two singles.

"I don't believe in jinxes," Jones said, savoring his 16th victory. "The witch and *Sports Illustrated* were lucky for me."

Three weeks later Jones hurt his arm in an auto accident. He won only six more games all year, lost 11, and never did regain his form. In 1977 he was 6-12. "It was my mistake," Ruth apologized. "I made it a little too strong. And I read the Bible wrong. I put in cypress instead of cedar." (Cedar is associated with healing, as in Cedars of Lebanon, but cypress is the traditional material for coffins.)

That winter Marshall was fired, while Madlock and Monday signed lucrative contracts with new teams. "That's how my magic works," Revzen says. "It's not just games, it's life. What I did may not have had anything to do with it, but who knows?"

That autumn New Orleans station WWL asked Revzen to help the hapless Saints football team snap a nine-game losing streak. They had just lost to Minnesota 40-9 and Dallas 24-6. Ruth was in Cleveland at the time and bored ("Have you ever been to Cleveland?"), so she agreed. She wrote out the thought that the Saints would win and had all the radio listeners light candles for the game in Kansas City. Losing 17-10 after three quarters, the Saints rallied for a 27-17 win. Alas, the following Sunday the Ruth-less Saints lost 31-26 and ended the season with a 4-10 mark.

♉ Psyching Sutton ♉

That winter Revzen moved to Beverly Hills, California, where her next assignment came from Jim Hawkins of KABC. From May 28 to June 7, 1977, the defending champion Dodgers had won only two games and lost seven. She agreed to give it a try.

Don Sutton (14-8 that year) was scheduled to pitch against the Cubs. He had lost his last three games, but Ruth mixed a little potion, did "a sacrificial burning" and some spells, both off the air and on. "I explained how I was going to send out the concentrated energy and get the people of Los Angeles going. I willed it and visualized it happening. I call it

'thought form': 'Hey, guys, if you want to win the big money, win the pennant!' We call that 'American magic.' And it worked."

Sutton threw a three-hitter to win 4-2. "It was easy," Revzen said. Alas, the Dodgers, back on their own, lost their last two games to the Cardinals.

♋ Pulling Up the Red Sox ♋

On Thursday, September 2, Ruth got a call from the Red Sox, who seemed to be unraveling. They were trying to stay in a three-way race with Baltimore and New York but had fallen 4½ games behind.

They would be doing better, two fans from Salem wrote in the *Boston Globe*, if it weren't for the moon. Mark Bellerme and Murray Haber discovered that the Sox had played five times under a new moon and had been humiliated four times:

On May 25, Minnesota (fourth in the Western division) blasted 37 hits to win a doubleheader.

On June 24, the Sox tied it in the ninth and won in the tenth. But the next day they opened a nine-game losing streak.

On July 23, fourth-place Cleveland came from behind to win 9-8; the Sox went on to lose four out of five.

On August 22, Minnesota beat them again in the last of the ninth.

On September 2, against Texas (second in the West), Boston pitcher Ferguson Jenkins made a two-run error, and Carlton Fisk and Fred Lynn each missed home runs by a foot. Losing 6-4, Lynn came up in the ninth with two men on and two out and meekly fouled out, shoving the Sox into third, 4½ games behind the Yankees.

That night someone at Boston station WMEX grabbed a phone and put in an emergency call to Revzen, who agreed to do what she could.

The next day, September 3, Boston's Jim Rice hit one of his 34 homers to tie the game, and in the ninth it was Texas' turn to err, letting in the winning run.

On September 4, the Sox faced Gaylord Perry, whom they hadn't beaten in four years. Boston's Rick Burleson, who had hit two homers all year, hit his third on the first pitch of the game, and the Sox won easily, 8-4.

On September 5, the Sox flew to Toronto to face the last-place Blue Jays, but their plane was diverted to Niagara Falls, where they landed about 3 a.m. When their taxi broke down about 4:30, Lynn, Jenkins, outfielder Carl Yastrzemski, and pitcher Bill Campbell wearily thumbed a ride, arriving at dawn to doze for a few hours before struggling out for a twi-night doubleheader. Did the night's misadventure affect their play? Hardly. They won both games, 8-0 and 6-0.

Meanwhile, the Yankees, who had beaten Cleveland 13 straight times, lost a double header to them, and the Sox were only 2½ games behind.

On September 6, Labor Day, the Sox won 11-2, their fifth win in a row.

The Sox were happy. But Ruth was not. "Don't I get paid?" she wondered. "It's not a matter of being greedy, but unless you give something of your own, the magic cannot work." The Sox apparently developed a sudden acute hearing problem. There was no reply. "So I took the spell off," she said.

On September 7, Toronto, with an 11-game losing streak, was losing 2-1 against Jenkins, when Blue Jays rookie Gary Woods, just up from the minors, knocked in the go-ahead runs. In the eighth Lynn came up with a man on and a chance to tie it but hit into a double play. In the ninth Boston slugger George Scott (33 homers) also smacked into a DP to end the game. The Sox fell back to 3½ behind again. They would finish third for the year.

≋ Ron Cey's Magic Potion ≋

After Revzen's psychic cocktail, the Dodgers went on to win the National League West and prepared to play the Eastern champs, the Phillies, for the pennant.

But L.A.'s cleanup hitter, Ron Cey (23 homers), was in a slump. Muscular, mustachioed, bowlegged—affectionately known as "the Penguin" for the way he ran—Ron had gone to bat 41 straight times and 41 straight times had dragged his bat back to the dugout without a hit. His average had plunged from .260 to .241. "I was hitting the ball hard,"

Cey told me, "but they were all going at somebody. After awhile it gets to you, you begin to wonder who's going to catch the next line drive."

While Ron desperately took extra hitting practice, his wife Franny went to Revzen. Ron and Franny had met her a year earlier at a Halloween party (Ruth had come as the Bride of Frankenstein, riding in a hearse). "Please help," Franny begged. "We're worried."

Ruth agreed. Since the Cubs fiasco, she had been working on getting the bugs out of the potion. She sent Cey a cologne bottle of what she called "16 patented, FDA approved ingredients"—mandrake root, wild hyssop, juniper berries, cedar, etc.—all mixed under a full moon at a crossroad in the woods.

"I finally got it right. It took me a long time," she said. "I've always mixed perfumes. I've studied aroma therapy since I was old enough to read, going all the way back to the old Egyptian science of perfuming. How a person smells has a lot to do with how he feels about himself and how others feel about him.

"What's the first thing you do when you're born?" Revzen continued. "Breathe. Smell is a very vital sense. How many times have you passed a bakery, and that smell makes you hungry, even when you weren't hungry before? If you smell ammonia, you're going to wake up. Well, my potions make you wake up so you see clearer and concentrate better. You put it on certain glands, and it starts them secreting and stimulating you."

She told Ron to apply it three times a day to three spots on his throat.

In Game 1, in his first at bat against the Phils' best pitcher, Steve Carlton, Cey singled sharply, breaking his slump. On his third at bat he powered one over the left field wall for a grand slam to tie the game, though the Phils rallied to win.

By sheer coincidence, I telephoned Ruth the next day to ask about her Red Sox activities. She off-handedly noted, "Ron was using my potion last night." Of course I pricked up my ears.

"I make love potions," Revzen explained. "The herbs involved in it work. They get inside your skin, and they work. On one level, the smell will influence you and set the glands going. On the psychic level you believe in me, and it works. Ron knows it's going to work, and he wants

it to. It's psychological. But I don't believe that's as important as people say. You don't necessarily have to believe in it for it to work."

I wasn't the only one who had called Ruth. Jim Hawkins of KABC was also on the phone. To win the series, the Dodgers had to win three of the last four games, including the last three in Philadelphia, where the Phillies almost never lost. So before the second game Ruth did three hours of yoga. Cey lined out a single, stole a base, and made a great stop at third, as the Dodgers won 7-1.

The third game, in Philadelphia, was one of the most bizarre in play-off history. Cey's fourth-inning double tied the score 3-3, but in the eighth his wild throw helped the Phils take the lead, 5-3.

In the Dodgers' ninth, with two out and a man on, 38-year-old pinch hitter Vic Davalillo bunted for a hit. Another old-timer, 39-year-old Manny Mota, pinch-hit a fly that popped out of left fielder Greg Luzinski's glove as he hit the wall. One run was in, and Mota was on second as second baseman Ted Sizemore dropped the throw.

Next, Davey Lopes hit an easy bouncer to Mike Schmidt, one of the best third basemen in the game. The ball took an "inexplicable" bounce over Schmidt's glove, wrote Thomas Boswell of the *Washington Post*. Shortstop Larry Bowa barehanded the ball and whipped it to first as the big crowd screamed.

Umpire Bruce Froemming spread his palms—safe. Replays showed that Lopes was out by half a step, but apparently Froemming, with his eyes on the bag, couldn't hear the ball hit the glove because of the noise. A moment later, Bill Russell got the hit that won the game.

The next afternoon I jumped in my car and dashed to Philadelphia. In an intermittent downpour, Cey collected a single in two at bats against Carlton as the Dodgers won 4-1. The pennant was theirs.

In the clubhouse, while the Dodgers whooped it up and hoarsed around, dowsing each other with champagne, I sidled up to Cey, and asked about Revzen. "You know Ruth?" he brightened. I nodded. Did the potion work?

Ron studied his words carefully. "Well," he said at length, "I can't say that it helped. But on the other hand, I can't say that it didn't."

I hastily wrote a story and filed it to *The Sporting News*.

There be none of Beauty's daughters
With a magic like thee.

Lord Byron

≈ Cabalistic Voodoo ≈

Who was Ruth Revzen, and did her magic potions really work? I bought a plane ticket to Los Angeles to see Game 3 of the World Series and to find out more about her. It was after midnight when I drove up to her small second-floor apartment on a quiet side street off Wilshire Boulevard in Beverly Hills—"a real power center for me," Revzen called it—and stepped into a pleasant room filled with small tables, flowers, and bric-a-brac.

Ruth turned out to be a dark-eyed, fast-talking, attractive woman of 29. "I'm a fifth-generation psychic," she said. Her great-great-grandmother, from Bessarabia in the Ukraine, made magic mirrors and crystal balls. Her great-great-grandfather was a Cabalistic rabbi. The Cabala, a secrect teaching of Judaism that flourished in the Middle Ages, sought hidden, mystical meanings in every word, even every letter, of the Old Testament. (According to Los Angeles witch Louise Huebner, who was plying her craft for the Angels in 1977, each Hebrew letter has a numerical value from one to nine. Letters of the same value can be interchanged to form new words. Huebner says that in World War II, Syrian Jews, fearing a Nazi invasion, transposed the Hebrew word for "Syria" into "Russia," thus diverting the danger.)

"Cabalistic magic is the strongest in the world," Revzen said. "The Cabala starts with the fact that there is harmony, reason, in the universe. This order is understandable and controllable. You can tune into it and make things happen if you can catch the universal flow."

Ruth's mother was born with a caul, or membrane of skin, over her face, which is considered the mark of a psychic. Ruth believed that she, too, was born to her vocation. "I've got birthmarks on my female organs," she said, adding that she would menstruate every seven weeks. "My insides are all different."

Revzen learned numerology and Tarot cards at the age of four. "I also practiced yoga when I was a little kid; I practiced holding my heartbeat in the lotus position." She demonstrated for me by standing on her head with her feet crossed. Psychic thoughts often come to her at such times, she insisted.

At the University of Illinois, Revzen made the dean's list by letting a ouija board guide her in writing term papers. "I did a tremendous amount of research into witchcraft, tracing it back to its pre-Egyptian origins." She said she believed in a "God Force, the Tree of Life," which can be expressed in numerical, alphabetical, or musical terms—Pythagoras, for example, wrote of "the music of the spheres," and Aristotle wrote the first book on palmistry.

After graduating with honors, Ruth set out for New Orleans to study law at Tulane and also did card readings in the Bottom of the Cup tearoom. She was adopted by a voodoo cult—"Crazy people, *crazy* people!"—and learned their African secrets, watching their dances and chicken sacrifices. She told me she met the spirit of Marie Laveau, the legendary "voodoo queen" of the 1840s. "I was living in direct view of her grave. I had a formula for a potion come to me once through her." The combination of Cabalistic magic and voodoo, she believed, was "the most powerful [magic] in the world."

Revzen also considered herself a follower of the Nazarene. "I got my healing powers by opening up to Jesus," she said, adding emphatically, "Satanism has nothing to do with it. Satanism is sick; it's the reverse of Christianity."

When I visited, Ruth's living room was filled with tables and plants. "All my tables are altars. You have to look carefully and know magic to know what's going on in my house. One table has a Hermes scarf. There's an Egyptian Isis. And I use African gods—Bataya, Yemeya, Shango—the old gods, older than the Egyptians. These are the basics, when it was original—Anima, Yahweh, and the old Hebrews. Yahweh is the Hebrew 'I-am-what-I-am.' When I just say it, I get a chill." She told me that when she put a Hebrew Bible on the altar, the candle to Shango broke.

Organized religion opposes what she does, Ruth conceded. "The Old Testament priests were upset about a cult in Babylon called Baal worship. It was based on astrology, ghosts, witches, or whatever you want to call it. You would buy charms from them, and you wouldn't have to go to the temple and keep the Sabbath and pray. The Hebrew religion was strict; Baal worship was a lot more fun—get naked, have festivals,

get drunk, have orgies. You want a good crop? You don't have to plant the seed and harvest. All you do is make love, show the crop what to do.

"That's a pretty hard religion to put down," she continued. "The authorities couldn't allow a religion like that. So there are many things in the Bible putting down soothsayers, fortunetellers, and witches. It's simple economics: If they want the people to come to them, they have to put down the other religion."

Revzen said she had also studied Tibetan Tantric magic, the art of drawing energy from others, especially from young people, "sort of vampirism on a spiritual level." Kids at baseball games send out a tremendous amount of energy: "Tantric energy is what team spirit is all about. The crowd is cheering, and the players get all that energy from them. Of course you have to have ability to start with." (Older people may also be tapped into. I once heard novelist Pearl Buck describe an incident that happened to her in India. She said people walked for miles to see the famous writer and just sat at her feet, silently absorbing her energy. At the end of the day, she said, she felt drained of her strength.)

She didn't believe in Native American gods, Revzen said, but she once did a Navajo sun dance. On a Halloween weekend in Magnolia, Texas, the town was holding a festival to raise money when rain clouds appeared. "So we danced. Wild. Rib movements and like that. Wild drum beats. A few people danced naked. Some of the girls started jumping into the fire. The people were afraid it would turn into an orgy, but of course it didn't. But it did create vibrations. All of a sudden it got still." The rain stopped, and the festival went on.

After three years in New Orleans, Ruth returned to Chicago and read palms at R.J. Grunt's restaurant. She used her grandmother's system, 32 cards from a regular bridge deck. Whenever she faced a problem, she said, she'd frequently go to the cards on a table in her living room and cut the deck. "I used to not like to listen, because I didn't like what the cards said. But they've always been right."

I asked her to do a reading for me. She held my hands and began talking fast, apparently using psychic impressions as much as, or more than, actually reading the lines in my palms. Then she shuffled the cards and began flipping them at a fast pace, speaking rapidly as the thoughts

tumbled out faster than the cards were turned. She described my children and their problems, though she had never seen them or heard me mention them. "Your daughter Diane...."

"Why did you say Diane? How did you know her name was Diane?"

"How did I know? I just said Diane. I don't know why I said Diane. I just did. It just comes. If I focus, I can do it, but it's beyond any analytical process."

As for the future, Ruth saw me going to a French-speaking country—I did go to Geneva, but it was several years later. She thought I would go into the building or construction business; four years later I began investing in real estate, which may satisfy that prediction. She also predicted I would become heavily involved with someone named Linda. It's been more than 20 years now, I'm happily married, and so far no Linda has come into my life. (Psychics say timing is difficult in foretelling the future; they may see something coming but can't say just when.)

A believer in health foods, Revzen wrote *A Fairy Tale Cook Book* for children. It's filled with recipes like "Cinderella's Pumpkin Pie" and "Witches' Garden Greens." She recommends sugar. "Sugar is a powerful force. It sends things up the nervous system, sort of a quick rush." She ate a lot of chocolate chip cookies, she said.

Sugar or no, I found Ruth Revzen to be bursting with energy. "I'd love to make love all night and dance all day," she said. "I have so much energy, it's got to go some place!" However, she added, "If I'm not in love but involved sexually, it will hurt my powers."

On the subject of other psychics, Revzen was skeptical. Many, she felt, bilked the unsuspecting public with phony readings. "There's one reader in Chicago I'd like to have banned. She lives in the ghetto, and people give their welfare checks to her. She charges 10 dollars, and she makes money, but I've never seen her be right on a reading yet. There are people all over who make a living telling little old ladies about their dead husbands. I'm not one of those Gypsy con artists. It's like any other business: When you try to screw people, you'll get it right back. If your own life is messed up, you're not in shape to read anyone else's."

Occasionally, Ruth said, she gave seances. "But only for a very

practical purpose. A friend of mine had $100,000 buried in his house. He wanted to find it, and we did. If there's a reason to talk to a spirit, I'll do it, but never for entertainment. And you have to have a spirit of fun about it. The attitude makes the power. If something is fun, there's more energy in it. Of course I get upset if it doesn't work. You wonder what went wrong. It might just be that there's something wrong with me today. But we can figure out why and flow with the universe the next move."

Ruth picked up some money betting on the third Muhammad Ali-Ken Norton fight. But she wouldn't predict the outcome of sports events, ever since "a nasty man in Chicago" used her predictions to make a killing. She said he ended up paying with a serious eye infection.

"I may not have a lot of money," she told me, "but I have absolutely no debts. I have everything I want. I'm free. I'm living on my savings now. I'm free to do whatever I want."

I wanted more details on her potions, or as Revzen calls them, "body spirits." "I called up Marie Laveau, on my ouija board, with Isis, Circe, Aurora, and Diana, and produced my first body fluid, the incarnation of all these women."

Excitedly, she turned her kitchen into a lab. She chose Chicago, she explained cryptically, because "it's a Capricorn city." "I spent my life savings on 40 acres of juniper berries in Arizona and 1,000 old bottles from the Nippola perfume company, which had originated during Prohibition as a front for a bootleg liquor operation."

Ruth was guarded about her exact ingredients. She experimented with hundreds, all mentioned in the Old Testament. She said she favored a fixative that's found only in a mussel that lives 200 feet down in the Dead Sea. "Some of this stuff is ridiculously expensive."

Sometimes she'd mix them under the full moon, sometimes under the new moon. "Every hour and every day is supposedly sacred to a different energy force."(Even today in the American South, people plant root crops on the waning of the moon, leafy crops on the waxing. And there is some evidence that the moon does affect the chemical makeup of plants.)

"This stuff is strong—very strong," Ruth warned me. "Perfume is

technically three percent perfume, 97 percent alcohol. Well, this stuff is 97 percent perfume." Mixing the ingredients made her sick at times. In order to win FDA approval, she was required by the government to alter her formula. "It was giving everybody a rash," she admitted. Sanitary regulations required that the potions be mixed by a laboratory in New York. The lab returned them to Ruth, and she bottled them while chanting incantations.

One of Ruth's potions, "Majick" ("a nice little psychic vitamin"), was concocted of jasmine and blended when the moon was in Cancer. "Goodness," she said, was made from the essence of roses, cherries, hyacinth, and geraniums. "Success" had the scent of sandalwood for protection, sage for wisdom, and magnolia for fighting spirit—only ambitious people should wear it, Ruth warned.

Of course, her most popular potion was "Love." When Revzen's potions were test-marketed in Cleveland, "Love," the most expensive at $22 a quarter-ounce, was the fastest seller. Revzen told me that "Love" could be worn by men or by women. "Its ingredients come from King David's Song of Songs, plus a voodoo sex potion. But it is not a sex potion—that would be too powerful." (Ruth *did* have a sex potion, but said it was too potent to be put on the market. She saved it, she said, for herself and a few friends.)

Even Ruth found "Love" efficacious. "The first time I put it on, I literally bumped into Engelbert Humperdinck on the street in Chicago. He felt the psychic energy happening, dragged me off to a concert, and I spent the better part of an evening with him. I mean, here's a man who is a sex symbol for millions of American women, and my love potion attracted him!"

The encounter, she said, "gave me energy to call up the Henri Bendel specialty store in New York. They told me to come right in. I said I couldn't, that I was a witch and it was my busy season, but I'd be in later." She took 300 bottles and sold out in three weeks.

Revzen opened her own shop in Beverly Hills, selling her newest potions, "Witch's Essence" for women and "Warlock" for men. Perhaps, she theorized, football players need a different potion than baseball players. "Football is more instinctive; baseball is more intuitive. A foot-

ball player might need pepper and mace. But you have to give a baseball player things that wake up the mind, like juniper berries and phenyl."

This is the potion that Ron Cey got.

)(**The 1977 World Series**)(

Cey was not doing well at all.

In the first two Series games in New York, he faced the yawning reaches of left field in Yankee Stadium, dubbed "Death Valley," where long drives die as outs. Cey was 0-for-3 as the Yankees won the opener in the 12th, 4-3.

The next night Ron did get a homer in four at bats as the Dodgers won 6-1. He was hitting the ball hard, but his drives were being caught.

In Game 3 in Los Angeles he was 0-for-3, and a single off his glove by New York's Bucky Dent set up the winning run as the Dodgers lost.

In Game 4 against Ron Guidry, Cey was 0-for-4, though he was robbed of a game-tying homer.

The Dodgers won the fifth game 10-4, though Cey went hitless again. His drought had now reached 14 straight at bats.

Following Game 5, Ruth Revzen and I went to the theater to see Neil Simon's "Second Avenue." Ruth took the play, which was about New York, as an omen that the Yankees would win. As I prepared to fly home, she asked if I planned to attend both games in New York. I said I had business and would have to skip Game 6, but planned to attend the seventh game. "I think you should go to both," she advised.

I ignored her advice—and missed one of the great performances in World Series history, as Reggie Jackson blasted three home runs in three swings to overwhelm the Dodgers and win the Series then and there. There was no Game 7.

Cey ended the Series with a .190 average. The potion must have been a hoax after all, I concluded.

Only later did I learn the truth. Afraid of publicity and the ribbing he might take if the story got out, Cey had stopped using the potion after talking to me in Philadelphia. I was sorry to see his slump return and regretted that I might have had something to do with it. But the result

was a fortunate, if unplanned, scientific control for the experiment. We now had the following data for Ron Cey:

	AB	H	AVG
End of regular season	41	0	.000
Playoff, with potion	13	4	.308
Series, without potion	21	4	.190

That was the end of Ruth's sports activities until the following August, when she got a surprise call from Franny Cey again. The Dodgers were locked in a close race with the San Francisco Giants, Ron's batting average had dropped to .261, and the team was half a game behind as it began a 13-game homestand. Would Ruth help out one more time? She shipped the Ceys another bottle.

In the first game, August 24, Ron got a double and two singles as the Dodgers beat the soon-to-be Eastern champion Phils, 5-4. On the 25th he got three more hits as Los Angeles triumphed, 6-5. Cey kept hitting, and the Dodgers kept winning. They won nine and lost four, and Ron batted .404 with three home runs for the homestand. The Dodgers left town three games ahead of the Giants and were never behind again.

It's what you learn after you know it all that counts.

Earl Weaver

C H A P T E R   3 6
Weaver's Witch Doctor

IN SEPTEMBER 1977, I FOUND MYSELF IN NAIROBI for a United Nations conference, and I looked up John Agunga. I found him through the sports department of the *Nairobi Nation*, where a nice young man smiled deprecatingly, saying that educated Kenyans don't believe in such things. ("They still come," Agunga said, adding that they'd wait until after dark when no one would see them.)

I took a taxi to a housing development of small stone duplexes near the light towers of the Nairobi stadium. During the British regime, many of Kenya's future leaders were spawned there. Children were playing jacks, napping on mattresses on the ground, or tending braziers on which lunch cooked amid curling smoke. Their eyes followed me as I checked the house numbers.

Agunga ushered me into his two-room apartment with a bare concrete floor, plus a kitchen area. In the sitting room were a bed curtained off from the rest of the room, a bare table, chairs, shelves, and a framed magazine illustration of the magician. Here he would see up to 20 clients a day, curing everything from barrenness to lunacy to snake bites. Agunga apparently lived alone, though he said he had eight wives living in eight different villages.

Could Agunga pick the winners of 15 NFL games on the coming weekend? He gladly agreed. The results, alas, were not good: He got four right and 11 wrong. But he remained confident. Would he like to try again with the Baltimore Orioles? "Of course," he replied.

First Agunga wanted to see how they would finish if he did nothing. At the time, September 8—unknown to either of us, since there were then no current U.S. papers in Nairobi—the Orioles were in third place, 4½ games behind the Yankees.

To get psychic impressions, Agunga would often lie down on the bed and go to sleep for 15 minutes, and the answer would be written on his mind as on a blackboard. This time, however, he went into trance, using an African samsa, or marimba, a small cigar-box size instrument that he held it in his lap, picking at the strings with his thumbs and

thumping the bottom with thimbled fingers. It produced a sound somewhat like a Caribbean steel band. As he played, he chanted to his grandfather, Agwambo, part in English, part in Swahili.

After a minute or two, Agunga stopped and jotted down three numbers: seven, nine, three. They added up to 19. Divided by the three teams
in the race—New York, Boston, and Baltimore—he announced that New
York would win by 6½ games, with Baltimore second.

For 100 Kenya shillings ($12), Agunga agreed to an experiment. He
was given the choice of either helping Boston or Baltimore, but by now
he was a fan of "Blantimyre," as he pronounced it, and said his powers
wouldn't work for any other team.

Agunga took some bottles and cans from a shelf behind his sofa,
where he kept his love potions and other medicines, and poured some
large black granules onto a table from a ketchup bottle. These, he said,
were bits of bone and other things. From a large dried-milk can, he
pulled a bird's wing. A moth flew out of the can, and he watched it alight
on a chair. He said that, as the feathers had been changed into a moth,
so too could he change the outcome of the pennant race.

Sitting with a carved stick between his knees, Agunga opened a
small coffee can and shook out three piles of black powder. He mixed
this with the granules, put the mixture into the palm of his hand, lifted it
to his mouth to taste, then walked to the window and blew it away,
chanting in a whisper as he did so. He waved a tassel of hairs from an
animal's tail and blew more powder out the door, continuing to pray.
When he came out of his trance, he put his cans back on their shelf and
announced that he was done.

That evening, September 8, in faraway Detroit, unaware of the bolt
that had just been shot their way from deepest Africa, the Orioles shut
out the fourth-place Tigers on a four-hitter by Jim Palmer, his 15th win of
the year.

On September 9, in Baltimore, the O's beat fifth-place Cleveland,
7-1. Rudy May pitched a two-hitter for his 16th win, a career high.

The next day Baltimore led 4-0 going into the ninth, but Cleveland
tied it, and went ahead in the 11th on a homer by John Lowenstein. But
a walk and hits by the Orioles' Pat Kelly, Eddie Murray, and Doug

DeCinces brought in two runs for victory.

On September 11, Ross Grimsley (14-10), KO'd in his last four starts, beat the Indians 9-5 as the O's moved to only three games behind. Exulted manager Earl Weaver: "I've got so many hot bats I can't get them all in the lineup!" Agunga was now four-for-four.

On September 12, the O's beat last-place Toronto 6-3 for Palmer's 16th victory and were only 2½ games behind.

On September 14, the Orioles played a doubleheader against last-place Toronto. In the first game, losing 5-2, the O's scored four unearned runs in the ninth. A bases-loaded walk scored the winning run. They won the second game 4-2.

On September 15, Weaver complained that a rolled-up tarpaulin might injure a player, and when the umps refused to move it, led his team off the field. The umps forfeited it to Toronto, the only game the O's had lost since Agunga intervened.

Back home the next day, Palmer faced the third-place Red Sox, who had bombed him twice that year. In the first Baltimore's Andrew Mora got a triple when Bernie Carbo caught his foot in the fence. Ken Singleton hit a chopper that Thomas Boswell of the *Washington Post* said "would have sliced foul 99 times in 100." It bounced within two inches of the chalk and into the left field corner as both runners scored. Three times Palmer got out of two-on, two-out situations, the final time striking out Jim Rice and winning it, 6 -1.

September 17: Weaver put five rookies in the lineup, including pitcher Dennis Martinez, who defeated Bill "Spaceman" Lee, 11-2. It was Baltimore's ninth straight win, excluding the forfeit loss.

Over the same stretch the Yankees' record was 7-3 while the Red Sox went 5-4. Baltimore had climbed over Boston into second and trailed the Yanks by two games. On September 15, the O's lost 10-4, their first real defeat since Agunga had cast his spell.

Over the final two weeks, the Birds won 10 and lost five. Alas, the Yankees matched them game for game. From September 8 on, Baltimore played the hottest baseball in the league but couldn't make up the ground. They finished tied with Boston, 2 ½ games behind New York.

Too bad I hadn't seen Agunga one week earlier.

♈ **Postscript** ♈

In January 1999 I returned to Nairobi, but Agunga had moved back to the shores of Lake Victoria. I eventually found another witch doctor, a muscular retired railroad engineer of 55, who owned a small general store, selling groceries and potions, including something he said was "better than Viagra." He agreed to help the Arizona Cardinals (9-6), the NFL Wild Card team, win the 1999 Super Bowl. I bet him $75—$15 down, plus $5 for a sacrificial rooster.

As I watched and photographed, he did his incantations over the rooster, then slit its throat and with the blood wrote a spell for Arizona on an eggshell.

I promised to send him clippings and $15 for each of the Cardinals' victories. I emphasized that they were heavy underdogs, especially against Minnesota (15-1) the coming Sunday. "Don't worry," were his final, smiling words.

Alas, Arizona was badly beaten, which may prove that a) some witch doctors are better than others, or b) witch doctors have bad and good days, or c) as my son suggested, it was a bad rooster.

... And now about the cauldron sing
Like elves and fairies in a ring.

Shakespeare,
MACBETH

CHAPTER 37
A Witch Among the Angels

IN 1977 THE EXPERTS were saying the Angels should realize their destiny at last. Owner Gene Autry had opened his saddlebags and handed out $5.2 million for Oakland outfielders Joe Rudi and Don Baylor and Baltimore second baseman Bobby Grich.

Yet the campaign opened ominously again. Rookie shortstop Mike Miley became the latest Angel to die in a flaming crash. Grich suffered a herniated disc lifting an air conditioner, and Rudi broke his hand; both missed the second half of the season. By July, five Angels were out with injuries. The pitching staff was reduced, pundits said, to "Tanana and Ryan and two days of cryin'." Then Frank Tanana developed a sore arm and wouldn't win a game for a month. That left Nolan Ryan (14-10).

"I can't understand what happens to this club," catcher Andy Etchebarren shrugged. "It's a jinx or something. I've been here two years, and we've had more injuries in that time than in the 10 years I was at Baltimore."

Baylor was playing but was hitting only .234, and the fans were boo-ing him. Bobby Bonds was so tired he couldn't swing a 37-ounce bat and had to switch to a 32-ounce model.

The Angels were floundering in fifth place, 14 games behind the division-leading White Sox and 8½ behind fourth-place Texas. On August 2 the Yankees walloped them 9-3, on 19 hits, for the Angels' fifth loss in six games. In that stretch they went 21 straight innings without a run. Four of the defeats had been at the hands of the A's, the worst club in the division.

"We'll try anything," general manager Harry Dalton said grimly.

"Anything?" wondered Dick Miller of the *Los Angeles Herald-Examiner*. He got on the phone and called Louise Huebner, the official witch of Los Angeles County. Would she help? Huebner said she would.

....Silver swirling smoke,
Thick enough to make you choke,
Mingles with the sound of bells
As a witchy casts her spells."

Louise Huebner,
NEVER STRIKE A HAPPY MEDIUM

ŏ The Official Witch of Los Angeles County ŏ

Louise Huebner was probably the most famous witch in North America, leader of a super-coven, "The Magic Circle," of 4,000 members. "A good witch," one pundit had written, "and very pretty too, with flowing, raven hair and a great figure." In photos she projected a pixie-like Barbra Streisand twinkle.

Louise had written numerous books: *Power Through Witchcraft, The Witches' Cookbook, Love Spells From A to Z, Your Lucky Numbers*, and her autobiography, *Never Strike a Happy Medium*. She also had a record album, "Seduction Through Witchcraft." She lectured and cast spells for colleges and other groups; the University of Washington had awarded her an honorary degree. She wrote a syndicated column, conducted her own TV series, and had been featured in *Time, Life, Cosmopolitan, Genesis, Gallery*, and *Ladies Home Journal. Life* called her "the good witch of the west" and said she did nothing but good.

"There is no such thing as black magic and white magic, evil spirits and good spirits," Huebner agreed. "There is only energy."

In 1968, in a ceremony in Hollywood Bowl, Huebner was declared "the official witch of Los Angeles County" by county supervisor Ernest E. Debs. In return, she had cast a spell to raise "the levels of romantic and emotional vitality" throughout the county and presented Debs with a magical golden horn to ensure his personal sexual vitality.

Louise also conducted a daily horoscope show on Los Angeles station KLAC. She worked in a dark studio lit only by a flickering candle and one small nightlight to read commercials by. One night, as she lit a flame to increase the sexual vitality of Long Beach, the small booth suddenly caught fire and filled with billowing smoke and incense. There was a lot of excitement before they got the fire out.

But when Louise put "official witch of Los Angeles County" on her stationery, Debs decided to revoke her witchhood. It had all been a publicity gag, he told her. Huebner replied that the county had been happy to have the publicity. Did he want her to de-spell the entire county? And what about his own magic horn? He didn't offer to return that, did he? She had a signed proclamation, and she jolly well intended to keep it.

Huebner kept her letterheads, Debs his golden horn, and Los Angeles County, presumably, its "romantic vitality." Louise enjoyed the fray thoroughly. She dedicated her next book to "Isis, the moon goddess, and Ernest E. Debs, the county supervisor."

Salem, Massachusetts—Laurie Cabot's hometown—was more hospitable. Louise had paid the mayor a visit before Cabot came on the scene, sweeping into his office dressed in black lamé "to match her hair," as UPI wrote. Hizzoner gave her a broom and a scroll proclaiming her Salem's official witch.

Once, in Italy, driving with her husband, Mentor, Louise suddenly visualized a truck coming toward them in their lane over the brow of a hill. She screamed just in time for him to swerve and miss a real truck.

Louise once dreamed of giving birth to twins and nine months later did so. And "three times a year," she said, "I dream I am dancing nude in a beautiful multi-lighted fountain." She added that didn't have any idea what that meant.

"The mysterious bond between lovers" can attract luck and success, Huebner had written. "An energy exchange celebration that is offered as a token to the gods" will expand a person's consciousness.

The best time for an orgy, according to Huebner, is the dark of the moon or the full moon, especially at the equinoxes (March 21 or September 23), "when the earth is surrounded by wild vibrations." There must be nine, 11, or 13 guests—or double or triple or seven-fold, "but never one more or less." Otherwise you may unleash powerful evil forces, "so plan your orgy with care." As she described it, all the participants stand in a circle and each person lights a red candle to the god Pluto. Next, "let the place be filled with laughter." The witch rings a pewter bell three times, and "psychic inspiration will direct the group activities from there on."

Huebner told me she prayed to different gods for different powers. Mercury controls a lover's secret subconscious; Mars is for sheer sex appeal—"puts that extra zing in your zap." Venus is for joy; Uranus helps find "a wild new lover" (the technique is to burn 11 blue candles for seven minutes at midnight). Saturn will bring a lover back, and Isis helps "in desperate cases."

She recommended worshipping Neptune "just before each sexual union." She also suggested a love cake or a "passion drink" of rum, honey, and lime juice for two.

Best of all, if you can catch one, is a demon—"a wild force of energy." According to Huebner, he's easy to spot with his glinty yellow eyes, pointy ears, twisted horns, toothy fiendish grin, gnarled skinny arms, scraggly tail, and wings. He's the cause of leaky faucets, lost keys, and pimples. He may be ferocious and diabolical, "but a demon-made love affair can be fun with no hangups." A demon, she said, is captured in a magic circle using three red candles, white chalk, garlic, cloves, and a fistful of roses. Once caught, he may rant and wail, or try to make a deal—if he does, you should demand "the supreme grand passion."

Not all witches are sexy. Huebner estimated that there were 7,000 across America, many of them overweight, middle-aged, "with flopping beads and boobs" and "not too itty-bitty bottoms." Her own Magic Circle members, she said, pooled their psychic energies and projected them "for the good of the club."

This was the woman Dick Miller had chosen to help the Angels.

♈ The Witch Pinch Hits ♈

Miller had not picked an easy schedule. The Angels had one game coming up against the Yankees, three against the Orioles, two at Kansas City, and a series in Boston, all of them battling for their division titles.

Huebner alerted the Magic Circle. Then she gave medals to owner Gene Autry and general manager Harry Dalton. "They'll be drawing on a reservoir of psychic and spiritual energy," she explained, and Autry and Dalton must return some of it by rubbing their medals at 9 p.m. when the moon is fullest. A side effect, she added, "is an improvement in sexual activity."

"I'm not sure I believe in witchcraft," Dalton said. "But do I have to wait until 9 o'clock?"

Bobby Bonds, however, reacted with alarm. Offered one of the medals, he snapped, "Don't let it touch me. That's voodoo."

Don Baylor wanted one for his wife's charm bracelet. "Don't touch it!" Joe Rudi warned. "That's the devil."

The players received their medals on August 3 just before the Yankee game, in which California's Nolan Ryan would face New York's rookie ace, Ron Guidry. "AT LAST—WITCH TO RELIEVE ANGELS," the *Herald-Examiner* headlined beside a large picture of Louise gazing beautifully over a row of lighted candles.

In the second inninng, Angel Ron Jackson walked, Baylor hit a double, and Dave Chalk singled. Then two banjo hitters, Rusty Torrez (.156) and Terry Humphrey (.227), knocked them in with a fly and a double.

Meanwhile, Ryan didn't have his fabled fastball. He struck out only three men and was nicked for nine hits. The Yankees tied it, but in the eighth California's Gil Flores singled, and Bonds lashed a home run to win 5-3.

On the 5th the Angels faced the Orioles. Tanana's arm was still sore, and he was still trying to win his 13th game, which had eluded him for a month. "The signs are favorable for Frank," Louise announced. "The moon will be in Leo. That's a dramatic sign dealing with sports and gambling." Tanana, a Cancer, had his natal moon in Aries. "He is extremely potent." But, she added, "any female influence would be a naturally debilitating element. Females short-circuit his natural physical capacity. He is extremely romantic and is his own worst enemy, because his passion draws females."

However, she insisted, "the Angels will be automatically connected into psychic energy. I will be at home. At 9 o'clock I will enter a quiet room and light a candle. I will sprinkle a heavy circle of salt around myself. I will write out this message: I will use the Magic Circle energy for good. I will contribute my share as demanded. I am an important creation within the cosmos."

How did the game come out? "That wicked, wicked witchcraft worked," Miller wrote the next day.

Tanana's elbow was still hurting. "I haven't had a good breaking pitch all year, except in maybe three games. But they kept swinging at it tonight, and it wasn't even in the strike zone." Frank gave up only three hits—only one of them a solid hit—struck out seven, and beat the Orioles

5-0. Bonds whacked another home run, and the team trotted off the field as the organist struck up "That Old Black Magic Has Me In Its Spell."

Tanana had not met Louise in person, although, he said, "I've been out with a few girls I thought were witches afterward." Anyway, "whatever she did tonight, I hope she does it every night." "THANK YOU, WITCH LOUISE," the *Herald-Examiner* agreed.

On August 6 the Angels faced the Orioles again. The *Herald-Examiner* headline next day told it all: "CURSES! ANGELS WIN ANOTHER FOR THE WITCH!" Bonds slugged another homer in the first, Baylor hit a three-run homer in the third, and the team won, 9-5.

California had won all three games with Huebner, outscoring its opponents 19-8. With Bonds and Baylor hot, wrote Chuck Dyrdal of the *Herald-Examiner*, the Angels "could be making a belated move.... The foundation is once again being laid for what figures to be a contending club."

The next day California faced Jim Palmer, the league's biggest winner in each of the past two seasons and working on another 20 victories in '77. The Orioles couldn't lose another if they expected to stay close to the streaking Red Sox and ahead of the on-rushing Yanks.

The best the Angels had was lefty Dave LaRoche, who had won only seven games so far. Losing 3-0 in the sixth, California's Thad Bosley, fresh off the injured list, doubled. Tony Solaita walked, Baylor singled Bosley home, Chalk blooped a double to score Solaita, and rookie Rance Mulliniks, replacing Grich, hit a solid single for two runs to put the Angels ahead. An inning later Bonds slugged a two-run homer, and the Angels won their fourth straight 6-3. They had now cut 6½ games from Chicago's lead.

"I can't explain it," Bonds admitted. "We still have a shot at the pennant. If we can pick up five or six more games this month, we'll only be four or five out [of first place] going into September, and you can make that up easily."

Rookie manager Dave Garcia smiled and nodded. "I want these guys in the frame of mind that when they leave home each day, they think they can win. If they play up to their capabilities, Greta Garbo could manage them."

Coming up was a doubleheader at Kansas City, where the Royals had won 13 straight. Ryan was to pitch the first game, but "there's really no life to my arm," he admitted. "It's going through a dead stage now." Moreover, he would be pitching in beastly 100-degree weather.

"Mr. Ryan will have the strength of 4,000 men," Huebner predicted.

"I didn't have anything from the first inning on," Nolan recalled. Still, he pitched no-hit ball for five innings.

California scored four runs in the second. "The witch may have had something to do with that," Miller wrote. Ron Jackson was picked off base, but the Royals' infielder dropped the ball. Then followed a walk and four singles, "three of them just out of reach of the fielders' gloves."

But Huebner "must have stopped rubbing after the fifth inning," Ryan joked later, because he gave up two hits and was taken out with the Angels ahead, 4-0.

In the seventh Kansas City loaded the bases with one out, but pinch hitters Amos Otis and John Wathan went out meekly as California won.

Who would pitch the second game? The overworked staff was dec-imated. In desperation, Garcia's eye lit on Wayne Simpson, a tall 28-year-old (5-8, 5.31 ERA). Simpson had spent 10 years bouncing around the minors and majors; he hadn't pitched more than seven innings in a game all year, and his last major league shutout had come way back in 1970. He would be facing Paul Splittorf.

"How effective is the witch's magic?" Miller asked rhetorically the next day. Simpson pitched his greatest game in eight years—7⅓ innings of shutout ball—and the Angels won again 7-2. They routed Splittorf with 11 hits. Bonds hit another of his now daily homers, and Flores pounded four hits, including three doubles. California had now won six straight, its longest streak since 1974. "Stunning," Miller gasped. "Louise Huebner... is making believers in conservative Orange County." She had better mix up more magic brew, Miller advised, because "the Angels were forced to use up virtually all of ther psychic and spiritual energy last night."

Cracked Louise: "I haven't been this tired since I flew to Transylvania on an economy model broom."

"Slowly, hope is returning to the Angels," wrote Don Merry of the

rival *Los Angeles Times*. The witch had been the *Herald-Examiner's* gimmick, and the *Times* had been ignoring the whole thing. But "a certain feeling of optimism has been gaining momentum," Merry admitted.

In the last six games, the Angels had outscored their opponents 38-17. Could they keep going like this and win the pennant? "If we go into September five or six games out, we can do it ourselves," Bonds said. "If we're any further back, we'll have to pray for help."

However, Bonds still denounced Huebner as a Satanist. "Some of the players were ridiculing [the magic]," Louise said later. "They said it was devil worship and voodoo. In general, they were very insulting." She had tried to help them, but felt there was "something very seriously the matter with the entire group. Individual people have things going for them, but united [they're] chaotic and terrible.

"I wasn't too thrilled with being involved with them," she continued. "I felt a terrible drain on me. And I felt I shouldn't have used the energy of the Magic Circle, because the Angels were not sincere and honest. I felt I used the members' energy for a group that didn't participate or give anything back. So I just pulled out of it. I got mad at them. I put the curse back on. After all, I'm not Mary Poppins. I don't *have* to help anybody."

∽ After the Witch ∽

Unaware of Huebner's decision, the euphoric Angels boarded their plane to Boston to meet the Red Sox, the leaders of the A.L. East. Tanana would be rested and ready to go against Luis Tiant.

The Red Sox had a nine-game winning streak going, ever since pinch hitter Bernie Carbo had slammed a 10th-inning homer against the Angels' Dyar Miller a week and a half earlier.

Boston knocked Tanana out of the box, but Bonds hit another homer and the Angels took a 10-8 lead in the seventh. Then Boston's Dwight Evans singled and Carbo stepped in to pinch-hit against Miller. It had just entered Garcia's mind that Carbo had hit a homer off Miller in a similar situation 10 days earlier, when Carbo hit the first pitch over the wall, his 13th homer of the year, to tie it up. A few moment later, two walks and a single by Carl Yastrzemski won it 11-10. "It was Carbo's bat

that did them in," nodded Laurie Cabot, who had energized the bat in Cleveland a year earlier.

The Angels won the next day 7-3, but then, says Louise, "they went back to their old ways." In New York they lost three out of four by scores of 10-1, 9-3, and 15-3.

Dick Miller would laugh later that the whole witch story had been just a big "put on"; he himself had never believed in it, he scoffed.

O.K., let's look at the record. Let's see how the Angels did in the six games before Huebner, the six games with her, and the six immediately after:

	Wins	Losses	Runs For	Runs Against
Before Huebner	1	5	16	26
With Huebner	6	0	42	16
After Huebner	2	4	30	55

All the brave talk about the pennant was gone. Ryan won only three more games and lost six to finish 19-16. Tanana was 2-2 the rest of the year. Simpson never won another game in the majors.

The Angels finished 28 games behind the Royals.

Undaunted, that winter Autry lured outfielder Lyman Bostock (.336), the second-best hitter in the league, from Minnesota for $2.2 million. Bostock had a disastrous beginning in '78 and offered to give his salary to charity until he felt he was earning it. By September he had raised his average to .296 when he was riding home from a night game in Chicago. A car pulled up next to his at a stoplight and a man emptied his pistol at his estranged wife, sitting next to Bostock. One of the bullets hit Lyman, killing him instantly. The Angels' Curse was back again.

♉ One More Tragedy ♉

The California Angels finally won a division title in 1979, the team's 18th year in the league. In the clubhouse celebration, pitcher Jim Barr punched a toilet seat, broke his hand, and was out of the playoffs. The Angels lost to Baltimore three games to one.

In 1982 Reggie Jackson hit 39 homers and Rod Carew led the hitters

at .319 as the Angels edged the Royals for the division flag. In the American League Championship Series against the slugging Milwaukee Brewers the Angels won the first two games. No team had ever won the first two and then lost a League Championship Series. The Angels did.

Their next shot was 1986, when they fell just one strike short of winning their first and only pennant, under veteran manager Gene Mauch, perhaps the unluckiest manager in modern times. Mauch, a chain-smoking veteran, had managed 26 years; his teams won almost 2,000 games, yet he never won a flag. In 1964, he suffered one of the worst humiliations ever to befall a big league manager when his Phillies, sporting a 6½ game lead with only 12 games to play, lost 10 in a row to finish in a tie for second.

In 1982, in Mauch won the division title but ran up against the Angels' Curse in the playoffs against Milwaukee, which beat California to clinch its first-ever pennant. So when Mauch led the Angels into the playoffs again in '86, sentimentalists were pulling for the popular veteran to win a flag at last after 25 years of trying.

Facing the Red Sox in the ALCS, California took a three-games-to-one lead. The Angels' ace, Mike Witt, started Game 5 in Anaheim, ready to wrap it up. He was winning 2-1 in the sixth when Boston's Tony Armas sprained an ankle in center and Dave Henderson replaced him. Since joining the Red Sox in midseason he had batted only .196, riding the bench much of the time.

With one man on base, Grich drove one to the fence. Henderson leaped, but the collision knocked the ball out of his glove and over the fence for a homer. On the bench after the inning he sat dejectedly alone. In the seventh he struck out feebly on four pitches.

With Boston losing 5-2 in the ninth, Bill Buckner, a former Cub, got an infield single. Jim Rice struck out, but Don Baylor drove a two-strike, two-run homer to narrow the score to 5-4. With Henderson up and one man on, the Red Sox had only one more out left in their season. Victory banners blossomed over the upper deck railings, police with attack dogs crouched at gates to charge onto the field, and Angels in the dugout poised on the top steps to run out and hug their teammates.

At this point Mauch called in his best reliever, righthander Donnie

"Gas Can" Moore (21 saves), to get the final out. Moore was nursing a sore shoulder, but he quickly got ahead on the count 1-2. Hendu took ball two. Moore threw a fastball, and Dave gave an awkward swing and lifted what one reporter called "a gasping foul."

Henderson fouled off another fastball. In the California dugout, Reggie Jackson hugged Mauch. One more strike to go.

Moore, who had been making Henderson look foolish with fastballs, decided to give him a split-finger. It broke low and outside, and Henderson swung. "When I hit it, I knew it was gone," he said later. He did a 360 in the air on his way to first. The homer put the Red Sox in front, 6-5. Suddenly they had a season again.

Miraculously, the Angels tied it the ninth, but in the 11th the Sox loaded the bases with Henderson up again. He hit a line drive to left-center, and what proved to be the winning run scored. The Angels lost the last two games without a fight.

Moore carried the heartache of that one bad pitch for the rest of his life. Despondent, in 1989 he shot his wife and himself to death, the latest victim of the Angels' Curse.

*He capers, he dances, he has eyes of youth, he writes
verses, he speaks holiday, he smells April and May.*

Shakespeare,
MERRY WIVES OF WINDSOR

                CHAPTER 38
                   The Two Faces of Steve

THIS IS THE STORY OF THE TWO STEVE STONES: Steve Stone, failure, and
Steve Stone, superstar.

Stone was a 33 year-old journeyman, who had been bouncing
around the big leagues with a lifetime record of 78 wins and 79 losses.

Better known as a connoisseur of fine food, fine wine, fine cars, and
fine women, he nevertheless called himself "the best Jewish pitcher
since Sandy Koufax." (He was virtually the only one, along with Kenny
Holtzman.) Intelligent, witty, puckishly handsome, a poet and restaura-
teur, Stone was one of the few ballplayers into psychic phenomena and
not embarrassed to say so.

He learned early that men are capable of seemingly incredible feats.
His grandfather, who had vowed to see young Steve bar-mitzvahed, suffered 14 heart attacks, four of them major. "The emergency squad would
come and take him away and say, 'This is it.' But I hadn't been bar mitz-
vahed yet, so it wasn't it." The old man clung to life until the big event
took place; only then did he pass away. Said Stone: "He did something
there was no way he should have been able to do."

Steve grew up around Cleveland and went to games with his father.
He gorged on cotton candy, snow cones, peanuts, and hot dogs "and led
the league in throwing up."

In 1969 Steve signed with the San Francisco Giants' farm team at
Fresno. Fresno was in the heart of the wine country, and Steve "sipped
his way across the Napa Valley." Between sips he won 12 games and
lost 13.

The following year was spent in Amarillo and Phoenix. After one
bad game he walked the streets until 5 a.m., came back to the hotel, and
wrote his first published poem, "Today's Hero." Cheers can quickly turn
to boos, he penned.

In 1971 the Giants brought Stone up, though manager Charlie
Fox told him frankly he'd never be a big leaguer because he read
too much and smoked a pipe. "I knew early on I'd never be one of

the boys," Steve sighed.

Fox also told him he didn't have the stamina to pitch a complete game. "And I didn't. There are a lot of people out there telling you you can't do things. They put restrictions on you. I was starting to believe I couldn't be a starting pitcher. The worst thing that can happen is for you to start believing the tags they put on you."

The Giants won the division title, but Steve's record was only 5-9. The next year he posted a good 2.98 ERA, but the Giants fell to next-to-last, and Steve had another losing year, 6-8.

The Giants waived him to the White Sox, where he went 6-11 with a 4.24 ERA as the White Sox also finished next to last.

"Steve, old buddy," he told himself one day in the bullpen, "you had better develop an alternate source of income." He loved to eat ("You can't be Jewish and not love food"), so he decided to learn the restaurant business. That winter he worked for free, waiting tables, cutting meat, tending bar, and at last went into partnership in a chain he called Lettuce Entertain You.

That's when he met Ruth Revzen, who was reading palms at R.J. Grunt's, one of the restaurants in the chain. Both were 26, single, and Jewish, and he asked her to hold a seance for him and his family.

The next spring, as Steve was leaving for Florida, Ruth suddenly told him to get his teeth fixed, that something was wrong with the right side of his mouth. He scoffed; he'd just been to the dentist. A few days later a tooth broke off on the right side, and a new dentist found decay under the filling. "Too bad you didn't come to me earlier," he said; "now I have to do a root canal."

In '74 Stone was 8-6 with the last-place Cubs. He read Sandy Koufax's autobiography five times. Koufax convinced him "how mental this game really is. You can actually will yourself to win."

That fall Ruth issued another warning: She saw an auto accident coming up at midnight. "Oh, great," he groaned. That night, as he was going under an overpass, something suddenly put him on guard that a blind intersection was coming up on the right. A split-second later another car ran the red light, but, forewarned, Steve hit the brakes and screeched to a stop. Shaken, he drove to his apartment, parked in the

garage, and called Revzen. "Was it midnight?" she asked.

"No," he said, "seven minutes before. You missed it by seven minutes."

"Go get the car fixed," she replied.

"But it wasn't scratched."

"Have it fixed," she repeated and hung up.

Next morning Steve found that a hit-and-run driver in the garage had put a three-foot gash in the door overnight.

Steve told me he had seen dozens of psychics, from charlatans to the very talented. "Ruth, to me, is the best in the country," he said. "I've seen her progress in her field. Now she's at the top. I can't believe there's anybody better."

The next season, 1975, Steve had his best record yet, 12-8, though the Cubs remained in last place.

In '76, Stone was on the field the day Ruth put the hex on Randy Jones. But he suffered a rotator cuff injury, the kind that has ended many a career, and fell to a 3-6 record. But the next year Steve was back with the White Sox. Smiled general manager Roland Hemond, "It's the first time I ever signed a player in a tux at the Pump Room."

On April 21 Stone was dining at a restaurant in California when he looked up in surprise to see Ruth, who had moved to Beverly Hills. "Ruth!" he cried. "How did you find me?"

"I had a feeling," she smiled.

Steve was scheduled to pitch that night. "I didn't like his arm," Revzen remembered. "I felt something was wrong with it. I didn't want him to pitch. I was afraid he was going to hurt himself."

"It did feel a little twisted," Steve agreed later.

That night, he said, "I couldn't get loose in the bullpen. But then, just as Ruth entered the park — boom!—a transformer short-circuited and knocked out the lights on the first-base side of the field. They had to call the game, and I was saved. I was a believer after that."

Stone also started to win. In a velvet dinner jacket with ruffled shirt and a stunning woman at his side, he also became a familiar figure at all the best restaurants on the American League circuit. His "dining adventures" included boiled lobster at Bishops in Boston, rack of lamb at Le

Francais in Chicago, liver dumpling soup at Karl Ratzsh's in Milwaukee, popovers and beer-cheese at Normandy Inn in Minneapolis. In Anaheim, Charley Brown's served "average food—but, oh, what women!" But his favorite restaurant was Dorothy's in Cleveland, which served "the best matzoh ball soup this side of Tel Aviv. I also love the prices." Dorothy was Steve's mother.

Steve drank apple daiquiris at Stephenson's in Kansas City and knew all the best wines—1974 BV Georges de Latour Private Reserve, 1975 Puligny-Montrachet. He recommended opening the 1970 Gevrey-Chambertin early: "A good burgundy needs time to breathe, like a reliever warming up."

Meantime Steve was also winning games. He equaled his previous high of 12 victories, then won his 13th. But suddenly he lost his stuff, failing four times to win number 14.

On September 9 Stone returned to Los Angeles, and Ruth offered him some of her potion. "I finally got some new stuff" after the Randy Jones experience, she assured him.

To one reporter Steve denied that he used it—"I didn't want any of the other guys asking me out," he grins. But to another he said he "splashed" it on. "It's a good thing she gave it to me, because I didn't have my good stuff at all." He beat the Angels that night 4-1. His final won-lost for the year: 15-12, his best season so far, as the White Sox finished third.

In '79 Steve was with pennant-bound Baltimore, but by midseason he was only 6-7. When he was announced to pitch, the fans booed. "It took 10 of my baseball cards to get one of anyone else." The newspapers urged manager Earl Weaver to send him to the bullpen. "I was the only weakness in what was a great year for our team. I was having negative thoughts about my pitching, my environment, about everything. I was 0-3 in fights with the manager. Everything I was doing seemed counterproductive. I realized I had to change my thinking. I felt I had to make the situation turn around.

"I began to realize my mental approach was wrong," Stone continued. "I had been going out there trying not to lose, rather than being determined to win. I had to take on a positive approach. I sat down and

tried to convince myself that I was better than a .500 pitcher."

A hypnotist named Harvey taught him to meditate on the opposing batters before each game. Pat, a faith healer, concentrated on his arm. He shaved his mustache, switched gloves, got new spikes, changed his number from 21 to 32 (Koufax's old number), and read *Winning Through Intimidation*. He also had breakfast each day at a pancake house with sportswriter Peter Pascarelli.

Pitching coach Ray Miller also helped. He told Steve to work faster. "When you take longer, psychologically maybe you're not that confident. He helped me tremendously."

Something worked. Steve won his last five games to finish with an 11-7 record. He brashly predicted that he would win 18 games in 1980.

♉ A Rolling Stone ♉

Stone started the 1980 season with three losses in his first five starts but won his next four to bring his record to 6-3. Then he ran into trouble. Both third-place Milwaukee and seventh-place Cleveland knocked him out of the box, though he wasn't charged with either loss. (He noted that he and Pascarelli had switched to steak and eggs for breakfast, instead of pancakes.)

When the Orioles flew to California to meet the seventh-place Angels, Steve looked up Ruth again. "How'm I gonna do tomorrow?" he asked anxiously.

"Well, the team's gonna win," she replied.

"I didn't ask you that. How'm I gonna do?"

"The team's gonna win," she repeated laconically, and added her prediction that his season was about to turn around.

The next night, June 8, Steve got knocked out again. The Angels, next-to-last that year, rocked him for five runs in four innings, his worst performance of the season, though the O's scored 13 runs to win the game.

It was the third time in a row he had been KO'd, and though his won-lost record was 6-3, his ERA was over 5.00. He called Ruth back. "Your season's going to turn around when you meet the team in green,"

she assured him. Her second prediction was a bigger shocker: "You're going to pitch in the All Star Game." With an ERA of 5.01, "I wasn't exactly All-Star material," Stone recalled. But Ruth just brushed his doubts aside. She agreed to help him, and "went into trance and opened up [psychically] and told him what to do, and he did it."

Revzen knew almost nothing about baseball, certainly nothing about the colors of uniforms. The only team to wear green was the Oakland Athletics, who would be the Orioles' next opponent, though Steve wouldn't pitch.

Stone had something else working for him. He picked up a copy of Shakti Gawain's book, *Creative Visualization*, and read it from cover to cover. "I had worked on this before," he said, "though not quite so graphically as at this particular time."

The next stop was Seattle. Steve decided to visualize pitching a complete game. "I hadn't thrown one all year, the bullpen was tired, and I feel that anything you can imagine, can happen." So he imagined the scoreboard after the coming game, with the Orioles on the long side of the score. Then he imagined Miller springing out of the dugout to shake his hand, a ritual that always signified a complete game.

It worked. Stone did hurl nine innings, yielding only one run, to win. "For the first time it all became clear. It was as if a TV picture had been jumping around and I finally figured out how to adjust the horizontal."

Back home in Baltimore five days later, he faced his former tormentors, the Angels. That afternoon he took the phone off the hook, lay down on his bed, closed his eyes, and pitched the entire game in his head, facing each hitter four times, plus a couple of pinch hitters. He ended with Miller congratulating him on another complete game.

At the park that night, Miller warmed him up in the bullpen as he traditionally did, then the two trudged into the dugout side-by-side to await the start of the game. "How's my stuff?" Steve asked.

"It's O.K.," Miller replied.

"I feel good," Steve said. "I think I'll win it 5-2." He almost did, but an extra run that scored on an error made the final score 5-3. He struck out 11, by far his best total of the season.

Stone resumed his routine of the year before. Before his next start,

he began the day with a cup of Morning Thunder tea, followed by pancakes and a milkshake with Pascarelli. He drove the same route to the stadium in his Porsche, listening to the same soft rock tape. ("I'd play it for you now, but I'm afraid it would make me jump out of the car and start pitching.")

Stone pitched his third straight complete game and his first shutout, whipping Seattle 9-0. In his next start he told Miller he thought he'd beat Toronto 4-1. He did, with another complete game.

Moving to Toronto, Stone hurled seven shutout innings. His complete-game string was broken, but his ERA for the five games since his little talk with Ruth was 0.83. He was leading the league in wins with 11. *Sports Illustrated* and *People* magazine discovered him.

They couldn't keep him off the All-Star squad. "Honest," he protested, "I really didn't sell my soul to the devil." Stone visualized himself pitching the maximum three innings, allowing no hits and striking out six. "I couldn't look at this [National League] lineup as a group. As a group, it would have seemed too big a task. But one-by-one, I was able to handle nine guys."

For the game, in Dodger Stadium, Ruth made one of her rare visits to a ballpark to watch Steve do just what he said he would: He mowed down all nine men to face him, although he struck out only three, not six. He was the first man since 1966 to set down nine straight in the Classic. "I really had my good stuff. Every one of my pitches was working for me." He walked off the mound "just feeling as exuberant as I've ever felt."

After that Stone beat Kansas City, Milwaukee, Minnesota, and Milwaukee again, to run his string to 10 in a row and 15 for the year. "He snaps his curves and fires his fastball," the *Baltimore Sun* wrote. "He swaggers to the mound and can't wait to get that ball."

Weaver beamed. "There was never any doubt in my mind this guy could be a winning pitcher. If it wasn't for him now, we'd be a losing team."

"I'm like an Haut-Brion, a first-growth wine," Steve exulted. "It never gets the recognition of a Lafite Rothschilde or a Chateau Latour. But it can be very surprising."

I decided it was time to talk to Steve himself.

We are spinning our own fates,
good and evil.

Alfred, Lord Tennyson

♌ Why the Change? ♌

Stone was wadding up newspapers in his outstretched fist to strengthen his arm when I walked into the clubhouse the morning after his 16th victory. The papers all crinkled, he sprawled in a camp chair. "It's not Ruth, it's me," Steve said cheerfully. "She and I both realize that you're the captain of your own fate. I think that all a psychic can tell you is the tendencies of what's going to happen. But I think that you can really determine yourself what's going to happen to you."

The big change, Stone told me, "is due to immersing myself completely in a positive environment." The subconscious mind is the key to all success. "It doesn't reason as the conscious mind does; it's more like a blackboard which records every suggestion it is given. If you keep saying, 'Boy, I'm unlucky,' or 'I can't believe I'm so accident-prone,' your subconscious mind believes it, takes it in, writes it on the board, and consequently you continue to be unlucky or accident-prone." On the other hand, "if you continually say, 'I feel great. My arm feels wonderful. I'm gonna win this ball game. I don't see any way in the world this team can beat me,' and keep saying it over and over, eventually the subconscious mind is going to believe that. It erases the old, negative blackboard and replaces it with the new, positive one."

Steve had not tried Sylva Mind Control or Transcendental Meditation, and wouldn't say what worked best. "Everything works, or nothing works," he said, quoting Adam Smith's book *Powers of the Mind*. What Smith meant, Steve explained, is that if you want a technique to work, no matter what it is, it will work. It doesn't have to be visualization, and it doesn't have to be Ruth Revzen. "It can be your best friend making suggestions that are logical to him that you might not have thought about. The main thing is that you have someone who convinces you of a path to take. And if that path turns to success, then you begin to believe in that particular path. Three percent of all pitchers are at the bottom of the talent pool, and three percent are stars. The only thing that separates the other 94% is mental approach."

Some of the other Baltimore pitchers had started scratching their heads at Stone's dramatic improvement. Mike Flanagan, the best pitcher

in the league in 1979 at 23-9, was struggling with a 16-13 mark in '80. "I've talked to Mike, and I've talked to the other pitchers on the team," Steve said. "They ask me what I'm doing, and I tell 'em." Whether coincidence or not, teammate Scott McGregor went from 13 wins in '79 to 20 in '80; Jim Palmer went from 10 to 16.

Stone shied away from the term "meditation," which he said frightened some people. He called his mental state "quiet time, time you spend by yourself just thinking or letting your mind wander." Each day he was going to pitch, Stone said he visualized the newspaper the following morning showing his new won-lost record. Saturday, the day before I talked to him, his record was 15-3. He pitched that night, and sure enough, the Sunday paper had the new total, just as he had visualized it: Stone, 16-3.

"Guys laughed when I said before the season that I could win 18," he rejoiced. "Now I know I'll win 20, and I think I can win between 22 and 24."

Stone's next stop was Texas, where the fourth-place Rangers shocked him, knocking him out in three innings. I called Revzen to ask what had gone wrong. "It was his fault, not mine," she said. "He knows what he did wrong. He was a bad boy." She would not elaborate. But the suspicion was that Stone, the league's leading ladies' man, might have missed a curfew.

With Chicago as his next opponent, Steve called Ruth the Sunday before. She went into a trance so deep that she later couldn't remember what went on. He beat the White Sox 8-2 for number 17.

Next he beat the first-place Yankees in nine innings, 4-2. The O's, who had been 11 games behind New York a month earlier, were now only 2½ behind.

Five games later Steve beat the Yanks again, this time on only two hits.

Going for victory number 20 in Anaheim, he walked into the clubhouse with 36 bottles of champagne and told the clubhouse boy, "Ice 'em up, kid."

"Now there," marveled Miller, "is a guy who doesn't expect to lose."

"I had to win," Steve shrugged, explaining that he couldn't take the

champagne on to the next stop, "because champagne doesn't travel well." He not only won, he almost pitched a no-hitter, giving up his first hit in the eighth.

Stone's final record for the year: 25-7. The O's couldn't overtake the Yankees and finished three games behind, but Steve won the Cy Young award. That earned him a $100,000 bonus, the figure his agent had put in his contract on the million-to-one chance he might ever earn it.

Steve Stone had reached the mountaintop.

)(**The End**)(

The next year it was all over. The arm was finished. Stone had pitched 251 innings in 1980, the most of his life. He averaged 75 curves a game, more than any other pitcher in baseball. The doctors said he had an irritation of the medial epicondial tendon—in other words, a sore arm. Steve never pitched another complete game again. His record for '81 was 4-7, and in September the Orioles let the 33-year-old pitcher go. But he had left a guidebook to stardom for any other pitcher who wanted to follow it.

Some people scoffed at Steve's ideas, but not at his success. And if he could do it, why couldn't every pitcher?

Baseball is 80 percent mental, Stone said, shaking his head. "Yet, while every team has a trainer to care for the body, none has a specialist to administer to the mind."

Others don't have to do it his way. "It's a personal matter. You have to arrive at a set of things that's comfortable for you. If you do do that— pick up a few tricks, things that can help you—I have to believe that everybody can be successful in whatever field they're in."

Today Steve is the color man on Cubs TV broadcasts. "If you visualize any type of success you want in any area of your life, you can make everything come to you. And it will come to you. There's absolutely no doubt about that."

CHAPTER 39
The Broken Bat

IN OCTOBER 1990 THE RED SOX were making a gallant run against the defending division champs, the Toronto Blue Jays.

Picked to finish fourth or fifth in the spring, the Sox had survived several key injuries. DH Dwight Evans injured his back in spring training and played hurt all year. Relief ace Jeff Reardon had a ruptured disk and was out for two months. Outfielder Mike Greenwell hurt his ankle, and his average fell to .238, though he pulled it up to .297 by the end.

In May the Sox traded relief star Lee Smith for Tom Brunansky, a righthanded power hitter. But Bruno hurt his shoulder in June, went for a stretch of 34 at bats without a hit in July, and was benched in September for weak hitting. By September 28 he was batting .267 with only 10 home runs—he should have had 20 or 30 based on past performances. And the team was in revolt against manager Joe Morgan.

The worst blow fell September 4, when pitcher Roger Clemens (20-6) was disabled with tendonitis and a fluid build-up in his pitching shoulder. The pain was so great he couldn't even play catch.

Still Boston clung to a one-game lead September 28, when second-place Toronto arrived for a two-game series. Boston station WZLX decided that the infamous "Curse of the Bambino" was afflicting the Red Sox. It put in a call to the Crystal Chamber, a witches' boutique in Salem, and asked to speak to Shawn Poirier (pronounced PAW-ree-er), a male witch. "The curse has to be lifted," the caller pleader.

"Let's try," Shawn said.

Poirier was a tall man in his late 20s with dark hair and eyes and a dark mustache. He wore all black, including a long purple-lined cape, when he gave psychic readings in his shop, across the street from Laurie Cabot's Crow's Haven Corner. The two are rivals for the active market in crystals, spells, potions and the like, sold both to tourists and regular clients.

A Cape Codder, Poirier claimed to be a third-generation witch (he says "witch," not "wizard"). "I've always been trained as a psychic," he

told me across a table in the back room of his shop. "As a child I felt centuries old in a young body." When he watched Walt Disney programs, he could instinctively tell how they would turn out.

Poirier said he followed the "old" religion. "To me, a witch is just a wise person, who takes others to see their places in the diverse scheme of the universe."

Police had just asked him about the murder of a girl in Kingston, Rhode Island. He described a basement where the body could be found and described the murderer—"a little man, bald, heavy around the belly, with glasses," who was later arrested.

"Right now," Shawn told me, "we're sending out thoughts of world peace, a nightly thing we do, covering the whole world with a healing web."

As for the Red Sox, Shawn recalled, the evening before the game he did his regular radio broadcast from his apartment. He and two female witches, Lupe Mannon and Rachel Cody, lit candles and went into the meditational alpha state. They did some incantations, "and visualized, or sent the Red Sox positive energy." They said things like, "I see them pulling together as a team, flying ahead full force. I see their bats striking like the thunder of Thor," the ancient Viking god. The witches wanted the players to be "quick as deer and fast as light."

Meanwhile, across the street from Fenway Park, at the Twins souvenir store, a fire suddenly broke out next to a poster of Babe Ruth. Firefighters extinguished the blaze, but there was no sign of how it started.

That night Brunansky slugged a two-run homer, his 11th of the year. He also made a sliding catch in right field against Fred McGriff, Toronto's home run champ (34 homers), saving a possible inside-the-park homer. In the bottom of the ninth, losing 5-4, the Red Sox tied the score, loading the bases with rookie Jeff Stone up for his first at bat of the year, against Toronto's relief ace, Tom Henke (32 saves). Stone slapped a single against the drawn-in infield, and the Red Sox moved two games in front. They had three games to go, one more against Toronto and two against the third-place White Sox.

Saturday's game would be on national TV, and fans across New

England crossed their fingers that Clemens might be able to pitch. If not, Joe Hesketh (1-5) would have to start. While fans lined up early for tickets, Clemens went out to his backyard to toss some pitches "just to see where I stood."

At 12:30 Shawn Poirier arrived at Twins, along with several hundred people. They arranged themselves in a circle near the pillar still dark from the flames of the previous night's fire. They brought various charms—a Babe Ruth doll, a Red Sox uniform, an African voodoo belt. Someone brought a three-foot rabbit's foot.

One of those in the crowd was Bill "Spaceman" Lee, who had played for the Sox the fateful 1978 season, when they lost the playoff to Bucky Dent and the Yankees.

Poirier says he "sent out healing to the guy with the shoulder problem." (Shawn was not a baseball fan and didn't keep up with sports news.) Then he took a Red Sox shirt as a symbol of the team, put the curse, or negative energy, into the shirt, tore it in half, and tossed the tatters to the crowd, who "totally destroyed it." Shawn picked up another shirt and invested it with "energy and good luck."

Then he held aloft a broken bat and intoned: "This is a symbol of victory. May the powers of the universe and the love of the fans and the energy of the players come together so that the Red Sox may fly again." Then he handed it to Lee.

Meanwhile, Morgan was pacing the dugout, still uncertain whether Clemens could start or not. At last Morgan, Clemens, and pitching coach Bill Fischer gathered to take the long walk to the bullpen, where Roger would warm up. The crowd stood as one person and roared. "The biggest thing for me was when I heard the crowd and the way they were supporting me," Clemens said later. "When the crowd gets behind you like that, it almost makes you feel you're invincible."

"Roger was positive, 100 percent, that there was nothing wrong with him," Morgan reported.

Clemens ran a few wind sprints in the outfield, then doffed his jacket and wound up for his first pitch. It sailed high over the catcher's head. He tried another, and this one was on target.

"How do you feel?" Morgan asked nervously.

"I can't believe this," Roger exclaimed. "I feel great!"

Tony Pena, the regular catcher, trotted out to complete Clemens' warmups. He too was impressed. "He hadn't pitched in a month, and he came out and had control like that!"

"It doesn't matter how many innings I pitch," Roger said; "I'm going to shut them out." They walked back to the infield as more cheers swelled from the stands.

The first batter was Mookie Wilson, the former New York Met who had hit the fateful ball that Bill Buckner fumbled to defeat the Sox in the 1986 World Series. Roger's fastball cracked into Pena's mitt like a rifle shot that could be heard throughout the park. Wilson went out. Then Clemens struck out Kelly Gruber and McGriff to end the inning.

Lee watched a couple of innings, then went to his car, threw the broken bat in the trunk, and drove home to Vermont. He was on I-93, listening on the radio, when Brunansky smacked a home run to give Clemens a 1-0 lead.

Roger left the game after six innings. He had given four hits, two walks, and no runs. He struck out five.

"I never believed he could do what he did today," Fischer marveled. "I've never seen anything like it in my life. If he told me he could walk on water, he could walk on water."

In the bottom of the inning, Brunansky came up with two men on and smashed another shot over the wall, his 13th of the year.

In the eighth Bruno came up again. "Throw him a low fastball," Lee prayed under his breath. A moment later he heard the announcer cry: "A fastball... a drive deep to center..." It was the third homer of the day for Brunansky, who became the first man to hit three in one game at Fenway since Jim Rice 13 years earlier.

"I can't explain it," Tom said. "I wasn't thinking about hitting a home run, I was just trying to get some good pitches."

The Red Sox won 6-5.

Did Shawn's witchcraft give the team a psychological lift? I asked both Fischer and third baseman Wade Boggs about it. Both said they hadn't even known about the ceremony across the street until I told them.

After Toronto beat Hesketh 10-5 on Sunday, Chicago came to town. Boston beat them 4-3 as Bruno made a fine catch. On Tuesday Brunansky hit a double off the wall and scored the run that tied the game 2-2, though Boston lost it in the 11th on Ozzie Guillen's clutch hit.

If the Red Sox could win the last game of the season on Wednesday, it would mean the pennant, no matter what Toronto did against Baltimore.

Brunansky's triple knocked in the first run. In the third, he was caught in a rundown, but kept the defense throwing at him long enough for another run to score, and when Chicago threw the ball away, Tom scored himself to make it 3-0.

Chicago got two runs back, and in the ninth put two men on with two out and Guillen up. Ozzie slashed a low, twisting drive into the extreme right field corner. Bruno raced for it, dove, gloved the ball, slid into the grandstand railing, and held on. The Red Sox—and Shawn Poirier—had won the title.

Lee, meanwhile, remembered the broken bat in his trunk. He went out to the car, lifted the lid, and took out the bat. It was a Tom Brunansky model.

PART VII

THE FUTURE

The ball no notice takes of ayes or no's,
But left or right, as strikes the player, goes.
But He who threw thee down upon the field,
He knows about it all—HE knows—HE knows.

THE RUBAIYAT OF OMAR KHAYYAM

For I dipp'd into the future, far as human eyes
    could see,
Saw the Vision of the world, and all the wonders that
    would be.

Alfred, Lord Tennyson

CHAPTER 40
Sport's Next Frontier

BASEBALL, LIKE ALL THE OTHER SPORTS, has coaches to develop the body, but few to develop the non-physical side of the game. As the invisible energy chronicled above shows measurable results, the race will be on to sign "psychic coaches."

All other things being equal—physical, mental, coaching, equipment—victory may go to the side that makes best use of this still underused tool.

Western sports now routinely employ hypnotists and psychologists to enhance performance. Once sniggered at as unmanly, they are now commonplace. Many players now "visualize" in advance the results they want to achieve. But the larger subject of opening up the mind to even greater powers is still largely taboo, both in the locker rooms and in the sports departments of our newspapers.

When a psychic sends energy to a team, is it as palpable as the vitamins the players ingest or the lift they get from a locker room pep talk?

In the late 1980s Dr. Helmut Schmidt of San Antonio's Mind Science Foundation did exploratory tests on football players. He hoped to find out if athletes have PK, or psychokinesis, the ability to cause physical changes by mental power alone. Can a gambler "will" the dice to come up a certain way? Can a bridge player "pull" good hands toward him? (Teammates swore that Carl Yastrzemski could.) Can a hitter straighten a curveball ever so slightly? Can an outfielder "will" a fly ball to stay up a split-second longer until he can reach it? Schmidt calls this "applied luck."

Laboratory statistics, based on rolling thousands of dice, suggest that it may be possible.

Precognition, the ability to foretell events, is another area Schmidt studied. When a football passer leads a receiver, how does he know, before he releases the ball, which way his target will break? Is there a special channel of communication that flashes between them? When a batter "guesses" curve, is he tuning into a channel that even he doesn't suspect?

Rosemary DeWitt and I were given permission to administer some of the standard Duke University tests to members of the Washington Bullets—this was in the 1970s, when the team was an NBA powerhouse. Some players declined, but most were generous in giving us an hour or so. They rolled dice and guessed symbols on a deck of psi cards as another player mentally sent the images to them. (My daughter scores above average on this.)

Our data were too meager to have any statistical significance. But some day researchers might follow up with better tests to the mutual benefit of both the researchers and the athletes.

Dr. Schmidt, who retired in 1992, reports some football players have been "quite successful" in changing a pendulum's swing.

He has also conducted experiments with a circle of lights that seem to rotate left or right depending on a random generator. Players tried to make the lights move one way or the other by mental power alone. The results were "pretty successful," Schmidt says.

At the Naropa Institute, a Buddhist center for meditation and martial arts in Boulder, Colorado, Schmidt found two teachers who he claimed were "very gifted" at PK. However, as a practical matter, he says psychokinesis "has a very small effect," although there are other possible applications, such as developing mental toughness during a losing streak.

A big problem is finding teams that will experiment. Schmidt's football team, which wants to be anonymous, gave each player a 10-minute test with the lights. However, when the team started losing, "the management did not encourage it any more."

Since Schmidt retired, he says he knows of no other researchers seeking similar sports applications in this country and only one abroad, in Freiburg, Germany. The U.S. Olympic Committee also knows of no one doing work in this field. Too bad, Schmidt says. "You could have something dynamic."

Salem's Laurie Cabot would like to see all clubs, both farm teams and parent teams, send their players to her courses. "It should be a group learning process, where they could rev up their own energies. They could be terrific." She would like to help any team "on the QT" to teach

players how to project their own psychic energy. It should be scientific with careful controls, Cabot says. "Let's see if there's anything to it or not. If not, let's throw it out. But if there is, let's use it to help people in many different activites."

Does it give one side an unfair advantage over the other? Not if both sides are free to employ it.

Gamblers may try it out before management does. Warning: The psychics I've talked to say they won't do it if unworthy motives are involved; others say they can't do it under such conditions.

These are psychic vitamins, not psychic steroids. Many of the persons in these pages say the most they can do is to help a player tap the full potential of his abilities, but they cannot create a superman who isn't there. "It won't make me into a great piano player," Cabot says. "I'm a lousy piano player."

Cabot invites serious researchers to put her powers to the test: "If there is anything there, fine, use it. If not, throw it out." Eventually, she believes, every team will be using psychic powers. The idea excites her: "It could make the Olympics into super games."

Men willingly believe what they want to believe.

Julius Caesar

APPENDIX
The Biorythm Hoax

FOR A WHILE IN THE 1970S THE BIORHYTHM theory was trendy. It was one of the first things I set out to investigate. I selected 1,039 sports feats to study, covering baseball, football, tennis, boxing, track and field, and swimming.

The theory was propounded by two doctors from Vienna and Berlin around the end of the 19th century. They said we all are subject to a 23-day physical cycle, beginning on the day we are born. The first 11½ days are up, when energy is high, the next 11½ down, when we are recharging the batteries. The days when we cross from one to the other are supposed to be critical, when the body is neither one nor the other; these are supposed to be accident-prone days.

A second, 33-day, mental cycle was also deduced, and later a third, a 28-day emotional cycle, based on the moon's orbit.

Using a "biolator," or special calculator, I could quickly tell where any athlete was on his cycles. Results were pretty much as expected. Let's take some examples of physical highs and lows:

Babe Ruth's 60 home runs in 1927: 27 came on physical highs, 29 during lows, and four on crossing days. Nine came on triple lows on all three cycles.

Roger Maris' 61 home runs in 1961: 23 highs, 35 lows, and three crossing days. (I had long since lost the biolator when Mark McGwire and Sammy Sosa broke the record in 1998).

Hank Aaron's first 500 home runs: 45% were hit on highs, 49% on lows, and 6% on crossings.

Or take what many consider the seven greatest baseball events of all-time:

1. When Bobby Thomson swatted the "shot heard 'round the world" to win the 1951 pennant, he was down physically.

2. Don Larsen's perfect World Series game in 1956 was pitched on a crossing day.

3. When Joe Oeschger and Leon Cadore battled 26 innings to a 1-1 tie in 1920, both gladiators were down.

4. Bill Mazeroski's *sayonara* home run that sank the Yanks in the 1960 World Series was hit on a down day for Maz.

5. When Harvey Haddix hurled 12 innings of perfect ball in 1960, he was down that night.

6. We finally found a high when Carl Hubbell struck out six American League sluggers in a row in the 1934 All Star Game. But (7) Carlton Fisk was down on all three cycles when he won the sixth game of the 1975 Series with a 12th-inning home run.

A few other examples:

Seven hits in one game: Cesar Gutierrez and Wilbert Robinson had crossing days; Rennie Stennett was up.

Four home runs in one game: Chuck Klein and Gil Hodges were up; Lou Gehrig, triple down; Mike Schmidt, double down, physically and emotionally.

Twelve RBIs in one game: Jim Bottomley, crossing.

Six stolen bases in one game: Eddie Collins, 1912, twice—down the second time, triple down the first.

Nineteen strikeouts in one game: Nolan Ryan, up; Tom Seaver, down; Steve Carlton, triple down. (Information not available for Roger Clemens' two 20-strikeout performances.

No hitters: Bob Feller, 3: down for all three. Sandy Koufax, 4: down for three, with a supposedly dangerous triple crossing for the fourth. Nolan Ryan, 4: up for three, down for one. (Information not available for the last three he pitched.)

Back-to-back no-hitters: Johnny Vander Meer, 1939: down for both.

Double no-hitter, 1917:Fred Toney was up, Jim Vaughn, down.

≈ Negative performances ≈

These ran closer to biorhythm predictions. Some samples:

Jack Chesbro's 1904 wild pitch to lose the pennant: triple down.

Fred Merkle's 1908 "boner": triple down.

Mickey Owen's 1941 World Series passed ball: down.

Fred Lindstrom's 1924 World Series error: down.

Dodger Willie Davis' three errors in one 1966 Series inning: triple up.

Other sports generally mirrored the baseball findings. Boxing, though, was an exception. Winners of heavyweight title fights tended to be up physically, while losers were usually down. But it was the other way around for Wimbledon tennis finalists. World records in track and field and swimming stuck close to the expected, divided between ups and downs.

A surgeon friend told me he believed in biorhythms and used them to schedule operations. However, he felt they behave more like menstrual cycles; that is, they vary slightly among individuals, and they can be altered by illness and injury. This is an avenue for further study.

I published my results in 1977. Since then almost nothing is heard of biorhythms any more.